"Why do my eyes hurt?"

"You've never used them before."

THE BASICS

THE SOUL-MATE MYTH
THERE IS NO ONE

ONEitis:
An unhealthy romantic obsession with a single person. Usually accompanied by unreciprocated affection and completely unrealistic idealization of the said person.

ONEitis is paralysis. You cease to mature, you cease to move, you cease to be you.

There is no ONE. This is the soul-mate myth. There are some good Ones and some bad Ones, but there is no ONE. Anyone telling you anything else is selling you something. There are *lots* of 'special someones' out there for you, just ask the divorced / widowed person who's remarried after their "soul-mate" has died or moved on with another person they insist is their *real* soul-mate.

This is what trips people up about the soul-mate myth, it is this fantasy that we all at least in some way share an idealization of – that there is ONE perfect mate for each of us, and as soon as the planets align and fate takes its course we'll know that we're '*intended*' for each other. While this may make for a gratifying romantic comedy plot, it's hardly a realistic way to plan your life. In fact it's usually paralyzing.

What I find even more fascinating is how common the idea is (and particularly for guys) that a nuts & bolts view of life should be trumped by this fantasy in the area of inter-sexual relationships.

Men who would otherwise recognize the value of understanding psychology, biology, sociology, evolution, business, engineering, etc., men with a concrete awareness of the interplay we see these aspects take place in our lives on a daily basis, are some of the first guys to become violently opposed to the idea that maybe there isn't "someone for everyone" or that there are a lot more ONEs out there that could meet or exceed the criteria we subconsciously set for them to be the ONE.

I think it comes off as nihilistic, or this dread that maybe their ego-investment in this belief is false – it's like saying "God is dead" to the deeply religious. It's just too terrible to contemplate that there maybe no ONE, or there maybe several ONEs to spend their lives with. This western romanticized mythology is based on the premise that there is only ONE perfect mate for any single individual and as much as a lifetime can and should be spent in constant search of this 'soul-mate.' So strong and so pervasive is this myth in our collective consciousness that it has become akin to a religious statement, and in fact has been integrated into many religious doctrines as the feminization of western culture has spread.

I think there's been a mischaracterization of ONEitis. It's necessary to differentiate between a healthy relationship based on mutual affinity and respect, and a lopsided ONEitis based relationship. I've had more than a few guys seeking my advice, or challenging my take on ONEitis, essentially asking me for permission to accept ONEitis as legitimate monogamy.

"But Rollo, it's got to be OK for a guy to have ONEitis for his wife or girlfriend. After all she's the ONE for him, right?"

In my estimation ONEitis is an unhealthy psychological dependency that is the direct result of the continuous socialization of the soul-mate myth in our collective consciousness. What's truly frightening is that ONEitis has become associated with being a healthy normative aspect of a long term relationship (LTR) or marriage.

I come to the conclusion that ONEitis is based in sociological roots, not only due to it being a statement of personal belief, but by the degree to which this ideology is disseminated and mass marketed in popular culture through media, music, literature, movies, etc.

Dating services like eHarmony shamelessly marketeer and exploit exactly the insecurities that this dynamic engenders in people desperately searching for the ONE "they were intended for." The idea that men possess a natural capacity for protection, provisioning and semi-monogamy has merit from both a social and bio-psychological standpoint, but a ONEitis psychosis is not a byproduct of it. Rather, I would set it apart from this healthy protector/provider dynamic since ONEitis essentially sabotages what our natural propensities would otherwise filter.

ONEitis is insecurity run amok while a person is single, and potentially paralyzing when coupled with the object of that ONEitis in an LTR. The same neurotic desperation that drives a person to settle for their ONE whether healthy or unhealthy is the same insecurity that paralyzes them from abandoning a damaging relationship – This is their ONE and how could they ever live without them? Or, they're my ONE, but all I need is to fix myself or fix them to have my idealized relationship.

This idealization of a relationship is at the root of ONEitis. With such a limiting, all-or-nothing binary approach to searching for ONE needle in the haystack, and investing emotional effort over the course of a lifetime, how do we mature into a healthy understanding of what that relationship should really entail? The very pollyanna, idealized relationship – the "happily ever after" – that belief in a ONE promotes as an ultimate end, is thwarted and contradicted by the costs of the constant pursuit of the ONE for which they'll settle for. After the better part of a lifetime is invested in this ideology, how much more difficult will it be to come to the realization that the person they're with isn't their ONE? To what extents will a person go to in order to protect a lifetime of this ego investment?

At some point in a ONEitis relationship one participant will establish dominance based on the powerlessness that this ONEitis necessitates. There is no greater agency for a woman than to know beyond doubt that she is the only source of a man's need for sex and intimacy. A ONEitis mindset only cements this into the understanding of both parties.

4

For a man who believes that the emotionally and psychologically damaging relationship he has ego-invested himself is with the only person in his lifetime he's ever going to be compatible with, there is nothing more paralyzing in his maturation. The same of course holds true for women, and this is why we shake our heads when see an exceptionally beautiful woman go chasing back to her abusive and indifferent Jerk boyfriend, because she believes he is her ONE and the only source of security available to her. Hypergamy may be her root imperative for sticking with him, but it's the soul-mate myth, the fear of the "ONE that got away" that makes for the emotional, almost spiritual, investment.

The definition of Power is not financial success, status or influence over others, but the degree to which we have control over our own lives. Subscribing to the soul-mate mythology necessitates that we recognize powerlessness in this arena of our lives. Better I think it would be to foster a healthy understanding that there is no ONE. There are some good Ones and there are some bad Ones, but there is no ONE.

Religion of the Soul-Mate

What you've just read was one of my earliest posts back on the SoSuave forums from around 2003-04. I was finishing my degree then and had the Fallacy of the ONE graphically illustrated for me in a psychology class one day. I was in class, surrounded by (mostly) much younger students than myself, all very astute and as intellectual as they come for mid twenty-somethings. At one point the discussion had come around to religion and much of the class expressed being agnostic or atheist, or "spiritual, but not religious". The rationale was of course that religion and belief could be explained as psychological (fear of mortality) constructs that were expanded to sociological dynamics.

Later in that discussion the idea of a 'soul mate' came up. The professor didn't actually use the word 'soul', but rather couched the idea by asking for a show of hands as to how many of the class believed "there was a special someone out there for them?" or if they feared "the ONE that got away." Damn near the entire class raised their hands. For all of their rational empiricism and appeals to realism in regards to spirituality, they (almost) unanimously expressed a quasi-Karmic belief in connecting with another idealized person on an intimate level for a lifetime.

Even the Frat guys and hook-up girls who I knew weren't expressly looking for anything long term in their dating habits still raised their hands in assent to a belief in a ONE. Some later explained what that ONE meant to them, and most had differing definitions of that idealization – some even admitted to it being an idealization as the discussion progressed – yet almost all of them still had what would otherwise be termed an irrational belief in 'predestination' or, even amongst the least spiritual, that it's just part of life to pair off with someone significant and there was "someone for everyone".

This discussion was the catalyst for one of my awakening realizations – despite all odds, people largely feel entitled to, or deserving of, an important love of their life.

Statistically and pragmatically this is ridiculous, but there it is. The feminized Disney-fi-cation of this core concept has been romanticized and commercialized to the point of it becoming a religion, even for the expressly non-religious. The Shakespearean longing for the ONE, the search for another soul (mate) who was destined to be our match has been systematically distorted beyond all reason. And as I'll elaborate later, men will take their own lives in the delusion of having lost their soul-mate.

Soul-Mate Men

This perversion of the soul-mate myth is attributable to a large part of the feminized social conventions we deal with today. The fear of isolation from our imagined soul-mate, or the fear of having irrecoverably lost that 'perfect ONE' for us fuels so much of the personal and social neuroses we find in the contemporary matrix of our society. For example, much of the fear inherent in the Myth of the Lonely Old Man loses its teeth without a core belief in the Soul-Mate Myth. The fear of loss and the delusions of Relational Equity only really matter when the person men believe that equity should influence is their predestined ONE.

The feminine imperative recognized the overwhelming power the Soul-Mate Myth had over men (and women) from the beginnings of its rise to ascendancy as the primary gender social imperative. Virtually all of the distortions of the core soul-mate dynamic evolved as a controlling schema for men. When it is soul-mate women who are the primary reward for a soul-mate necessitous man, there are a lot of opportunities to consolidate that power upon. To be clear, don't think this is some fiendish plot of a fem-centric cabal socially engineering that soul-mate fear into men. Generations of men, raised to be oblivious to it, willingly and actively help perpetuate the Soul-Mate Myth.

Soul-Mate Women

Although Hypergamy plays a large role in determining what makes for an idealized soul-mate for women, they aren't immune to the exploitations of that core fear. Though it's more an unfortunate byproduct than an outright manipulation, I'd argue that in some ways hypergamy intensifies that neurosis. An Alpha Widow knows all too well the languishing associated with pining for the Alpha that got away – particularly when she's paired off long-term with the dutiful, Beta provider after her sexual market value (SMV) declines.

For women, the soul-mate represents that nigh unattainable combination of arousing Alpha dominance matched with a loyal providership for her long term security that only she can tame out of him.

Hypergamy hates the soul-mate principle, because the soul-mate is an absolute definition, whereas hypergamy must alway test for perfection. Hypergamy asks, "Is he the ONE? Is he the ONE?" and the Soul-Mate Myth replies, "He HAS to be the ONE, he's your soul-mate, and there's ONLY one of those."

Building the Mystery

Due to this core concept and soul-mate mythology, both sexes will seek to perfect that idealization for themselves – even under the least ideal of conditions and expressions.

We want to build our intimate relations into that soul-mate idealism in order to relieve the fear and solve the problem, and most times so badly that we'll deftly ignore the warnings, abuses and consequences of having done so. For women the impact of the most significant Alpha male is what initially defines that soul-mate idealization. For men it may be the first woman to become sexual with him or the one who best exemplifies a woman he (mistakenly) believes can love him in a male-defined orientation of love.

However, these are the points of origin for building that soul-mate ideal upon. This ideal is then compounded upon with layers of investments in the hopes that this person "might actually be the one fate has prescribed for them." Emotional investment, personal, financial, even life-potential investments and sacrifices then follow in an effort to create a soul-mate. In the absence of an ideal, one must be created from available resources.

This process is why I say the Soul-Mate Myth is ridiculous – it's psychologically much more pragmatic to construct another person to fit that ideal than it ever will be to "wait for fate to take its course." People subscribing to the myth would rather build a soul-mate, consequences be damned. So women will attempt to Build a better Beta, or tame down an Alpha, while men will attempt to turn a whore into a housewife, or vice versa.

One of the most bitter aftertastes of having awakened to the red-pill truth is abandoning old paradigms for new. I've described this before as akin to killing an old friend, and one friend that needs killing is exactly this mythology. Disabusing yourself of this core fear is vital to fully unplugging yourself from the old paradigm, because so much of fem-centric social conditioning is dependent upon it.

Dropping the Soul-Mate Myth isn't the nihilism a lot of people might have you believe it is. If anything it will free you to have a better, healthier future relationship with someone who is genuinely important to you – a relationship based on genuine desire, mutual respect, complimentary understanding of each other and love, rather than one based on a fear of losing your ONE and only representation of contentment in this life. In any relationship, the person with the most power is the one who needs the other the least.

This is a foundation of any relationship, not just intersexual ones, but family, business, etc. relationships as well. It is a dynamic that is always in effect. For my own well being and that of my family's, I need my employer more than he needs me, ergo I get up for work in the morning and work for him. And while I am also a vital part for the uninterrupted continuance of his company and endeavors, he simply needs me less than I need him. Now I could win the lottery tomorrow or he may decide to cut my pay or limit my benefits, or I may complete my Masters Degree and decide that I can do better than to keep myself yoked to his cart indefinitely, thereby, through some condition either initiated by myself or not, I am put into a position of needing him less than he needs me. At this point he is forced into a position of deciding how much I am worth to his ambitions and either part ways with me or negotiate a furtherance of our relationship.

The same plays true for intersexual relationships. Whether you want to base your relationship on 'power' or not isn't the issue; it's already in play from your first point of attraction. You are acceptable to her for meeting any number of criteria and she meets your own as well. If this weren't the case you simply would not initiate a mutual relationship.

THE CARDINAL RULE OF RELATIONSHIPS

In any relationship, the person with the most power is the one who needs the other the least.

This is a foundation of any relationship, not just intersexual ones, but family, business, etc. relationships as well. It is a dynamic that is always in effect.

For my own well being and that of my family's, I need my employer more than he needs me, ergo I get up for work in the morning and work for him. While I am also a vital part for the uninterrupted continuance of his company and endeavors, he simply needs me less than I need him. Now I could win the lottery tomorrow or he may decide to cut my pay or limit my benefits, or I may complete my Masters Degree and decide that I can do better than to keep myself yoked to his cart indefinitely, thereby, through some condition either initiated by myself or not, I am put into a position of needing him less than he needs me. At this point he is forced into a position of evaluating my necessity to his future ambitions and either part ways with me or negotiate a furtherance of our relationship.

The same plays true for intersexual relationships. Whether you want to base your relationship on 'power' or not isn't the issue; it's already in play from your first point of attraction. You are acceptable to her for meeting any number of her criteria and she meets your own as well. If this weren't the case you simply would not initiate a mutual relationship. This is the first comparison we make with another individual – call it 'sizing up' if you like – but we make innate (and often unconscious) comparisons about everything and in the case of initial attraction we decide if the other person is acceptable for our own intimacy.

This principle isn't so much about 'power' as it is about control. This might sound like semantics, but it makes a difference. It's very easy to slip into binary arguments and think that what I mean by the cardinal rule of relationships is that one participant must absolutely rule over the other – a domineering dominant to a doormat submissive. The problem with our modern interpretation of power is to think of it in extreme, absolute terms.

Control in a healthy relationship passes back and forth as desire and need dictate for each partner. In an unhealthy relationship you have an unbalanced manipulation of this control by a partner. Although control is never in complete balance, it becomes manipulation when one partner, in essence blackmails, the other with what would otherwise be a reinforcer for the manipulated under a healthy circumstance.

This happens for a plethora different reasons, but the condition comes about by two ways – the submissive participant becomes conditioned to allow the manipulation to occur and/or the dominate initiates the manipulation. In either case the rule still holds true – the one who needs the other the least has the most control. Nowhere is this more evident than in interpersonal relationships.

Too many people who I've counseled and read my blog assume that this Rule means that I'm advocating the maintaining a position of dominance at the expense of their partner's best interests; far from it. I do however advocate that people – young men in particular – develop a better sense of self-worth and a better understanding of their true efficacy in their relationships (assuming you decide to become involved in one).

Don't get me wrong, both sexes are guilty of manipulation; Battered women go back to their abusive boyfriends/husbands and pussy-whipped men compromise themselves and their ambitions to better serve their girlfriends insecurities. My intent in promoting this Rule is to open the eyes of young men who are already predisposed to devaluing themselves and placing women as the goal of their lives rather than seeing themselves as the *prize* to be sought after. Compromise is always going to be a part of any relationship, but what's key is realizing when that compromise becomes the result of manipulation, what is in effect and developing the confidence to be uncompromising in those situations. This is where a firm understanding of the cardinal rule of relationships becomes essential.

There's nothing wrong with backing down from an argument you have with your girl-friend, but there is something wrong when you continually compromise yourself in order to 'keep the peace' with the understanding that she'll withhold intimacy as a result of you holding your ground. That is a power play, also known as a '**shit test**'.

She initiates it thus becoming the controlling party. No woman's intimacy (i.e. sex) is ever worth that compromise because in doing so you devalue your own worth to her.

Once this precedent is set, she will progressively have less respect for you – exactly opposite of the popular conception that she'll appreciate your compromising for her and reward you for this. And really, what are you compromising in order to achieve? Set in this condition, you're appealing for her intimacy. That isn't genuine desire or real interest in you, it's a subtle psychological test (that all too many men are unaware of) meant to determine who needs the other more. There is no more a superior confidence for a man than one with the self-understanding that he will not compromise himself for the recog-nized manipulations of a woman, and the fortitude to walk away knowing he has in the past, and will in the future find a better prospect than her. This is the man who passes the shit test. It's called 'enlightened self-interest', and a principle I wholly endorse.

TRUTH TO POWER

Denying the utility of Power, vilifying it's usages, is in itself a means of using Power.

Real change works from the inside out. If you don't change your mind about yourself, you wont change anything else. Women can change their hair color, their makeup, clothes, breast size, and any number of cosmetic alteration on a whim, or as they can afford them, but the constant discontent, the constant inadequacies they complain of are rooted in their self-perceptions, not how others really perceive them.

This is an outside-in mentality; hoping the external will change the internal, and it's just this mentality that lesser men apply to themselves – the only difference being the application.

The Average Frustrated Chump (AFC for lack of a better term) has the same problem as the vain woman (OK, really any woman) – a lack of true self-understanding of their own problem. It's very difficult to do self-analysis and self-criticism, particularly when it comes to questioning our own beliefs and the reasons our personalities are what they are. It's akin to telling someone they're not living their lives 'correctly' or that they're raising their children 'wrong'; only it's more difficult because we're doing the telling about ourselves to ourselves.

Self-estimation (not self-esteem) **never** happens spontaneously, there always has to be some crisis to prompt it. Anxiety, trauma and crisis are necessary catalysts to stimulate self-consciousness. A breakup, a death, a betrayal; tragically, it's at these points in our lives that we do our best introspection, we have our 'moments of clarity' and yes, discover what abysmal, simpering chumps we've allowed ourselves to be molded into.

Denial

The first step to really unplugging from our preconditioning (i.e. the feminine Matrix) is recognizing that this conditioning has led to the beliefs we think are integral to our personalities. The psychological term for this is called 'ego-investment'. When a person internalizes a mental schema so thoroughly, and has become conditioned to it for so long, it becomes an integral part of their personality. So to attack the belief is to, literally, attack the person. This is why we see such a violent reaction to people's political, religious, inter-social/inter-sexual, inter-gender, etc. expressions of belief – they perceive it as a personal attack, even when presented with irrefutable, empirical evidence that challenges the veracity of those beliefs.

One common frustration that Game-aware Men express is how difficult it is to open an AFCs eyes as to why he's not hooking up, why he's not getting dates (or 2nd dates if he is), why he's constantly getting 'lets just be friends' (LJBF) rejections, etc., and all the flaws in what is really ego-investment internalizations. As I'm fond of saying, it's dirty work unplugging chumps from the Matrix, and this is made all the more difficult when a person is in a categorical state of denial.

People resort to denial when recognizing that the truth would destroy something they hold dear. In the case of a cheating partner, denial lets you avoid acknowledging evidence of your own humiliation. Short of catching a spouse in bed with your best friend, evidence of infidelity is usually ambiguous. It's motivated skepticism. You're more skeptical of things you don't want to believe and demand a higher level of proof. Denial is unconscious, or it wouldn't work: if you know you're closing your eyes to the truth, some part of you knows what the truth is and denial can't perform its protective function.

One thing we all struggle to protect is a positive self-image. The more important the aspect of your self-image that's challenged by the truth, the more likely you are to go into denial. If you have a strong sense of self-worth and competence, your self-image can take hits but remain largely intact; if you're beset by self-doubt (a hallmark of self-righteous AFC thinking), however, any acknowledgment of failure can be devastating and any admission of error painful to the point of being unthinkable. Self-justification and denial arise from the dissonance between believing you're competent, and making a mistake, which clashes with that image.

Solution: deny the mistake. Attribute it to an outside element (women won't play by "the rules") rather than resort to introspection (maybe I'm wrong about "the rules"?).

Therefore we see AFCs tenaciously cling to a moralistic sense of purpose in their methods which is only reinforced by popular culture in our media, our music, eHarmony, our religion, etc.

Articles of Power

The term Power has a lot of misapplied connotations to it. When we think of Powerful people, we think of influence, wealth, prestige, status and the ability to have others do our bidding – all of these are not Power. As much as we'd like to convince ourselves that women are attracted to *this* definition of Power, this is false. Because what I've described as aspects of Power here are really manifestations of Power.

Here's a cosmic secret revealed for you:

Real Power is the degree to which a person has control over their own circumstances. Real Power is the degree to which we actually control the directions of our lives.

When we allow our thinking, our personality disorders and our mental schemas, combined with their accompanying behaviors, to determine the course of our decisions, we relinquish real Power. The man who succumbs, by force or by will, to the responsibilities, liabilities and accountabilities that are required of him by society, marriage, commitment, family, fatherhood, career choice, the military, etc. leaves him very little influence over the course of his own life.

The painter Paul Gauguin is one of history's most powerful men. At middle age Paul was a "successful" banker, with a wife and children and by all appearances, a man of great merit and considerable wealth. Then one day Paul decided he'd had enough and wanted to paint. He left his wife, children and his money, and decided he would become a painter. He cast off his former life to live the life he chose, he had the power to assume control of it. Eventually he died in Tahiti, but not after having one of the most interesting of lives and becoming a world renowned painter.

You may think, what a horrible man he was to abandon his responsibilities to selfishly pursue his own desires, but the fact remains that he had the Power within himself to do so that most men would shudder to even consider. So entrapped are we in our self-expectation and self-imposed limitations that we fail to see that we have always had the keys to our own prisons – we're just scared shitless to use them.

This Power is the root of that all important term 'confidence' we toss out every time we tell a 19 year old chump what women really want so he can get laid. It's this ability to make our own decisions, right or wrong, and to confidently own them that separate us from "other guys." It's this self-guided Power that evokes a seemingly irrational confidence to Spin Plates, to date non-exclusively, to assert ourselves and to be unafraid to make ourselves the *prize*, and it's just this Power that women want to be associated with.

Lack of this Power is exactly what makes master Pick Up Artists (PUAs) revert to some of the most pathetic AFCs once they become involved in an LTR. They sell women on this idealization and the perception that they possess this Power only to discover the AFC insecurities these behaviors were meant to cover up once they've bought the act. This isn't to devalue PUA skills as effective behavior sets, rather it's meant to illustrate the behaviors that should be manifest as a result of effecting a real personal change. It should be that adopting a positive-masculine mental schema prompts these PUA skills as a result. Instead we have the cart before the horse in a mad rush to get that all important pussy we've been deprived of for so long, by masking our deficit in real Power and understanding with rote memorized PUA techniques hoping that by practicing them they'll turn into "natural game" and we'll mature enough to initiate a lasting personal change.

We'll return to this later.

THE DESIRE DYNAMIC

You cannot negotiate genuine Desire.

This is a very simple principle that most Men and the vast majority of women are willfully ignorant of. One the most common personal problems I've been asked advice for in the past 10 years is some variation of "how do I get her back?" Usually this breaks down into men seeking some methodology to return his relationship to an earlier state where a previously passionate woman couldn't keep her hands off of him. Six months into a comfortable familiarity and the thrill is gone, but in truth it's the genuine *desire* that is gone.

It's often at this stage that a man will resort to negotiation. Sometimes this can be as subtle as him progressively and systematically doing things for her in the hopes that she'll reciprocate with the same sexual / intimate fervor they used to have. Other times a married or long term couple may go to couples counseling to "resolve their sex issues" and negotiate terms for her sexual compliance. He'll promise to do the dishes and a load of laundry more often in exchange for her feigned sexual interest in him. Yet, no matter what terms are offered, no matter how great an external effort he makes so deserving of reward, the genuine desire is not there for her. In fact, she feels worse for not having the desire after such efforts were made for her compliance. Her desire has become an obligation.

Negotiated desire only ever leads to obligated compliance. This is why her post-negotiation sexual response is often so lackluster and the source of even further frustration on his part. She may be more sexually available to him, but the half-hearted experience is never the same as when they first met when there was no negotiation, just spontaneous desire for each other.

From a male perspective, and particularly that of an uninitiated beta male, negotiation of desire seems a deductive, rational solution to the problem. Men tend to innately rely on deductive reasoning; otherwise known as an "if then" logic stream. The code is often something like this:

I need sex + women have the sex I want + query women about their conditions for sex + meet prerequisites for sex = the sex I want.

Makes sense right? It's simple deductive pragmatism, but built on a foundation that relies on a woman's accurate self-evaluations. The genuine desire they used to experience at the outset of their relationship was predicated upon a completely unknown set of variables.

Overtly communicating a desire for reciprocal desire creates obligation, and sometimes even ultimatums. Genuine desire is something a person must come to – or be led to – of their own volition. You can force a woman by threat to comply with behaving in a desired manner, but you cannot make her *want* to behave that way. A prostitute will fuck you for an exchange, it doesn't mean she *wants* to.

Whether in a monogamous marriage, LTR or a one night stand (ONS), strive for genuine desire in your relationships.

Half of the battle is knowing you want to be with a woman who wants to please you, not one who feels obligated to. You will never draw this genuine desire from her by overt means, but you can covertly lead her to this genuine desire. The trick in provoking real desire is in keeping her ignorant of your intent to provoke it. Real desire is created by her thinking it's something she wants, not something she has to do.

IMAGINATION

A woman's imagination is the single most useful tool in your Game arsenal. Every technique, every casual response, every gesture, intimation and subcommunication hinges on stimulating a woman's imagination. Competition anxiety relies on it. Demonstrating Higher Value (DHV) relies on it. Prompting sexual tension relies on it. Call it "Caffein-ating the Hamster" if you will, but stimulating a woman's imaginings is the single most potent talent you can develop in any context of a relationship.

This is the single greatest failing of average frustrated chumps; they vomit out everything about themselves, divulging the full truth of themselves to women in the mistaken belief that women desire that truth as a basis for qualifying for their intimacy.

Learn this now: Women **never** want full disclosure. Nothing is more self-satisfying for a woman than to think she's figured a Man out based solely on her mythical feminine intuition (i.e. imagination).

When a man overtly confirms his character, his story, his value, etc. for a woman, the mystery is dispelled and the biochemical rush she enjoyed from her imaginings, her sus-picions, her self-confirmations about you are gone. Most guys with a Beta male mindset classically do exactly this on the first date and wonder why they get LJBF'd promptly af-ter it – this is why. Familiarity is anti-seductive. Nothing kills Game, organic passion and libido like comfortable familiarity. Despite their common filibuster tactics, women don't want to be comfortable with a potential (or proven) sex partner, they need their imagina-tions stoked to be excited, aroused and anxious to want sex with a potential partner.

In an LTR there's an even more critical need to keep prodding that imagination. I would go so far as to say it's imperative for a healthy relationship, but then you'll ask, how do you go about that when your LTR girlfriend or wife already knows your story and the familiarity becomes cemented in?

The easy answer is never let it be from the outset - the health of any LTR you might entertain depends and survives on the frame you enter into it with. The foundations of a healthy LTR are laid while you're single and dating non-exclusively. I've yet to meet the guy who's told me he's getting more frequent, more intense sex after his LTR / Marriage / Live-in situation was established.

The primary reason for this is the relaxation of the competition anxiety that made the urgency of fucking you with lustful abandon in your dating phase an imperative to get you to commit to her frame. That's the crux of the matter that so many guys fail in, they surrender the frame *before* they commit to an LTR. They believe, (thanks to their feminine conditioning) that commitment necessitates, and is synonymous with, acquiescing to her frame control. Combine this with anti-seductive familiarity and the growing commonness of your own value because of it, and you can see exactly why her sexual interest wanes.

So what do you do to prevent that?

First and foremost, understand that whose frame you enter into an LTR sets the foundation of that LTR. If you find yourself buying into an "it's women's world and we just live in it" mentality where your default presumption is that commitment means she wins by default, you lose and that's just how it is, don't even consider an LTR. She enters your world, not the other way around.

Secondly, you need to cultivate an element of unpredictability about yourself prior to, and into, an LTR. Always remember, **perfect is boring**. Women will cry a river about wanting Mr. Dependable and then go off to fuck Mr. Exciting. In an LTR it's necessary to be both, but not one at the expense of the other. Too many married men are terrified to rock the excitement boat with their wives or LTRs because their sex lives hang in the balance of placating to her and her already preset frame. She must be reminded daily why you're fun, unpredictable and exciting, not only to her, but other women as well. This requires covertly, tactfully, demonstrably implying that other women find you desirable. Women crave the chemical rush that comes from suspicion and indignation. If you don't provide it, they'll happily get it from tabloids, romance novels, The View, Tyra Banks or otherwise living vicariously through their single girlfriends.

By playfully staying her source of that rush you maintain the position of stimulating her imagination. Married men, who were defeated before they committed, don't think that elements of Game apply to marriage out of fear of upsetting their wives frame, when in fact being cocky & funny, neg hits and many other aspects of Game work wonderfully.

Just kicking her in the ass or busting her chops, playfully, is sometimes enough to send the message that you're fearless of her response. You can break her frame with cockiness and the imaginings that come with it.

Breaking from an established, predictable familiarity is often a great way to fire her imagination. Married guys will report how sexual their wives become after they get to the gym and start shaping up after a long layoff (or for the first time). It's easy to pass this off as looking better makes women more aroused (which is true), but underneath that is the breaking of a pattern. You're controllable and predictable so long as you're pudgy and listless – what other woman would want you? But start changing your patterns, get into shape, make more money, get a promotion, improve and demonstrate your higher value in some appreciable way and the imagination and competition anxiety returns.

SCHEDULES OF MATING

There are methods and social conventions women have used for centuries to ensure that the best male's genes are selected and secured with the best male provisioning she's capable of attracting. Ideally the best Man should exemplify both, but rarely do the two exist in the same male (particularly these days) so in the interest of achieving her biological imperative, and prompted by an innate need for security, the feminine as a whole had to develop social conventions and methodologies (which change as her environment and personal conditions do) to effect this. Not only are men up against a female genetic imperative, but also centuries-old feminine social conventions established and adapted from a time long before human beings could accurately determine genetic origins.

I've detailed in many of my blog posts that mate selection is a psycho-biological function that millennia of evolution has hardwired into the psyches of both sexes. So internalized and socialized is this process into our collective unconsciousness that we rarely recognize we're subject to these motivators even when we repeatedly manifest the same behaviors prompted by them (ex. women having a second kid with the Alpha Bad Boy).

It's simple deductive logic to follow that for a species to survive it must provide its offspring with the best possible conditions to ensure its survival – either that or to reproduce in such quantity that it ensures survival. The obvious application of this for women is sharing parental investment with the best possible mate she can attract and who can provide long term security for her and any potential offspring.

Thus women are biologically, psychologically and sociologically the filters of their own reproduction, where as men's reproductive methodology is to scatter as much of his genetic material as humanly possible to the widest pool of sexually available females. He of course has his own criteria for mating selection and determining the best genetic pairing for his reproduction (i.e. "she's gotta be hot"), but his criteria is certainly less discriminating than that of women (i.e. "no one's ugly after 2am"). This is evidenced in our own hormonal biology; healthy men possess between 12 and 17 times the amount of testosterone (the primary hormone in sexual arousal) women do and women produce substantially more estrogen (instrumental in sexual caution) and oxytocin (fostering feelings of security and nurturing) than men.

That stated, both of these methodologies conflict in practice. For a woman to best ensure the survival of her offspring, a man must necessarily abandon his method of reproduction in favor of her own. This then sets a contradictory imperative for him to pair with a woman who will satisfy his methodology. A male must sacrifice his reproductive schedule to satisfy that of the woman he pairs with. Thus, with so much genetic potential at stake on his part of the risk, he wants not only to ensure that she is the best possible candidate for breeding (and future breeding), but also to know that his progeny will benefit from both parent's investment.

Side note: One interesting outcome of this psycho-biological dynamic is men's ability to spot their own children in a crowd of other children more quickly and with greater acuity than even their mothers. Studies have shown that men have the ability to more quickly and accurately identify their own children in a room full of kids dressed in the same uniforms than the mothers of the child. Again, this stresses the subconscious importance of this genetic trade off.

These are the rudiments of human sexual selection and reproduction. Obviously there are many other social, emotional and psychological intricacies that are associated with these fundamentals, but these are the underlying motivations and considerations that subconsciously influence sexual selection.

Social Conventions

To counter this subconscious dynamic to their own genetic advantage women initiate social conventions and psychological schemas to better facilitate their own breeding methodologies. This is why women always have the "prerogative to change her mind" and the most fickle of behaviors become socially excusable, while men's behavior is constrained to a higher standard of responsibility to "do the right thing" which is invariably to the advantage of a woman's reproductive strategy . This is why guys who are 'Players', and fathers who abandon mothers to pursue their innate reproduction method are villains, and fathers who selflessly sacrifice themselves financially, emotionally and life decision-wise, even to the benefit of children they didn't father, are considered social heroes for complying with women's genetic imperatives.

This is also the root motivation for female-specific social dynamics such as "lets just be friends" (LJBF) rejections and women's propensity for victimhood (as they've learned that this engenders 'savior' mental schemas for men's breeding schedules – Cap'n Save a Ho) and even marriage itself.

Good Dads vs. Good Genes

The two greatest difficulties for women to overcome in their own methodology is that they are only at a sexually viable peak for a short window of time (generally their early 20s) and the fact that the qualities that make a good long term partner (the Good Dad) and the qualities that make for good breeding stock (Good Genes) only rarely manifest themselves in the same male. Provisioning and security potential are fantastic motivators for pairing with a Good Dad, but the same characteristics that make him such are generally a disadvantage when compared with the man who better exemplifies genetic, physical attraction and the risk taking qualities that would imbue her child with a better capacity to adapt to it's environment (i.e. stronger, faster, more attractive than others to ensure the passing of her own genetic material to future generations). This is the Jerk vs. Nice Guy paradox writ large on an evolutionary scale.

Men and women innately (though unconsciously) understand this dynamic, so in order for a woman to have the best that the Good Dad has to offer while taking advantage of the best that the Good Genes man has, she must invent and constantly modify social conventions to keep the advantage in her biological favor, and in accordance with her pluralistic sexual strategy.

Reproductive Schedules

This paradox then necessitates that women (and by default men) must subscribe to short term and long term schedules of mating. Short term schedules facilitate breeding with the Good Genes male, while long term breeding is reserved the Good Dad male. This convention and the psycho-social schemas that accompany it are precisely why women will marry the Nice Guy, stable, loyal, (preferably) doctor and still fuck the pool boy or the cute surfer she met on spring break. In our genetic past, a male with good genes implied an ability to be a good provider, but modern convention has thwarted this, so new social and mental schemas had to be developed for women.

Cheating

For this dynamic and the practicality of enjoying the best of both genetic worlds, women find it necessary to 'cheat'. This cheating can be done proactively or reactively.

In the reactive model, a woman who has already paired with her long term partner choice, engages in a extramarital or extra-pairing, sexual intercourse with a short term partner (i.e. the cheating wife or girlfriend). That's not to say this short term opportunity cannot develop into a 2nd, long term mate, but the action of infidelity itself is a method for securing better genetic stock than the committed male provider is capable of supplying.

Proactive cheating is the Single Mommy dilemma. This form of 'cheating' relies on the woman breeding with a Good Genes male, bearing his children and then abandoning him, or having him abandon her, (again through invented social conventions) in order to find a Good Dad male to provide for her and the children of her Good Genes partner to ensure their security.

I want to stress again that (most) women do not have some consciously constructed and recognized master plan to enact this cycle and deliberately trap men into it. Rather, the motivations for this behavior and the accompanying social rationales invented to justify it are an unconscious process. For the most part, women are unaware of this dynamic, but are nonetheless subject to it's influence. For a female of any species to facilitate a methodology for breeding with the best genetic partner she's able to attract *and* to ensure her own and her offspring's survival with the best provisioning partner is an evolutionary jackpot.

Cuckoldry

On some level of consciousness, men innately sense something is wrong with this situation, though they may not be able to place why they feel it or misunderstand it in the confusion of women's justifications for it. Or they become frustrated by the social pressures to 'do the right thing', are shamed into martyrdom/savior-hood and committed to a feigned responsibility to these conventions. Nevertheless, some see it well enough to steer clear of single mothers, either by prior experience or observing other male cuckolds saddled with the responsibility of raising and providing for – no matter how involved or uninvolved – another man's successful reproduction efforts with this woman.

Men often fall into the role of the proactive or reactive Cuckold. He will never enjoy the same benefits as his mate's short term partner(s) to the same degree, in the way of sexual desire or immediacy of it, while at the same time enduring the social pressures of having to provide for this Good Genes father's progeny. It could be argued that he may contribute minimally to their welfare, but on some level, whether emotional, physical, financial or educational he will contribute some effort for another man's genetic stock in exchange for a mitigated form of sexuality/intimacy from the mother. To some degree, (even if only by his presence) he is sharing the parental investment that should be borne by the short term partner. If nothing else, he contributes the time and effort to her he could be better invested in finding a sexual partner with which he could pursue his own genetic imperative by his own methodology.

However, needless to say, there is no shortage of men sexually deprived enough to 'see past' the long term disadvantages, and not only rewarding, but reinforcing a single mother's bad decisions (bad from his own interest's perspective) with regard to her breeding selections and schedules in exchange for short term sexual gratification. Furthermore, by reinforcing her behavior thusly, he reinforces the social convention for both men and women. It's important to bear in mind that in this age women are ultimately, solely responsible for the men they choose to mate with (baring rape of course) and giving birth to their children. Men do bear responsibility for their actions no doubt, but it is ultimately the decision of the female and her judgment that decides her and her children's fate

BUFFERS
Rejection is better than Regret.

While sifting through some of my past posts on the SoSuave forum it hit me; over 90% of what I advocate there can be reduced to overcoming a fear of rejection. 90% of the dilemmas AFCs find themselves in, and a majority of men's concerns, with the opposite sex find, their roots in the methods and means they use to reduce their exposure to female rejection. These are buffers meant to reduce the potential for this rejection of intimacy.

Men of course aren't the only ones who use buffers – women have their share as well – but I think it would be much more productive for guys to recognize this propensity in themselves and see the methods they use, and often ego-invest in their personal psychologies, to buffer themselves against rejection.

Virtually every common problem guys deal with finds its basis in these buffers:

LDRs - Long Distance Relationships. A guy will entertain an LDR because it was based on a previous acceptance of intimacy and being no longer convenient (due to distance) the guy will cling to the "relationship" because it's a buffer against potential rejection from new women instead of accepting the relationship as being finished and maturely re-entering the dating pool. It's a perceived "sure thing", even if only rarely rewarding.

Playing Friends - Usually after an LJBF rejection where the perception is the potential love interest "might" later become an intimate with time and qualification. No matter how misguided, the time and effort spent by a guy in proving himself as the would-be "perfect boyfriend" is a buffer against further rejection by new potential females, which is then further compounded by a moralistic sense of duty to be an actual *friend* to his LJBF girl. In essence, his buffer against further rejection is his misplaced dedication to the LJBF girl. Another variation of this is the Cap'n-Save-A-Ho dynamic.

Emails, IMs and Texts - I should also add lengthy phone conversations to this list as well, but really any technology that seemingly increases communication serves as a buffer (for both genders) the more it limits interpersonal communication. The rationalization is that it keeps him in constant contact with his sex interest (which in and of itself is a mistake), but only serves as a buffer against her rejection. The latent perception being that it's easier to read a rejection (or hear one) than to potentially be rejected in person. A lot of guys will counter this with how texts and IM's are just how this generation plies it's Game. The difference I'd argue is that when digital communication becomes your preferred method of interacting with women, it's a buffer.

Facebook & Online Dating - This one should be fairly obvious for the same reasons as above – Online dating is perhaps the best buffer ever conceived – particularly for less than physically ideal women. In fact it's so effective that businesses can be built upon the common insecurities and fear of rejection of both sexes.

Objectification of Gender - This might be less obvious, but both sexes objectify one another. Naturally when we think of this, the popularized notion is that men objectify women as sex objects, but women have a tendency to objectify men as "success objects" for the same reason. It is easier to accept rejection from an object than it is to take it from a living, breathing, human being. This is why we refer to intergender communication as a "game." We "score" or we get "shot down" not personally or emotionally rejected; the buffer is in the language and mental approach.

Idealization of Gender - This is the myth of the "Quality Woman." The buffer operates in perceived self-limitations based on a search for an ideal mate. Thus a tendency to fixate on one woman (ONEitis) or one type of woman (a gender Archetype) develops. By limiting to, and/or fixating on one woman (or type) the potential for rejection decreases, while insuring that any real rejection will come only from what will later be deemed non-qualified women. Rejection = 'Low Quality Woman' and is thus disqualified. This works in a similar fashion to the objectification buffer in that the woman delivering the rejection is reduced to an object.

Scarcity Mentality - The "Take What I Can Get and Be Glad I Got It" mentality acts as a buffer in that it works opposite of the Idealization buffer. Deprivation is motivation, and by sticking with the "sure thing" as the "only thing", the potential for new rejection is then eliminated.

Older Women, Younger Women - I should also include certain body types in this category as well, but the buffer is in certain types of women being less likely to reject a man due to their personal circumstances. The Cougar dynamic debate has been done into irrelevancy now, but the buffer is that older women, acting in accordance with their conditions, will be more inclined to accept the advances of younger men. In the same vein, very young girls will be more apt to accept the advances of older men due to naiveté and fat women are easier to become intimate with due to sexual deprivation. In and of themselves these preferences aren't buffers per se, but an internalized preference for particular women develop by associating that particular type of woman with the minimization for potential rejection.

Leagues - This is the opposite of a "high standards" buffer which could be grouped with Scarcity. There is the woman some guys actually fear because she is perceived to be so much more socially valuable than the average guy estimates himself. Think of a hot, statuesque, corporate director who runs marathons, travels a lot, has good friends, dresses well, etc, etc, etc. The average frustrated chump tells himself "wow is she out of my league I would just get shot down because I would need to possess A, B & C to be her social status / physical status equal for her to even be interested". Ergo, the internalized idea of Leagues is a useful rationalization buffer against rejection.

Pornography - I realize this will draw some fire from the masturbation / no-masturbation set, but porn (as men use it) is a buffer against rejection. Porn doesn't talk back, porn doesn't need a few drinks to loosen up nor does porn require any social skills to produce rewards. It's convenient, immediate, sexual release that requires nothing more than a PC and an internet connection (or a magazine if you prefer the analog means). We can argue the obsessive-compulsive aspect of it, or the "my girlfriend and I enjoy porn together" reasoning, but for the single guy the root reasoning is its facility as a buffer. I should also add that it's this very facility that makes women hate it (when they do). Porn gives a guy his reward for free; a reward that should be her single best agency is rendered valueless when a man can get off to an infinite variety of sexual experience at the click of a mouse. It's unlimited access to unlimited sexual availability without the stress of learning methods to earn it from women as a reward.

These are really just a few notable examples, but once you become aware of how buffers manifest you'll begin to see how and why they are useful against rejection. Buffers are generally the paths of least rejection that become ego-invested "preferences." Buffers aren't so much about those "preference" as they are about the rejection aversion motivations behind them.

At this point you might be thinking, "Well, what the hell, I don't want to feel rejection, why not employ buffers against it?" The main reason for embracing rejection is that rejection is better than regret. Scan back through this short list of buffers; how many of these have become greater, longer term problems for you than a briefly painful rejection would've been? Buffers also have a tendency to compound upon themselves in that one tends to dovetail into another, or more, until you no longer realize that they were originally rejection prevention methodologies and gradually become associated with your genuine personality. After a long enough period, buffer become "just how I am."

Lastly, experience teaches harsh, but it teaches best. Rejection, real, raw, in your face rejection stings like a bitch. It must be something so intolerable that human beings will devise countless social and psychological constructs in order to avoid it. However, there is no better teacher than getting burned by the stove. As a Man, you are going to face rejection in far more facets of your life than just dealing with a woman. The buffers you learn in one aspect of your life will be just as encumbering when they're transferred to another aspect of your life. All of these buffers listed, and many more, become indicators of how you confidently deal with adversity. Some make you look like a Beta male pussy, others are subtle and nagging parts of an internalized personality, but dependence upon them incrementally reveals your real character to a woman. Are you Alpha enough to take a rejection on the chin, smile and confidently come back for more? Or will you run, will you block yourself, will you hide with convenient buffers?

COMPENSATION

One of the higher orders of physical standards women hold for men is height. There are countless threads in the manosphere community that address this, but I think that for the better part it's not difficult to observe this in the 'real world'. I should also add that this is one characteristic that is central to the Social Matching Theory in that humans are sensitive to asymmetrics and imbalances.

Now, before I get told in so many ways that this isn't always the case or the "not all girls are like that" exceptions to the rule, let me start by saying that this isn't the point of this section. I don't want to debate the logistics of why women prefer a taller mate or the tendency for like to attract like in this respect. What I'm on about is really the root of the infamous "short man's disease." That's right, you know who I'm talking about; the ultimate in compensation for inferiority, the dreaded 'short man's disease.'

You know the guy. About 5' 6", pounding out the weight on the bench press. Bad ass attitude, hangs with the bigger guys (which is pretty much all of them) and throws his ego around. What a tool, right?

But if you think this is only limited to short men, you're making a mistake. You see, in so many ways we all compensate for deficiencies. I once read a thread on another "non-community" forum that saw fit to start a topic asking why men lie and it got me to thinking why any of us lie, man or woman. At the time I'd also been fielding a lot of questions regarding issues we kind of take for granted after having discussed them to death in the manosphere; one of those being the nature of personality and one's ability to change their own or have it changed by circumstance, or often both. I think it's a tragic miscalculation on our part to think of personality as static, unchangeable or to question the ingenuousness of that change, but more tragic is the doubting of ourselves for that change.

One simple truism that a lot of people love to use as their convenient escape clause is the JBY (just be yourself) notion. This of course is just what ones says as advice when they really don't know what else to say. Given that though, what is it that makes a personality shift 'genuine'? Any number of us probably know an individual who began acting differently at some point in their life. This can be the result of some kind of tragedy or trauma (think PTSD) or it can be that the individual felt a need to change their fundamental way of thinking and made the change of their own accord. Usually in these cases we think of them as posers or try-hards, trying to be something they're not. They reflect this change in their appearance, their regular practices, their friends or the people they associate with, attitudes, behaviors etc. And this is what's jarring for people who knew their prior personality.

What makes us doubt the sincerity of a personal change is what's at issue. If their change is something we agree with or generally think of as positive, we are less inclined to doubt the ingenuousness of this change. But when their change conflicts with our own interests, when it dramatically clashes with what we've come to expect of that individual, this is where we doubt their sincerity. We say "dude, stop trying to be something you're not", we tear it down, we fall back on JBY platitudes because it clashes with our interpretations. And in this doubt, we fish for reasons as to why a person would want that change; essentially, what are they compensating for? It may be funny to presume someone driving a monster truck down the highway is making up for a small penis, but the root of that 'compensating' is what makes us feel uncomfortable in our own internal compensating.

It's a difficult enough task for an individual to critically assess their own personality, and even more so to effect a change in it, but the final insult is to have other's doubt the veracity of it. What others fail to see is that at some point in the development of their own personalities, they themselves had to compensate for deficiencies, discontentments and prompts to grow and mature. This is a gigantic hurdle for most average men wanting to transition to being something more. I like the term positive masculinity, but the crux of all that is the ingenuousness of the actual change. Why are you changing?

There is a saying that average frustrated chumps (AFCs) are like a bunch of crabs in a barrel. As soon as one is about to climb out there are always half a dozen ready to pull him back in again. Add to this a self-doubt from societal conditionings that tell him to stay the same, not to aspire to more, he's doing it right, and it's amazing that any AFC progresses beyond what he was. This has been termed the 'Societal Cockblock'; they tell him he's compensating, and in a way they're right, but for the wrong reason. PUA skills, psychology, Positive Masculinity are all compensations for deficiencies. They go beyond behavior modification – that's the easy answer. PUAs teach a set of behaviors and scripts to be aped in order to mask a deficit. These are easy pickings for the JBY apologists because they are actions that generally don't match a person's prior personality. They're not "really" like that, so they're posers, or worse, they've been duped by guys hawking the PUA brand of self-help tools. What they don't see is the genuine desire to change and the reasons for it.

When we compensate, we improvise, we fake it till we make it; but who determines when we've stopped faking it? You do. I read all kinds of articles doubting the realized capacity a person has to adopt 'natural Game' into their personality. It's an internalization process for sure, but there has to come a point of transition where a Man's default response *is* his Game response. That's who he *is* now.

ALPHA

What you're about to read here is not going to make me any new friends. I know because any discussion of what constitutes Alpha Male characteristics in a Man always becomes clouded by the self-perceptions of how well we think we align with them. The 'community', the 'manosphere', the new understanding of gender relations that's picked up momentum for the last 12 years has always generated it's own terminologies for more abstract concepts. The danger in this is that these terms lack real, universal definition.

For purposes of illustrating a concept these terms are usually serviceable – we have a general understanding of what makes for a 'Beta' or a Herb, or a man who falls into a sublimated 'provider' mentality. Even 'Alpha' in a specific context is useful as an illustrative tool, when the subject isn't directly about 'Alpha-ness'. It's when we try to universally define what constitutes the qualities and attributes of an Alpha male that the sparks start to fly. So before you continue on reading further, think about what you believe makes a man Alpha.

Got it in your head now?

Good, now put all of that aside, purge that from your head, and read the next few paragraphs from the perspective that you don't know anything about Alpha.

The Alpha Buddha

I was first introduced to Corey Worthington, the Alpha Buddha, courtesy of Roissy and his post "Umm, sorry?" You can go ahead and look this up and read this from the Chateau's perspective, and I think the analysis is pretty good, but it might be easier for readers to simply search for "Corey Worthington" on youtube.

Corey Worthington was a teenage kid from Melbourne, Australia who made internet infamy by hosting a raucous house party, unbeknown to his parents, resulting in $20,000 of property damage. He was later interviewed by an attractive local news anchor who made efforts to shame him into self-realizations and apologies. It's probably better to simply watch the video (linked on my blog) to get an idea of Corey's Alpha cred.

I call Corey the Alpha Buddha not in the hopes that men will aspire to his almost Zen-like 'being' in Alpha, but rather to provide an example of Alpha in it's most pure form. He literally *is* Alpha, unclouded by pretense, afterthought, or conscious awareness of any influence that could have a hope of prompting introspection about his state.

Corey Worthington is a piss poor example of a human being, but he's a textbook example of Alpha. I could use a lot of adjectives to describe this kid, but "beta" wouldn't be one of them. What's funny, and a bit ironic, is this kid has probably never come across Mystery Method or "the PUA community" or even heard of 'peacocking' and he gets naturally what millions of guys pay small fortunes at PUA seminars to acquire over the course of a lifetime. He's a selfish little prick, but what makes him insulting to 'normal' men is his having the natural, internalized Alpha bravado that so many AFCs wish they had. If you could bottle and sell this Alpha essence, you'd be rich beyond imagine.

Right about now all of those self-affirming preconceptions you had about Alpha-ness (that I told you to stow away before reading this) are probably yelling to be let out of the mental box you put them in. ",..but, but Rollo, how can you possibly think this arrogant douchebag kid could ever be an example of anything remotely Alpha?!"

You'll be pleased to know I fully empathize your outrage. You work hard to be a "better man", you put in the self analysis, you paid your dues coming to terms with unplugging and reinventing yourself. You're a success, Corey is fuckup. Corey's not a better Man than you are, however, he understands Alpha better than you do.

Alpha is mindset, not a demographic.

Alpha is as Alpha does, it isn't what we say it is. There are noble Alphas and there are scoundrel Alphas, the difference is all in how they apply themselves.

There's a tendency to approach every "Alpha" argument from what a guy thinks is righteousness; ergo, his personal definition of Alpha is what appeals to his sense of virtue. He earned his Alpha cred, played by the rules, and by God people (women) should respect that. However, the sad truth is that prisons are full of Alpha males who simply channeled their drive toward destructive and anti-social endeavors. There are plenty of examples of indifferent Asshole Alphas who you wouldn't say are upstanding moral leaders at all, yet women will literally kill each other (or themselves) in order to bang them because they exude a natural Alpha-ness. Just as Corey does here.

There are Alpha drug dealing gang leaders, and there are Alpha husbands, fathers and leaders of industry. It's all in the application. Genghis Khan was Alpha as fuck, and a leader-of-men, but probably would be on most people's douchebag list for that era. Here's an illustration:

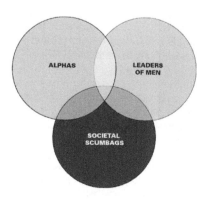

Guy's like Corey infuriate men who have invested their self-worth in the accomplishments of what they think ought to be universally appreciated and rewarded. So when they're confronted with a natural Alpha being undeservedly rewarded for brazenly acting out of accord with what they think the rules ought to be, they seethe with resentment.

The natural response in the face of such an inconsistency is to redefine the term 'Alpha' to cater to themselves and their accomplishments as "real men" and exclude the perpetrator. The conflict then comes from seeing his new definition of Alpha not being rewarded or even appreciated as well as a natural Alpha attitude and the cycle continues. Your respect (or anyone else's) for an Alpha has nothing to do with whether or not he possess an Alpha mindset. Three failed marriages and 100+ lays has nothing to do with a man having or not having an Alpha mindset. There are many well respected betas who've never had a passing thought of infidelity, or may have 300 lays either with prostitutes or because they possess fame or stunning good looks and women come to him by matter of course.

The take home message here is that you are not Alpha because of your achievements, you have your achievements because you are Alpha. You possess a mindset you either had to develop or it came naturally to you. I constantly field questions from young men asking me whether some action or behavior they displayed to a woman was Alpha, or Alpha enough. The real answer is that Alpha behaviors are manifestations of an Alpha mindset.

And just like Corey the Alpha Buddha, the introspect required to wonder if something was or wasn't Alpha wouldn't ever be a consideration enough to ask. You almost need to have a childlike understanding to really appreciate what Alpha really is. Kids get Alpha. Even the picked on, introverted, beta-to-be kid has a better understanding of Alpha than most adult men do because he lacks the abstract thinking required to rationalize Alpha for himself. Most men, by our socialization, and to varying degrees, lose this in-born Alpha mindset over time. The naturals, the Corey's of the world, have a better grasp on it's usefulness and re-purpose it; either to their adulthood advantage or their detriment.

Defining Alpha

I understand why guys, both of the red and blue pill variety have a problem with using the terms Alpha and/or Beta; depending on the perspective, terms that are definitive about what someone has an investment in make us uncomfortable. It's much more comfortable to put those issues into more subjective understandings because when we're objective about them we can't help the wondering about, or we doubt, our own status within that definition. Objective terms are very close to absolutes depending upon who's doing the defining.

From a generalized perspective, I feel that the terms Alpha and Beta are good reference points in assessing the characteristics that women find arousing (and attractive) in men for both short and long term mating strategies. However, I think that beyond these convenient terms, men need to be more realistic about how they apply to their own self-impressions in contrast with how women are interpreting the Alpha and Beta cues that they exhibit.

For the record, at points in my life I've personally been the worst, bottom scraping Beta, the douchebag Alpha rock star, and the strong (but lesser) Alpha father and husband. So it's with this in mind that I think guys shouldn't believe that their 'stars are set' and they'll never live up to the manosphere standard of Alpha.

Living Up

The reason that so many guys get so bent about what defines an Alpha is usually because they don't fit that general definition very well. So it's a logical ego defense to make necessity a virtue and redefine it to better suit their own conditions. It's exactly the same dynamic as the debate over Looks vs. Game. Game takes priority for those without Looks and vice versa. A personal definition of "what's Alpha?" becomes whatever plays to an individual guy's strengths, and women who can't appreciate them (i.e. all of them) are relegated to being less-than *quality* women. Sour grapes are sour, but deductively it makes sense; we want to be the embodiment of what we 'know' is attractive to women and others. The worst beta schlub you know thinks he's Alpha, because every woman he's ever known has defined and affirmed for him that being Beta is what women want.

Ethics of Alpha

The problem then is looking at the definition objectively.

In an objective light it's difficult to look at ourselves as not measuring up to an Alpha ideal. So it becomes the first recourse to cast suspicion on the whole idea of being Alpha at all. It's a pissing contest between immature men then.

Or is it? There is a LOT of observable, provable evidence that many so-called Alpha traits do in fact elicit very predictable, desired, favorable behaviors (usually breeding cues) in women. From an evolutionary psychology perspective Alpha is just as unprincipled, just as efficiently ruthless and uncaring as it's female counterpart – feminine Hypergamy.

So then the definition moves into an ambiguous moral ground; is it ethical to be / act Alpha? To be Alpha implies that you necessarily rise above a certain degree of common mediocrity depending upon the context – whether you do so like a guy from hotchickswithdouchebags.com or like a perfect "honorable" gentlemen is irrelevant, you still position yourself above "other guys". To some extent this is selfishness or implies a self-importance that questions moral tenets.

At this point I should also add here that women *never* doubt themselves on moral grounds for outshining their own competition in the sexual market place – they just do so covertly and with a polite smile, unburdened by ethical doubts. Hypergamy is its own excuse.

Alpha Selectivity

And that brings us to the subjectively deductive end of defining Alpha. Every sexual competitor seeks to disqualify their rivals from breeding opportunities. Most animals fight for territory or harem rights. Humans generally (though certainly not exclusively) do the same combat in the psychological. We seek to disqualify sexual competitors by calling into doubt the sexual credibility of a rival. "Yeah, he's really good looking, but that means he's probably gay" from a man, or "You think that blonde with the big boobs is hot? Girls who dress like that are usually sluts" from a woman are both psychological, sexually disqualifying forms of combat.

This also applies to the observably, provably, sexually successful male capable of OVERTLY flaunting his high sexual value with two (or more) concurrent women. He must be of low moral character to so flagrantly manipulate his multiple girlfriends, right?

His observable success, as a sexual competitor, conflicts with what a Beta believes should constitute a Beta-defined definition of Alpha-ness as it characterizes him personally. Thus, the polygamist either must be disqualified as a sexual competitor based on subjective (moral) grounds, or a guy is forced to alter his own definition of Alphaness and therefore his own self-estimate.

Every guy has *a* Game. Everyone thinks they are Alpha in their own way. Even the worst doormat Nice Guy, hammered flat by women for a lifetime, thinks his supplications or Cap'n Save-a-Ho mindset is the best way to win a woman's intimacy. He's invested in thinking he's unique in his understanding of how best to arrive at sex with a woman. Likewise, Alpha-ness is a moving target that's conveniently applied or disparaged based on personal circumstances.

Personally I believe Alpha-ness can, and does, have a concrete, objective definition. The problem arises when anyone asserts that they can definitively outline Alpha traits when it conflicts with the subjectiveness and ego-investments of those who define it personally for themselves.

So we get a wide variety of what makes a man Alpha – he's the guy of high moral character, princely ambition and integrity, as well as the self-important cad banging his wife and "their" girlfriend. They are *both* Alpha. Thus I would propose that while certainly contextual, objective Alpha-ness is NOT exclusive to social status or personal integrity, but rather an attitude of expressly manifested traits. These can be innate or learned, but the definition is not dependent on moral grounds (or a lack of).

A scoundrel and a champion can be equally Alpha or Beta in their own psyche.

THE ORIGIN OF ALPHA

"Safe sex, safe clothing, safe hairspray, safe ozone layer, ...too late! Everything that's been achieved in the history of mankind has been achieved by not being safe."
– Lemmy Kilmister, Mötorhead

A Rational Male reader Jeremiah presented me with a well worn question:

" My question is, Tomassi, do you think alpha traits are usually learned or genetically inherited? What percentage of modern men "get it" and of the men who "get it" how many of them have always "gotten it" and how many of them learned to adapt? It is hard to believe there are still naturals out there when feminism is being rammed up the anus of every man before he sprouts his first tooth."

I don't think distilling the essence of Alpha 'presence' in a Man is as subjective as most people feel compelled to qualify, enumerate or otherwise yammer on about in as personally identifying a manner as they can muster. In my estimation Alpha is a state of mind, not a demographic. The manosphere will endlessly debate the qualifications of what is Alpha, but I think for the most part, the influence of an Alpha mindset (whatever the qualifiers) is more or less agreed upon.

However, with this in mind, I think it's a perfectly valid question to ask whether an Alpha is born that way or molded into his Alpha mindset. This is actually the classic debate psychology has always put to its various schools of thought; Nature vs. Nurture – is a dynamic influenced by inherent, biological, environmental prompts or is that dynamic a learned, socialized and acculturated phenomenon? And of course the equally classic conflict comes from people attempting to define various dynamics in terms of absolutes, when to greater or lesser degrees a dynamic is influenced by both nature and nurturing elements.

While the Tomassi school of psychology is firmly planted in the nuts and bolts of behaviorism, it's also important to take into account that external influences can and too often do modify innate, inborn predilections – even inborn self-preservation instincts.

So with this in mind, my perspective on the origin of Alpha is that biology determines the starting point for Alpha, what happens to it from there is modified by a man's environmental conditions. Alpha 'energy', for lack of a better term, is to varying degrees, part of a male human's biologically determined "starting package"; from there, through social feedback, it's either refined and developed by his upbringing, acculturation and social affirming, or it's repressed, constrained and mitigated by his social environment.

When I was in art school one of my most influential teachers told me, "There are two types of artists; those who were born with a natural, innate gift for art, and those who lack that gift, but possess such a passion for art that it drives them to be good at it. The true masters are the artists that combine both natural talent and the drive that comes from a passion for it." I've always referred back to this model in my creative efforts, but I believe this model can be extended beyond just the artistic sense.

The Learned Alpha

Manosphere godfather, RooshV has an excellent breakdown of The Myth of the Natural that perfectly encapsulates the learning theory of Alpha. The premise behind this is that Alpha behavior, and consequently facility with women, comes as a set of modeled behaviors based upon trial and error:

If I were forced to agree on what a natural is, it would be a man who's a prodigy of sex— someone who gets laid way above other men with no formal instruction in game. This means he was not exposed to any 12 DVD "Cocky Humor" sets or seminars in a hotel room with three dozen other guys. You look at him and think, "Wow, he gets laid automatically. He was born to get laid!"

But he wasn't. Just because he didn't read a book doesn't mean he didn't learn through trial and error like you did, practicing his game on a large number of women. It doesn't mean that he wasn't conscious and deliberate with his behavior, incrementally improving his moves and tactics over a long period of time. He has experimented like you have experimented, and he has also connected his attempts with results to figure out what works and what doesn't.

He may not be obsessive about it enough to log his data into a spreadsheet, but he's mindful and aware of what he's doing. He understands the mechanism behind charm and can often turn it on or off depending on what he wants. He has learned the type of humor and story-telling that gets a positive response in women. The last thing you can say about him was that he was born into the world with the "automatic" ability to fuck a lot of girls.

Essentially what Roosh explores here is a very basic behavioral psychology premise – macro-psychological dynamics to micro-psychological schema are developed, deliberately or unconsciously, through a process of deductive trial and error management. Whether you're aware of it or not, everyone has Game to varying degrees. Every man you know has some concept of behaviors and mental attitudes he believes will best help him arrive at sexual intimacy with a woman. Even the worst Blue Pill Beta believes he has some idea of how best to get with a girl.

All of this proto-Game has been in a constant state of trial and error management since you were five years old and had your first interaction with the opposite sex on the kindergarten playground, right up to the point when you started reading in the manosphere and discovered the Red Pill. And you will continue to modify your old behavior and mental sets based upon the new information available to you after you adopt formalized Game.

In fact, in its rawest sense, the PUA community, the manosphere and all its permutations are really a meta-effort in behavioral modification by way of experimentation and information feedback.

For some this learning process comes easier than it does for others.

THE RATIONAL MALE

Again Roosh:

The reason he blows you away isn't because of his genetics, but because of how early he started. A unique set of circumstances threw him into the sex game years before you, during a time he was lucky enough to be surrounded by giggly schoolgirls. By the time you did your first approach, he had already practiced his game on hundreds of women.

While I do agree with this from a behavioral standpoint, this is where I have to depart from accepting Roosh's theory entirely. There are far too many biological and environmental determinants involved in developing an Alpha male to ascribe an Alpha status based solely on learned behavior. The simple, observable, fact is that a genetically better looking, more physically arousing male is going to statistically have more opportunities to experiment and develop his Alpha Game prowess than a less physically impressive male. In theory, a man with a more advantageous physical presence will "start earlier" in his process of deductively evaluating behaviors since his efforts will be more frequently encouraged by the women who are naturally attracted to his physique.

Unfortunately all of that assumes developing a behavioral set in a vacuum. There's literally a world of environmental conditions and variables that would predispose a man towards behavioral development of Alpha status or (more often) limit him from it. Roosh touches on this:

At this point you may be thinking, "Well, there have to be guys who were born with it. Look at Mozart!"

Nobody questions that Mozart's achievements were extraordinary compared with those of his contemporaries. What's often forgotten, however, is that his development was equally exceptional for his time. His musical tutelage started before he was four years old, and his father, also a skilled composer, was a famous music teacher and had written one of the first books on violin instruction. Like other world-class performers, Mozart was not born an expert—he became one.

I don't think this example excludes for a natural, innate talent, but it does help to illustrate the environment's role in molding a person by limiting or encouraging his behavioral development and ultimately his personality. In the Mozart example we see the success story (the story of a master artist) of a natural talent encouraged and developed to potential by favorable external conditions. Mozart was the perfect storm of natural talent and an ideal environment for nurturing it, thus giving him the advantage of an "early start" in his behavioral trial and error efforts.

My reader Jeremiah laments, *"It is hard to believe there are still naturals out there when feminism is being rammed up the anus of every man before he sprouts his first tooth"* and of course this is a negative example of an environment (deliberately) averse to nurturing an Alpha mindset. There's no shortage of examples, but feminization from a behavioral psychology perspective, is nothing less than a socialized effort in deliberate behavioral modification of men's natural drives and predilections to better fit the feminine imperative.

As men socialized in an all-encompassing, pervasive, fem-centric reality, we tend to see "Natural Alphas" as outliers because somehow, through some combination of innate gift and external development, these Men have developed themselves into an Alpha state despite the meta-environment we find ourselves in.

The Natural Alpha

A lot of people call my credibility into question when they read my holding Corey Worthington up as an example of an apex Alpha. Guys who believe that Alpha should necessarily mean "virtuous leaders of men" are understandably insulted by Corey's indifferent Alpha swagger. The 'Qualities of Alpha' debates aren't going away, but I think there's an overall consensus among the manosphere and legitimate psychologists alike that there is an innate (probably testosterone fueled) Alpha drive that manifests itself in human males.

No one has to teach the average, healthy, five-year-old boy how to be Alpha – he gets it on his own. In various contexts that 'lil' Alpha' wants to explore his surroundings, take risks, see what works and see what doesn't, even when the consequences may be endangering himself or destroying the thing he took apart to see how it worked. It may manifest as a boy attempting to ride wheelies on his bike or a kid tinkering with his dad's computer, but that unrefined, irrationally confident, Alpha swagger, is by order of degrees, an innate element unique to the male condition.

When a boy is unencumbered with an adult capacity for abstract thinking (ages 3-21 progressively) he is as Alpha as he will ever be. He is unapologetically Alpha and it takes a lifetime, and an entire world of feminized social conditioning to repress and/or crush that Alpha vigor and turn him into the pliable Beta the feminine imperative needs to insure its social primacy. This is precisely why the raw, irresponsible, irrepressible, obliviously un-self-aware Alpha energy of the Alpha Buddha/Corey Worthingtons of the world offend our sensibilities so well.

All of the Game theory, PUA techniques, even feminine-serving appeals to Man-Up! or any other effort designed to help men better mimic or internalize an Alpha behavioral or mind set, all of those efforts' latent purpose is to return a man back to that primal Alpha energy the five-year-old you had in spades.

THE CONTEXTUAL ALPHA

In March of 2012, James Hooker, a 41-year-old married father left his wife and kids for his 18-year-old-student. He resigned from his job at Enochs High School in Modesto, California over the scandal that shook up a community and put one mom on a crusade to save her daughter from a man she called a "master manipulator."

The girl, Jordan met her teacher as a freshman, but both maintain nothing physical happened until she turned 18. Hooker claimed he saw Powers as "just a student" and had no romantic feelings toward her at first, but when her 18th birthday came around, things changed.

They changed so much, in fact, that Hooker, left his wife and three kids (one of them a 17-year-old Enochs high school student as well) so that he could move in with Jordan.

Well, as is manosphere godfather Roissy's (now Heartiste) wont to do, the Chateau (Roissy's blog) boldly nominated James Hooker as Alpha of the Month.

As expected the post's comments got heated, but that's not the end of it. The SoSuave forum discussion thread created by the (sometimes overly) passionate members in response really gets down to the meat of the matter:

How "Alpha" will Mr. Hooker be seen by the general public?

How "Alpha" does the 18 year old's friends think he is? (If she has or had any at this point.)

What about new employment for the infamous Mr. Hooker? Will he take his 'soulmate' to work functions he may be required to attend?

There are probably loads of weird situations they will find themselves in. Or will they become a pair of social recluses?

Think about it. That dude isn't Alpha he's more of the Little Rascal's Alphalpha. Pathetic nerd.

Before I launch into my take on this situation I feel it's incumbent upon me to throw out this disclaimer; I do not condone Hooker's actions. At my time of writing this I have a daughter who will turn 15 in April and if there is any better indictment of the delusions of empowered single mothers and the inherent necessity of a strong, positive, masculine influence in a child's upbringing, of either sex, I can't think of it. Kids need the resolute, protective Fathers that far too many 'strong, independent women®' emphatically resist, run off, or covertly despise – only to further shame them for a lack of presence when an incident such as this occurs.

That said, I agree with the Chateau's assessment – Hooker is an Alpha, but only contextually so.

From Roissy seminal 16 Commandments of Poon (emphasis mine):

XII. Maximize your strengths, minimize your weaknesses

In the betterment of ourselves as men we attract women into our orbit. To accomplish this gravitational pull as painlessly and efficiently as possible, you must identify your natural talents and shortcomings and parcel your efforts accordingly. If you are a gifted jokester, don't waste time and energy trying to raise your status in philosophical debate. If you write well but dance poorly, don't kill yourself trying to expand your manly influence on the dance floor. Your goal should be to attract women effortlessly, so play to your strengths no matter what they are; there is a groupie for every male endeavor. Except World of Warcraft.

As a teacher, James Hooker is afforded a default status authority. To students in a classroom, being the teacher confers a contextual presumption of mastery and thus a de facto social proof is conferred upon that person. In that theater, in that environment, the teacher is Alpha. A uniformed police officer is perceived as Alpha in his given role, despite his personally being a chump when off duty.

As Roissy illustrates, Hooker was playing to his strengths. In virtually any other social setting he'd be perceived as a beta. The SoSuave forum and damn near every other casual observer peg this guy for the Beta-Symp he undoubtedly is, but in that classroom, to a 14 year old girl who gradually matures into an 18 year old woman, Hooker is Alpha, and probably the only Alpha she'd ever experienced.

How "Alpha" will Mr. Hooker be seen by the general public?

In all likelihood, he'll be more publicly reviled than legitimate sexual predators when the genders are reversed. The great unwashed masses in the pop culture narrative don't recognize the legitimacy of Alpha influence as it is. To them it's psychological manipulation, and to a calculated extent it really is, but the real question that nags them is *why* that manipulation is effective. They'll blame it on the naiveté of the girl, and her seeking a father figure, as well as the lasciviousness of Hooker, but what's really uncomfortable is *why* the Alpha influence works.

What about new employment for the infamous Mr. Hooker? Will he take his 'soulmate' to work functions he may be required to attend?

It's precisely because of Hooker's subscription to the soul-mate myth that he reeks of Beta. I have no doubt that he fluidly convinced himself of his noble intent narrative, casting himself as the savior for his adoring princess. White Knights are very prone to using their delusions of chivalry to rationalize good intent into the same behaviors they'd condemn in Players, PUAs or typical 'other guys' in general. To venture a guess I'd expect that Hooker buys his own bullshit, and because of this he hasn't given an afterthought to how it will affect his career, his relationship with his family, his kids or any future social circle.

As an extension of this, along with his teaching job, Hooker has lost his contextual Alpha cred. As his young chippy matures more, she'll begin to see that contextual Alpha status erode with every progressive shit test he fails – and removed from the environment that made him Alpha, fail he will.

Alpha is as Alpha does

In context, James Hooker parlayed enough Alpha mojo to land a solitary 18 year old girl; one he had to invest in for at least 4 consecutive years to consolidate on. In fact, I sincerely doubt he had any idea that he was situationally an Alpha to the point that he thought he could intentionally manipulate this girl with it.

There is a vast difference between the contextual Alphaness of Hooker and the subconscious Zen mastery of it in Corey Worthington – the Alpha Buddha. Both of these guys are an affront to the sensibilities of the "Alpha = Leader-of-Men" faction of Alpha definers, but both tap into a common root of Alpha energy that women naturally respond to.

It's discomforting to think that the brave Marine fighting in Mogadishu, commanding the noble respect from his country and peers taps into the same Alpha energy that makes a guy like James Hooker attractive to women. Same Alpha, different context.

Hypergamy is a cruel mistress.

Jerry Seinfeld dated and married his wife when she was 18. And while it caused a brief stir in the press, Jerry's wider Alpha appeal pushed this story out of the headlines. Elvis Presley, Jerry Lee Lewis, both were banging and/or marrying underage girls, but were given an Alpha pass then and now. As I stated, I'm not condoning it, in fact I find it deplorable, but I do understand why it occurs.

CHAPTER 2

PLATE THEORY

PLATE THEORY I

ABUNDANCE AND SCARCITY

Spin more plates.

This is the main premise behind Plate Theory. Imagine for a moment a plate spinner. They're kind of like jugglers, but require a real finesse and dexterity to maintain a spinning plate atop a long, thin stick.

Just like the plate spinner, a Man needs to have a lot of simultaneous prospects spinning together. Think of each plate as a separate woman you are pursuing. Some fall off and break, others you may wish to stop spinning altogether and some may not spin as fast as you'd like, but the essence of plate theory is that a man is as confident and valuable as his options. This is the essence of the abundance mindset – confidence is derived from options.

This principle is the key to solving so many of the problems that dog the heels of Beta AFCs and recovering AFCs. In fact I would say that this ideology should be the cornerstone to success for a man in many facets of life, not simply attracting and keeping women. A man with options has power, and from these options and this sense of power, a natural sense of confidence will manifest itself. A man without options becomes necessitous and this leads to a lack of confidence and a scarcity mentality. Necessitous men are never free.

As we progress through this section, keep in mind the Cardinal Rule of Relationships:

The Cardinal Rule of Relationships
In any relationship, the person with the most power is the one who needs the other the least.

When a man spins more plates, when he has irons in the fire, when he is pursuing multiple women simultaneously, when he has options equally worth exploring, a man will have a natural, subconscious (but not exclusively) understanding that if one prospect does not expand, others very well may. This understanding has manifestations in a man's behavior that women key on covertly. There are mannerisms and attitudes that a man with options will subconsciously convey to prospective women that they interpret, and give this man a value as a commodity to be competed for with other females.

On my blog and in the PUA community, men are taught to emulate this behavior since it is a key element in attraction and interest. Being Cocky & Funny is one such technique that trains a confidence behavior that (more often than not) essentially masks a deficit of options. In other words, C&F is a natural behavior for men with options that must be compensated for by those who don't. This is why the 'natural' Alpha male seems to exude C&F effortlessly while those without the benefit of more plates spinning (or the confidence in the ability of spinning more) struggle with simple things like eye contact or initiating approaches. This is also a fundamental principle in the "I don't give a fuck" mentality that pervades community technique – it's much easier to actually not "give a fuck" if you have other prospects going simultaneously.

Shotgun Logic

One very important benefit that Plate Theory provides for a man is that it greatly curbs the propensity for ONEitis both in and out of an LTR.

Outside of an LTR, most guys subscribe to what I call the Sniper mentality. This is the AFC that applies all of his time, effort and resources to patiently waiting out his target, waiting for that perfect opportunity to summon enough courage in the most precise of conditions to take his one shot at the girl, who by then is the focus of his ONEitis.

This process can take anywhere from a few weeks to a few years in extreme cases, but all the while he voluntarily sacrifices his most valuable of resource – potential opportunity. The man who subscribes to Plate Theory can more easily avoid this situation as he goes hunting for women with a Shotgun; scattering as much influence across the broadest area possible. While the AFC fishes with a single line and a single hook, the Plate Theorist fishes with a trolling net, selecting the fish worth keeping and tossing back those who aren't.

Inside an LTR, Plate Theory becomes more specified. The AFC placates and identifies with his partner because the balance has shifted to her advantage since he reinforces her understanding that she is his only source of intimacy. I can't think of a better recipe for ONEitis since he become progressively more dependent on her as his only source of intimacy.

The man who maintains, at the very least, the covert perception of options, either profes-sionally or on an intersexual level (i.e. social proof that other women will compete for him) maintains this power balance. Most successful men have an innate understanding of this and this explains their popular reservations for committing to marriage,

In an LTR (long term relationship), Plate Theory becomes a subtle dance of perception and recognizing how your partner interprets understanding a particular man's options, but regardless, it reduces a guy's tendency to regress into ONEitis in an LTR from his own self-perception and the confidence it inspires.

Natural Selection

Spinning more plates allows you more opportunity to select from the largest pool of prospective choices and date them or drop them as you see fit. This has two benefits. First, it serves as valuable, though non-committed, experience for learning what a man requires for his own personal satisfaction. Experience teaches harsh, but it teaches best and the breadth of experience serves a man well. Who's insight is more beneficial, the man who's sailed the world over or the man who's never ventured beyond a lake?

Secondly, opportunity and options make a man the *prize*. Rock stars, professional athletes and movie stars aren't irresistible to women because of their celebrity, but because they blatantly, and with the highest form of social proof, prove they have options that other women will jealously compete for as well as the confidence that this unconscious knowledge naturally manifests itself in them.

What Plate Theory is not

Critics of Plate Theory will often take a binary stance in their arguments with this idea stating that *"they could never be with more than one woman at a time out of respect for her"* or *"so I should just lie to her and see other girls on the side?"* to which I'd argue that these are feminized social conventions that attempt to thwart a man's options in order to establish and / or maintain women as the prime selectors in intersexual relations.

If it can be conditioned into a boy / man to 'feel bad' about seeing more than one woman at a time, or non-exclusivity in his relations with women, it only better serves the female-as-chooser dynamic. To be sure, women are naturally the filters for their own intimacies, but it is essentially men who do the sexual selection. The common trope that women do the sexual selecting is false – it's just that men's side of the sexual selection equation is a threat to feminine primacy in sexual selection. The latent purpose of social conventions that sublimate men's sexual choosing are designed to put selection of intimacy on a conditional basis that favors women, and as long as men will internalize this women will have a preconstructed social high-ground.

The way to circumvent this dynamic is brutal honesty and a commitment to truthful, non-exclusivity with the plates you're spinning. If you keep your options above board and are honest with any one girl and yourself about your choice to be non-exclusive, you not only remove the teeth from this convention, but you also reinforce yourself as a man with options (or at least perceived options).

Further, critics will offer "well gee, if I did that with any woman she'd push off and dump me" to which I'll refute – not if you establish this honestly from the outset. Most guys who've swallowed the 'female power' convention are too afraid or to preconditioned to even consider this as an option for seeing women. Letting a woman know, or covertly perceive, that you wont be exclusive to her pushes your commodity level up and implies options and potential success she'll compete with other women to be associated with.

That said, Plate Theory is also, most definitely not, a license to be indiscriminate with women. Just because you can spin a plate doesn't necessarily mean you should spin that plate. Some aren't worth spinning and a man with options should have no reservation about letting one go for a better one or two. In fact a man ought to be more discriminating in this regard since it affords him the best available from the largest selection.

PLATE THEORY II

NON-EXCLUSIVITY

Women would rather share a high value Man than be saddled with a faithful loser.

The following is a quote from a Rational Male reader:

"I just started applying Plate Theory, and I have to say with all honesty that this is probably the best thing I've ever done in my entire life. The feeling of having options is addictive; the whole idea that you don't come from a necessitous emotional state is genius, and in fact the more options you have, the more attractive you become to women (through the unconscious changes in your behavior), the more women become attracted to you, and the more options you have. Once you get it started, it's hard to stop it.

Recently I've been Spinning Plates with some success, but there comes a point when I risk one girl finding out about another. How do I handle this without the risk of losing one of my plates? Should I even bother with the effort of spinning plates that aren't as high a value as others?"

Real options are the cornerstone of confidence, so try not to think of it in terms of risk – as in you're risking the loss of "a great girl". Most guys get to a point where Game and plate spinning give them their first taste of real options to select from or fall back on when another doesn't pan out. The problem arises when they spin enough plates successfully to the point where they think they've maxed out to their "best" option and the old Beta mindset of the scarcity mentality returns. Most times a guy who newly practices Game and plate spinning never really spins plates per se; he uses it for the first monogamous opportunity that's been eluding him for so long and calls it quits, so he never actualizes and internalizes an abundance mentality.

Spinning Plates doesn't necessarily mean you're having sex with all of your plates.

It's more of a spreading out of your efforts across a wider pool of subjects. Some will reciprocate, and those you entertain. Others will not, or prove to be less desirable, and those you let fall. This isn't as difficult as it sounds once you've established your own resolve to be non-exclusive.

At some point a woman will attempt to corner you into exclusivity and this is where your resolve will be tested. Women love to say how they have Rules, well, you must have Rules as well. This means not shacking up with a woman, not slipping into any routine with her, not calling her more than necessary to set up another sporadic date, saving your weekends for women who've had a proven interest level in you (i.e. sex or physical intimacy) and relegating those who haven't to Tuesdays & Wednesdays.

This may seem like a lot of micromanagement, but once you put it into practice, in as pragmatic a way possible to accommodate your life, you'll find that the decisions you make regarding the plates you are choosing to spin will become automatic.

If you feel that you have something to lose with a particular girl, you're no longer spinning plates – you're thinking and approaching dating in terms of exclusivity. Long ago on the SoSuave forum the most enigmatic of members named POOK's came up with a great quote:

"Women would rather share a high value Man than be saddled by a faithful loser"

A lot of guys (and almost every woman) have a big problem with the truth of this because they take it too literally. POOK wasn't suggesting that you overtly declare that you'll be open to other options and that your girls should consciously be expected to accept this. Every woman takes this quote in this way, and with good reason because they don't want to seem like an easy mark. When it's on the table like that it unsurprisingly becomes an affront to their pride and self-worth. However, in practice, non-exclusivity has to be covert. It needs to be implied, not declared. Thus you see the truth in POOK's observation – women's behavior will bear him out. Imagination and competition anxiety paired with implied non-exclusivity are the cornerstones of successful plate spinning.

Become the commodity she's looking for.

A high value Man can spin plates, and sometimes those plates suspect there are, or *know* there are, other plates in his rotation. Women will tolerate this so long as he remains high enough value (or effectively presents that perception) to here from a sexual market value perspective. If not, hypergamy will move her along to another high value Man.

As I state in Plate Theory I, some plates fall off to be replaced by new plates. You must be willing and confident enough to let some of them fall. This is a tough reality for recovering chumps, new to Game, to accept. Deprivation has conditioned them to hang onto a "sure thing" and this becomes all the more difficult when the plate they happen to drop was the first woman they'd ever successfully applied Game to, or was hotter than any girl they'd previously been with.

As I mentioned earlier, you don't have to be sexual with every one of the plates you're spinning (this used to be called "dating" in the days before serial monogamy became the fashion). It's the potential in knowing that you could be, or that there are women on stand-by who will value your attention that prompts a competitive anxiety in women.

If you are sexual with some of the plates you're spinning, so much the better since you know that they're proven commodities and if one isn't performing as you'd like, you have the unconscious knowledge that others will, or you have the proven ability to generate more options for yourself.

Monogamy is a byproduct, not a goal.

One of the biggest obstacles guys have with Plate Theory is breaking themselves of this 'LTR-as-Goal' mentality.

Obviously I'm not anti-monogamy, however monogamy should never be a goal in and of itself; it should be a by-product of Plate Theory, but only when you've properly filtered through enough plates to understand how options play into confidence and controlling the frame. The frame you enter into a committed monogamy with is imperative to the health of that relationship.

If a woman is unwilling to be non-exclusive with you (i.e. "she'll leave me if I see other girls" fear) she isn't a plate to spin. This seems counterintuitive to a guy with an LTR-as-goal mentality, and it is, but the guy who can fearlessly, and honestly stay above-board with his intent is the one who'll be spinning more plates and dating within *his* frame.

Most guys (AFCs in particular) are deathly afraid of losing that ONE perfect girl and so never even attempt to spin more than one plate, much less have any others to compare her 'perfection' to in the first place. I've even seen PUAs do exactly this. They're so impressed with the success of newly perfected techniques that they settle for the ONE 'dream girl' and find that their attentions become valueless to her because she perceives she is his only option for intimacy, his script gets flipped on him, and he gets marginalized. It's not a failure in technique, but rather a failure in his mindset.

So what do you do to establish your plates and be truly, and successfully, non-exclusive with women?

Initially I'd suggest doing exactly what most women have perfected for the better part of their lifetimes – internalize an intentional ambiguity with women. Women practice Plate Theory by default – they play the coquette (hard to get), they know how to be ambiguous enough to keep their options open, but not so much as to let a guy's interest fail. They naturally know that we only chase what runs away from us. They never commit fully, but still keep the carrot in front of the donkey.

Women communicate *covertly*, with gesture, with looks, with veiled meanings – you have to communicate your intent to be non-exclusive *covertly*. Never *overtly* tell a woman you've got other plates than her spinning. Allow her to discover this by your mannerisms, your behaviors, and definitely by your availability to her.

Create value through scarcity, don't be so available to her, but just enough to keep her interest and allow her mind to consider that maybe you have other options. Even when you don't. Fomenting this anxiety is a *very* useful tool for you while you do get more plates to spin. Even the ambient confidence that comes from knowing you have a past, proven, ability to generate more sexual options for yourself will manifest itself in your personality and trigger this competition anxiety.

At some point a woman will resort to overt communications when she's run out of options in her covert communications tool set. This is the point the anxiety becomes unbearable and the need for security forces her to be overt.

This is usually the stage at which she's ask something direct like, "where is this going?" or "am I your girlfriend?" or she may even give you an ultimatum. See this for what it is, she feels powerless and this is a press to commit. This is the point at which you will end up as a "cheater" or you'll continue to spin plates.

You actually have a lot of options in this situation, in fact more than you will ever have with any individual woman. You can of course take the coward's path and just agree to exclusivity with her, but in doing so you lose all options (for as far as you're willing to commit) as she intently becomes your only means of intimacy. She becomes the broker for your options and sexuality, and you lose power, whereas before *you* were in control of your sexual availability.

You could continue to spin her as well, but bear in mind she's resorted to overtly confronting you about it and it wont be the last you hear of it. Depending on how long you've had her around, you may simply just let her drop. You might also keep her going, but let her cool a bit and come back to her in a few week's time. Again, this seems counterintuitive, but your attention will either wildly increase in her value of it or she'll simply bug out in which case it wasn't worth pursuing and you aren't wasting your time and effort on a woman with less than 100% interest level and desire.

Confidence is derived from options.

Don't think of plate theory as a filter so much as it is a means to reinforce confidence. If you were to step into the ring with a professional MMA fighter right now it'd probably be suicide for you. However, train for a few years, spar with other fighters and win a few bouts and you'll probably be confident enough in your past performances that you know you can hold your own in the ring. That's the idea, confidence derived from the options of non-exclusive women in hand, and from having successfully generated those options in the past.

It's not a numbers game, it's a non-exclusivity game. The goal isn't racking up as many women as humanly possible in order to sift through the throng and find that one little golden flower. In fact that's the key to disaster. There is no Quality Woman, that's an idealization. Some are better than others of course, but you don't find the perfect woman, you make the perfect woman. There is no needle in the haystack – that is Scarcity / ONEitis thinking – the point is to mold yourself and any woman who you do exclusively end up with into your own frame. This is a process that should come before you commit to exclusivity, not after. The world is filled with guys forever trying to catch up, control the frame and be the Man they should've been long before they entered an LTR. They spend the better part of their LTRs/Marriages trying to prove that they deserve their girl-friend's / Wife's respect when they'd have done better in letting her come to that conclusion well before the commitment through a healthy dose of competition anxiety.

PLATE THEORY III

TRANSITIONING

You cannot help anyone until you've first helped yourself.

The following was posted with permission from a consult I did.

"Hi Rollo, my name is Akash and I am big fan of your posts. They are always lucid, logical, and insightful.

I discovered the community about 5 months ago after yet another failed relationship characterized by highly AFC behavior on my part. I ended it with a tremendous amount of guilt as I felt that because she was a "good person" I ought to have made it work even though I wasn't in love with her. I am 27 years old.

Based on your posts I would really appreciate your advice on two issues:
(1) how to make the best use of my impending return to school in May for a second undergraduate degree and;
(2) how to overcome the cognitive dissonance I feel about pursuing women outside the confines of a committed relationship as I still suffer from social conditioning that tells me I will hurt women by pursuing primarily sexual relationships with them and so it is immoral to do so.

If you would like to post a reply on the forum, rather than by a PM, for the benefit of others that is fine with me. I wanted to direct these queries to you though as I believe I could benefit from your worldly wise opinion.

Sincerely look forward to hearing from you.

Best,
Akash"

The following was my response:

To begin with, you've only been involved in the "community" for the past 5 months so the first thing I'm going to tell you is that it takes time to mold your personality and unlearn mental schemas you've become conditioned to consider integral parts of your current personality. One of the biggest obstacles most men have with accepting the fundamentals of a positive masculine mindset is the attitude that personality is static and uncontrollable by them.

A lot of this "that's just how I am" mentality comes from this basic conditioning and needs to be addressed from the outset since this almost universally is an ego-investment on the part of a guy who's probably emotionally distressed, confused and/or frustrated.

Understand now that personality is ultimately what YOU determine it to be. This isn't to say that external factors don't influence personality; indeed these variables and outside influences are exactly the reason men such as yourself do seek out the community. However, it is you who determine what is comfortable for you and what will constitute the traits that makes your personality your own. You are most definitely not a blank slate, but you have the capacity to erase parts you don't like or are unusable and rewrite new parts that you like and prove efficient.

Issues

(1) *how to make the best use of my impending return to school in May for a second undergraduate degree.*

This all depends on what your own personal goals are. The best use you can make of this time is to devote yourself completely to achieving the purpose for which you decided to pursue a second degree in the first place. I can only assume you are working for this degree with a set outcome in mind, but is this what you truly want? I ask this because I know far too many men who've altered the course of their lives to better accommodate the women in their lives or to facilitate their insecurities and fear of rejection.

It's not an unfamiliar story to me to hear of how a guy opted for a certain university or a career path because he'd convinced himself that it would sustain a relationship that he was fearful of loosing or he felt was his "responsibility as a man" to be 'supportive' of *her* ambitions at the sacrifice of his own. The conclusion of this scenario, more often than not, ends with a bitter man, mad at himself with the long term results of his choices after the woman he'd striven so long to accommodate leaves him for another man who held fast to his own identity and ambition – which is exactly what made him attractive to her.

I'm not sure how or if this fits into your conditions, but let it serve as an illustration for reclaiming and remolding your own personality. Only you have the hindsight to assess why you've made certain decisions in your life. I'm only asking you to be as brutally critical of your true motivations for making them. Maybe it's time you review why you decided to pursue a second degree?

(2) *how to overcome the cognitive dissonance I feel about pursuing women outside the confines of a committed relationship as I still suffer from social conditioning that tells me I will hurt women by pursuing primarily sexual relationships with them and so it is immoral to do so.*

Any reasonably attractive woman knows you'd like to have sex with her. It's a primal, chemical instinct and to be bluntly honest, there's nothing wrong with it. In certain Islamic sects men are allowed to take "temporary" wives for a set period of time in addition to their "permanent" wives so long as they support them financially. Some Mormons practice open polygamy in a similar fashion. Some men marry and divorce multiple times (and support them congruously) – also known as "soft polygamy".

All of these practices are considered, to a greater or lesser degree, moral. The dissonance occurs when the rationalizations for a behavior conflict with the motivations for it and the associative psycho-social stigmas that get attached to it. Sorry for the $10 words here, but your feelings of guilt or hesitancy in a desire to explore multiple relationships is a calculated result of a very effective social conditioning with a latent purpose meant to curb a natural impulse.

Recognizing this is the first step to progressing beyond it and actually using it (responsibly) to your own advantage. As men, our biological impetus is a desire for unlimited access to unlimited sexuality with females bearing the best physical attributes. Ever wonder why pornography has been an ever-present element of human society for millennia? It simulates exactly this (virtual) access.

This is a rudimentary fact, and on some level of consciousness both men and women understand this. No amount of proselytizing or social conditioning will erase what God and evolution hard-coded into our collective bio-psychological desires and behaviors. Admittedly, social conventions have historically made a good run at limiting this drive, but it can never (nor should it ever) purge this, because in essence it is a survival-ensuring attribute for us.

I wont argue against the utility in the latent purpose of absolute monogamy. No other method proves more valuable in parental investment and developing a strong masculine and feminine psyche in a person than that of a committed, opposite sex, two-parent family.

I feel it's necessary to add here that I am thoroughly unconvinced that gender identity is exclusively a set of learned behaviors as many in the mainstream would try to convince us of. There is simply too much biological evidence and the resulting psychological/behavioral response to gender differences to accept this, making it vitally important that a child (and later a healthy adult) be taught a healthy appreciation for both the masculine and feminine influences in their psyches.

The genders were meant to be complimentary, not adversarial. I certainly would never condone infidelity based on just this principle alone since it seems the most beneficial for healthy adults. It's when this healthy monogamy becomes clouded by infantile, emotionality and insecure romanticisms, with the resulting expectations that are derived by them, that it becomes necessary for a man to cultivate an attitude of being the **prize**.

Adopting this mindset broadens his selection of opportunities for monogamy to his greatest advantage prior to committing to monogamy. In other words, if you are essentially sacrificing your capacity to pursue your biological imperative (unlimited access to unlimited sexuality), pragmatically, you'll want to choose a partner of the highest quality from the broadest pool of potentials you are capable of attracting.

The downside of this proposition is twofold. First, your ability to attract a sizable pool of quality 'applicants' is limited by factors you immediately have available. At 37, if all goes well, you'll be more financially stable and mature than you are at 27.

The 37 year old you will, in theory, be more attractive to a long term prospect than the 27 year old you.

Secondly, women's sexual value decreases as they age, meaning there is no guarantee that your beautiful, vivacious, 27 year old bride will remain so at 37. In fact the odds are she wont. All of this makes betting your biological imperative on monogamy critically important and thus deserving of the widest possible selection.

Men literally live and die according to their options, so it stands to reason they ought to entertain a prolonged period in their lives where they are open to exploring the most options they have access to while concurrently developing and improving themselves prior to making a commitment of this magnitude.

This is precisely where most men fail. They buy into, and internalize, psychological social contrivances (i.e. ONEitis) that are little more than effective means of embedding a self-expectation of accountability and liability to make this commitment, irrespective of maturity level or personal success (not simply financial success). The saddest ones, the AFC ones, are the pitiable men who carry these contrivances into marriage and even old age without ever understanding that they had more potential which they squandered due to an inability to see past these contrivances and learn to be selective based on experience.

A truly powerful Man jealously guards his most precious resources; his independence and his ability to maneuver. In other words his options and his ability to exercise them.

True power isn't about controlling others, but the degree to which you control the course of your own life and your own choices. Commitment to anything *always* limits this. When you step through one door, a hundred more close behind you. You're free to do what you want, right? You can always quit a job, divorce a wife, change your school, etc., but how many men do you know who are what they are today as a result of their own real doing, unfettered by how their choices impact their girlfriend, wife, kids, parents, etc.? By comparison, how many guys do you know who dutifully stick with a dead-end job that's slowly killing them because it's better than dealing with the consequences and backlash it would have on his family? Are they free to quit? Sure, but not without an impact on their families and relationships.

So where does this leave you? You have two paths as I see it. You can explore your options with multiple STRs and, should you decide to become sexually involved, do so while maintaining non-exclusivity with them. Put off and unlearn the expectations you've been conditioned to accept through (feminine beneficent) social contrivances and truly explore your opportunities while bettering your own conditions in anticipation for becoming monogamous at some later point.

Or, you can remain in your sense of moral doctrine (no shame in this) and still non-exclusively date and explore your options while you continue to better yourself with the caveat that you know you'll be limiting your depth of experience. I wont denigrate a decision to opt for this, but far too few religious men have the perseverance to stay objective in their decision to 'hold out' and overlook major character flaws in women they'd like to be their spouse in a furious rush to marry them and get to "the sex part." Better to fall short in conviction than make hurried decisions that will negatively alter your life.

Perhaps this isn't even what you're driving at? I don't know if it's a religious conviction or an internalized social contrivance that passes for one that's the cause of your hesitancy, but isn't it interesting that both are so closely associated? I know devout atheists who still believe in the fallacy of the ONE or the soulmate myth. Most women (and far too many men) look at me as if I'd denied the existence of God when I elaborate on why I think their eHarmony, induced fantasies of a soulmate are hogwash and psychologically damaging on a social scale.

Regardless, whatever your reasons, women should only ever be a compliment to a man's life, never the focus of it. When you start living for a woman you become that woman.

Never again compromise your own identity to receive the ever-changing approval she grants you. You have to be the **prize** at all times, not just while you're single. In fact, it's imperative that you remain so into an LTR. My suggestion to you is not to even entertain the idea of monogamy until you are established in your career for two years, after your college is complete. Play the field, do whatever, but do not commit even to a girlfriend.

Rather, make a commitment to yourself, promise yourself you wont allow yourself to let emotionality and conditioned expectations of monogamy dictate what your goals will be or how you'll achieve them.

It's called enlightened self-interest; you cannot help anyone until you've first helped yourself.

PLATE THEORY IV

GOAL-STATE MONOGAMY

Whenever a guy uninitiated to the concept of spinning plates reads the theory for the first time his first response is usually rejection of it because it conflicts with what I call a monogamy-as-goal mindset.

Understand, this is always going to be a tough stretch for any guy still plugged in to the feminine Matrix, but it's not limited to them, it's also the 'natural' guy who doesn't have much trouble attracting women. A male-specific, monogamy-as-a-goal mindset serves the feminine imperative, but it also has roots in our natural desire for security. So it makes anything even remotely like plate spinning counterintuitive.

The feminine imperative pounds into men's collective consciousnesses over the course of a lifetime that monogamy will cure loneliness, make them responsible, provide them with a constant supply of sex, and a host of other things that assures them it's "the right thing to do" and it's in their own best interest. This then leads the more option-less individuals to develop and practice Beta methods and rationales in accordance with what they believe (and have been told by) women is required of them in order to achieve their monogamous intimacy (i.e. the goal of everything).

So, understandably, when the principle of being non-exclusive is presented to them in a rational way (instead of a ridiculed way as it's normally passed off as) it conflicts with this perceived path to happiness in monogamy. The very idea that any man would be better off with more options in this arena of life, or could feasibly and logistically pull it off, seems foreign. As a counter to this he makes up rationales as to why it wont work or wont work for him.

Logistics

"I can't spin plates because I have too little time, I can't manage more than one girl without the other finding out, etc."

If you are indeed spinning plates in a healthy, upfront, non-exclusive way this should never be an issue. There are Game-aware Men with less time than most who manage 4-5 different girls in a week without having them consume all their leisure and business time.

I don't suggest that you go this route per se, because for the better part PUAs rely on a dishonesty in non-exclusivity. However, the reason they are capable of this is because they've perfected plate spinning effectively enough to have the plates spin themselves.

Most uninitiated Betas reason that they *must*, at all costs, apply a constant effort to each and every individual girl they encounter at risk of losing a "good one."

Besides this being indicative of 'soul-mate thinking', what they fear is losing a plate because they are unaccustomed to ever having had the leisure to do so. This is evidence of a scarcity mentality that is a result of their monogamy-as-goal preconditioning.

Plate Theory necessitates an attitude of fearlessness – not carelessness, fearlessness. When you're practicing Plate Theory your plates should call you. You are the **prize** and the Prince who's time is valuable and sought after. *You* should be the object of women's pursuit.

That said, you still have to make an effort to see them and keep the attention you do apply to them valuable, but this must be done with the attitude that if one plate falls you're confident in your other options or your ability to generate new options.

Personality Type

"I'm just not like that. I don't want to be considered a 'playah'. I could never do that to a woman. How can anyone be like that?"

This rationale is a common one and not limited just to chumps. There are plenty of otherwise confident, positively masculine men who'd still think they owe it to women to allow them to set the frame in their relationships without any fear of competition anxiety.

Players are men who're dishonest – they are not spinning plates because they are isolating each plate independent of the other, and this goes back to logistics. Of course you can't find time for anything else if all you do is *try* to coordinate each individual story with each plate for fear that they discover each other.

The plate spinning Man has no need for this, because he *never implies exclusivity to any plate*. Either they accept this or they're not a plate to consider. Done in a frank, honest, yet indirect way, you will not be a 'Player' and you will establish yourself as Man who's attention is worth a woman competing for.

Women would rather share a successful man than be saddled with a faithful loser, perfectly sums up Plate Theory vs. Monogamy-as-Goal mindsets.

Men in general gravely underestimate the power of female competition anxiety and how useful it really is. As I'll illustrate next, women are natural plate theorists – they are accustomed from a very early age to mitigate multiple sex-interests, they simply learn how to balance their indirect communications with that anxiety in their own plate spinning.

Anxiety in women is good for men. Even when they make no effort to use it or would never consider it if they knew it's usefulness it is always present. Everything a woman does on a daily basis is colored by competition anxiety. Make up, clothing, shoes (God, the shoes!), indirect communications with men and women, social contrivances, comparing and evaluating dates and possible suitors, everything is borne from this competitive desire to achieve security with the best possible guy and make damn sure the girl next door doesn't get him first.

This anxiety is analogous to men's consummate fear of rejection and all of the myriad rationales he'll create and the Buffers he'll devise to avoid it.

Bear in mind that monogamy is a dictate of the feminine imperative. It is the social contract that the feminine ultimately needs in order to quell a constant desire for security in a very chaotic world. When you are predisposed to monogamy-as-goal thinking, or trying to break yourself of this, understand that this is a tool of the feminine imperative.

That's not to discount the overall merits of monogamy, but it is to make you aware of how it's acculturated into men as a responsibility to providing monogamy. Men who find themselves in a state of internal conflict about abandoning monogamy-as-goal are really confronting a fundamental shift in their prior feminine conditioning.

PLATE THEORY V

LADY'S GAME

Female Plate Theory

For as often as I've mentioned women being natural plate theorists, I don't often go into detail about it. I think it's pretty well established that I completely disagree with idea that women will only fuck (or want to fuck) one guy at a time. I could outline several women I know from experience in this, but really, observing behavior will bear this out fairly predictably for most men. I will however agree that women are predisposed to, and are socially encouraged to, seek monogamy (once convenient), but as in all things female the talk rarely matches the behavior. Sexuality is a woman's first, best, agency and even the homeliest women know this – even when they're just complaining about other women using it.

The principle is that a woman's first priority is to seek out security, and even when confronted with the duplicity of women pluralistic sexual strategy, we'd be wise to bear this in mind when evaluating motives for behavior –their methodology is what's in question here.

There is an understandable confusion for guys in this respect. On one hand women present a constant facade that the fear of being perceived as a slut (i.e. concurrently fucking more than one guy at a time) is primary to their self-respect and respectability. However, this has to be tempered with the desire (both biological and psychological) to experience a variety of men in order to ensure the security/provisioning from the best among them. So in order to facilitate this women must practice a kind of calculated hypocrisy that is socially reinforced by the gender as a whole as well as some men (usually those so optionless as to excuse the behavior in order to get to her sexuality, or guys so conditioned that they overlook it as normal).

It is socially acceptable for a woman to blatantly spin plates.

Does this sound outrageous? While a woman who makes her sexual practices a bit too overt runs the risk of being perceived as a slut (which is dubious in this age as it is), most relatively attractive women covertly have a constant bullpen of starters ready to go to bat at any one time – these are also known as 'Orbiters'.

Orbiters are the attention providers, the "maybe" guys. It makes little difference in terms of available options which she chooses at any given time, the very fact that she has five or six of them pursuing her is enough to boost her sense of self-worth, her social status within her same-gender peers, and give her the confidence to drop any one of her plates at a moments notice for any reason knowing that 2 or 3 more guys (or 20 more on facebook) stand ready to take his place, no questions asked and prepared rationalizations at the ready.

Furthermore, this practice is socially reinforced by women doing the same thing and the social conventions constructed to excuse the behavior. It's the unspoken rule of a woman's prerogative; *a woman can always change her mind.*

This is a powerful tool for women – in any situation, if a woman doesn't choose to be sexual it is necessarily forced (or obligated), even when it's after the fact. Either the "Jerk" forced her, physically or emotionally, or she had thought she wanted to, but later reconsidered – it makes little difference. In all social situations the default is to side with the feminine, the "weaker sex" – women, from sympathy or empathy, and men, from a desire to eventually become intimate with them.

In either instance, the feminine prerogative is socially reinforced. That's important to understand because even by my focusing on it here as a male, my motives for doing so become suspect. That's how embedded this dynamic is – to question it risks ostracization. However, I also understand that for the greater part of women, this plate spinning dynamic isn't a conscious effort on their part. In fact I'd suggest that it's so thoroughly recognized that women default to it autonomously. Also, this is a good example of the first principle of power – when you have power, always feign powerlessness.

Free Reign

So, with a firm understanding that their behaviors will for the most part be excused, they are free to practice the feminine form of plate theory unhindered by social reprisal. The feminine plate spinning involves much more than sex though.

Remember, attention is the coin of the realm in female society. The capacity to command attention determines self-esteem, peer status, sexual selectivity, and a host of other factors in a woman's life, so spinning plates becomes more than just a "which guy am I gonna get with tonight" prospect. This dynamic and these factors are what makes women natural plate spinners. Even when a woman has no intention of ever becoming sexual with a "maybe" guy, his attention still has some value to her. It appeals to the long term prospective for security that's a continuous subroutine running in her hindbrain. This is the rudimentary psychology behind hypergamy.

Now, combine all of this with women's native language – covert communication – and it's natural for a man to assume that a woman will only ever become sexual with one guy at a time. This serves the latent purpose of keeping him in a kind of stasis. If he assumes women will only be sexual under the precondition of comfort and commitment she is free to spin plates (essentially weighing options) as she pleases and sample at will what she sees as in her hypergamic best interest at the time.

If the carrot looks good enough the guy will patiently pull the cart until such time as another, better carrot comes along. Either way he's in that stasis. If a guy were to see her social and psychological machinations for what they are, he'd never pull the cart – so it serves women best that men think commitment should always be required for intimacy, even in the face of her behavior directly contradicting this.

Plate Wars

Lastly, this social dynamic serves as a very effective weapon for women against each other. Competition anxiety between women is something men can exploit for their own plate spinning, but the reason it is useful is because women so readily use it against each other. For a woman to say another woman is a "slut" translates into an overt betrayal of this unspoken social contrivance. Essentially she's saying, "the rules are that women require commitment for sex, but here's one who'll never be worthy of any guy's commitment because she wont play by the rules you suckers think she will."

She is tacitly disqualified for a man's commitment and is, at least in the accusing woman's mind, a reduced threat in this feminine competition. She becomes exposed in the same game they're all playing and in being so, loses attention and therefore status and personal esteem.

It seems petty to guys, but it's really intra-gender warfare. Think of how many times an exceptionally attractive woman, that is completely anonymous to a group of women you happen to be with, will berate her based on appearance alone.

"She's must be a tramp if she dressed like that."

These are the same women who'll berate a man for basing his estimation of a woman on her outer appearance. This is manifested feminine competition anxiety. Ask a woman to name the most attractive female actress they can think of. Odds are it will be a woman (who as a guy you'd never think of) who presents the least threat of this anxiety.

Gentlemen, as I'm fond of saying, women will fuck. They may not fuck you, they may not fuck me, but they will fuck someone. The girl who bangs the hot guy at the foam party in Cancun on Spring Break within 5 minutes of meeting him is the same girl who wants you to believe that they'll only fuck one guy at a time and then after commitment. All women are sexual, you just need to be the right guy at the right time for the job.

PLATE THEORY VI

SCARCITY & ABUNDANCE

Plate Theory is for your benefit, not for women's.

That might sound harsh, but it's a method intended to increase your value as a commodity that works on two levels. First, the external – by practicing honest, non-exclusive dating you communicate to your prospective plates that you are in demand. I've gone so far as to tell men to foster this sense by never answering the phone from Friday to Sunday evening, even when they have no other plans.

The perception that your attention is sought after increases it's value – it's when men are too eager to get with a woman that their attention becomes worthless and interest levels decline. Nothing serves a man better than having 3 or 4 women competing for his exclusive attention and fostering in them that feminine competitive anxiety in as subtle and covert a way as possible. Make no mistake, it's a real art that women are all too familiar with themselves in their own inter-gender dealings. Women are natural plate theorists, they simply use their varying degrees of physical attractiveness to line their plates up.

Secondly, plate theory is for a man's own internal benefit. It's much easier for a man not to give a shit if he truly doesn't give a shit. It's far easier to deal with women on the basis of indifference when you have a subconscious knowledge that there are at least 3 other women who'll be happy to have your attention if one plays games with you.

The reason men fail most shit-tests women give them is because they subconsciously telegraph too much interest in a single woman. Essentially a shit-test is used by women to determine one, or a combination of these factors:

a.) Confidence – first and foremost
b.) Options – is this guy really into me because I'm 'special' or am I his only option?
c.) Security – is this guy capable of providing me with long term security?

By practicing Plate Theory, your mental attitude will be such (or should be such) that you will pass most shit-tests based simply on this practice.

Abundance thinking is the root of Plate Theory. A lot has been written about approaching women (and really life in general) from a position of Abundance. People often make the mistake of assuming that having a wide variety of choices tends to cheapen the commodity, and to a degree this is accurate, but it also allows for a better, learned awareness of which choice amongst the pool is common and which is of higher quality.

"...but Rollo, I'm so busy that I have no choice but to ignore and postpone. They sense it and seek me out. I worry that I'll create crazies. My weekends are jammed. At what point do we stop?"

This is a the best problem you can have. You've successfully flipped the script; you've gotten to a point where it becomes instinctive and your plates actively seek out your attention. By default, you're creating value by scarcity.

At what point do you stop? How old are you? If you're under 30 stay in the game. If you're over 30, stay in the game, but cool things off occasionally – the only time a man should even contemplate monogamy is after experiencing abundance. If you're inundated with women occupying your weekends, consider hooking up with a proven plate on a Thursday evening and reserve your weekends for your other pursuits.

Also, don't be afraid to clear your schedule to hang out with friends or do other things that interest you. Remember, scarcity increases value. Too many guys think that plate spinning is something that needs a constant effort, it doesn't. In fact applying yourself equally across all your active plates only pushes you closer to settling for one or two.

Most guys think that they have to continually spin their plates, you don't; if you're doing it correctly they'll spin themselves for you. The anxiety is that if you don't keep applying attention to any one plate she'll lose interest and fall off. Sometimes this is the case and you have to be prepared to accept it, some plates have to break in order to spin more, and that's OK. More often than not however, your scarcity will create value and mystique, thus they will pursue you for their affirmation.

Plate theory of course can be a means to an LTR, but bear in mind that it's essential that you practice it long enough and effectively enough to determine what a quality woman means to you and how to recognize her. As with most Game skills, the uninitiated will use them to some degree of success up to the point that he finds his idealized "girl of his dreams" and launch into a self-destructive LTR because his idealization was based on juvenile impressions rather than a mature understanding of what a quality woman's characteristics are. This is all due to a lack of concrete experience.

Spin plates for as long as possible, because once you do commit to an LTR, even with the tightest of Game you will lose a measure of the competitive anxiety that made your attentions valuable to any one woman. All your plates fall off *and* the girl you're engaged in an LTR with gets too comfortable. This is root of why men find that the woman they had hot sweaty monkey sex with when they were dating becomes more sexually reserved a few months after they're a couple. The competitive anxiety is relieved and therefore sexual frequency and quality is no longer a proving trait for her. That's not to say there aren't methods to stoke this anxiety in an LTR, but, by comparison to being single, the frame of the relationship doesn't have to be contested when she and you understand that she is your only source of intimacy and sex.

In a committed relationship, you simply cannot spin plates.

PLUGGED IN

AVERAGE FRUSTRATED CHUMP

In the "community" there's a lot of want for better terms. One of the major obstacles in the average guy's path to unplugging from his conditioned interpretations of gender relations is really coming to terms with the 'terms' we use. Somewhere on the net I'm sure there's a glossary of the common acronyms used in the "manosphere" outlining the various shorthand we use. Some of these terms have gone mainstream and I'm beginning to see even "legitimate" online journalists use LTR (long term relationship) or ONS (one night stand) somewhat regularly, meaning there's a common perception that others will already know what they mean.

The reason this is a obstacle for a lot of plugged-in guys is because it seems almost juvenile, like a tree house club for preteen boys. For me to draw comparisons of an acculturated, feminine social paradigm to the central plot of the Matrix movies, admittedly, that seems kind of silly. It's an apt comparison and a useful allegory when you understand the concepts behind it, but for a guy just coming to grasp it while being immersed in a feminine-primary socialization for his whole life, it doesn't click.

And predictably, women invested in that same socialization see the terminology as little more than little boys holed up in their tree house, throwing rocks at the girls below.

However, like any new developing science or art or technology there is always going to be a need to codify abstract concepts. We lack better terms so we're forced to create new ones to represent new concepts.

The AFC – average frustrated chump – was coined almost a decade ago with Mystery Method. It's seen a lot of modification over the years, becoming almost synonymous the use of the term Beta (beta male) or Herb (herbivorous male). In fact, although I use it often, I rarely read AFC in PUA blogs, forums or the 'community' at large.

Regardless of the terminology, the concept is really the crux of the term. Most AFCs, most guys looking in from the outside, can relate to the idea of what an average frustrated chump is – they can identify with it. Once they begin unplugging, the AFC idea comes into better focus and, usually with some discomfort, they realize how that term applies to themselves:

Qualities of an AFC

• **ONEitis** – First and foremost.

• **Subscribes to feminine idealizations**.

• **Supplication is supportive.** To comply with gender equalism she must increase, so he must decrease, relational equity is the basis of a rational relationship.

- **The Savior Schema** –reciprocation of intimacy for problems solved.

- **The Martyr Schema** – the more you sacrifice the more it shows devotion.

- **The 'Friends' Debt** – LJBF ("lets just be friends") and the pseudo-friendship as a means to prospective intimacy.

- Primarily relies on dating and social skills (or lack thereof) developed during adolescence and early adulthood

- A behavioral history that illustrates a mental attitude of 'serial monogamy' and the related insecurities that accompany it.

- A belief that women infallibly and consciously recognize what they want, and honestly convey this to them, irrespective of behaviors that contradict this. Uses deductive reasoning in determining intent and bases female motivations on statements rather than objectively observing behavior. Believes women's natural propensity is for rational rather than emotional thought.

- An over-reliance on rejection **Buffers**.

- **A belief in the Identification Myth**. The more alike he is, or can make himself, with his idealized female the better able he will be to attract and secure her intimacy. Believes that shared common interests are the *only* key to attraction and enduring intimacy.

- Believes and practices the "not like other guys" doctrine of self-perceived uniqueness, even under the condition of anonymity.

- Considers **LDRs** (long distance relationships) a viable option for prolonged intimacy.

- Maintains an internalized belief in the qualifications and characterizations of women that coincide with his ability (or inability) to attract them. Thus, he self-confirms the "she's out of my league" and the "she's a loose slut" mentalities on-the-fly to reinforce his position for his given conditions.

- Harbors irrational (often socially reinforced) fears of long term solitude and alters his mind-set to accommodate or settle for a less than optimal short term relationship – often with life long consequences.

The AFC will confirm a belief in egalitarian equality between the genders without consideration for variance between the genders. Ergo, men make perfectly acceptable feminine models and women make perfectly acceptable masculine models. Due to societal pressures he unconsciously self-confirms androgyny as his goal state.

This is anything but a comprehensive list. There are far more, but my intent here isn't to provide you with a list of criteria that qualifies an AFC ("you might be a chump if,.."), rather it's to give you some basic understanding to clarify the term, and round out the idea of what an AFC is.

Needless to say these mental schema are some of the impediments to unplugging, or helping another man unplug, from his old way of thinking. As I'm fond of repeating, unplugging chumps from the Matrix is dirty work. Expect to be met with a lot of resistance, but understanding what dynamics you may harbor yourself or those that a friend might cling to will help you in moving past the years of social conditioning. It's thankless work, and more often than not you'll also be facing a constant barrage of shit tests (from both women and feminized men) and ridicule in your efforts. Be prepared for it. Unplugging chumps is triagé – save those you can, read last rites to the dying.

In the next few sections I'll be explaining some of these plugged-in qualities in more detail.

PLAYING FRIENDS

Women have boyfriends and girlfriends. If you're not fucking her, you're her girlfriend.

"Rollo, how do I get out of the Friend-Zone?"

Never allow yourself to get into it.

Women have used the LJBF ("let just be friends") rejection for a hundred years because it serves an ego preservation function for her. To a greater or lesser degree, women require attention and the more they have of it the more affirmation they experience, both personally and socially. The LJBF rejection is a Social Convention that has classically ensured a woman can reject a man yet still maintain his previous attention. It also puts the responsibility for the rejection back on his shoulders since, should he decline the 'offer of friendship', he is then responsible for entertaining this 'friendship'.

This of course has the potential to backfire on women these days since the standard AFC response will be to accept an LJBF rejection in the mistaken hope of 'proving' himself worthy of her intimacy by being the perfect 'surrogate boyfriend' – fulfilling all her attention and loyalty prerequisites with no expectation of reciprocating her own intimacy.

I should also point out that this situation is analogous to men using women as "fuck buddies" – fulfilling all his sexual availability needs with no expectations of reciprocating commitment. Needless to say this merely positions the new "friend" into being the 'emotionally supportive' Beta counterpart to the indifferent Alpha she'll consistently bang and then complain about – also popularly known as the Emotional Tampon.

The LJBF rejection also serves as an ego preservation for her in that having offered the false olive branch of 'friendship' to him in her rejection she can also sleep that night knowing that she (and any of her peers) wont think any less of herself. After all, she offered to be friends, right? She is absolved of any feelings of personal guilt or any responsibilities for his feelings if she still wants to remain amiable with him.

Men get a LJBF rejection because of a process. These are the "friends first" mindset guys; the guys who put far too much emphasis on a solitary woman and wait her out until the perfect moment to attempt to escalate to intimacy, at which point her most comfortable rejection (Buffer) is to LJBF. This is made all the more easy for her because of the process the guy used to get to that point.

Sniper Mentality

Virtually all guys who get to the point of a LJBF rejection come to it because they fall in line with some variation of what I call a Sniper Mentality. They patiently wait for their one target, to the exception of all others, constantly attempting to prove their quality in doing so – meaning they emphasize a comfort level and try to be friends before lovers.

In essence they believe that desexualizing themselves will make them more attractive (by virtue of not being like "other guys") because they've bought into the idea that a woman must be comfortable with them first before they initiate intimacy. Once the AFC gets to a point where he's mustered enough courage to initiate, and he feels she 'should' be comfortable enough to appreciate him as boyfriend material, the Sniper takes his shot.

The problem with this process is that it bypasses essential stages of attraction and the necessary discomfort and sexual tension necessary for intimacy, and proceeds directly to a warm familiar, comfortable, (and ultimately anti-seductive) rapport, the exact opposite of arousal. If you think about this in terms of sex, this is the stage right after climax when she wants to cuddle, spoon and be wrapped up in her nice, secure oxytocin induced comfort.

This is the opposite of the testosterone fueled, sweaty, anxious and uncomfortable stage of arousal and intercourse before that release. So in terms of "friendship" and the Sniper Mentality, you've skipped arousal and gone straight to comfort. You're perceived as a stuffed animal she can hug and then put back on the bed. Thus, when that previously platonic stuffed animal uncharacteristically gets a hard-on and says "I think we ought to be intimate" her reaction is to think that everything you've done for her up to that point has been a grand ruse. "My God, all you wanted was sex this whole time?"

Her most predictable response is then the LJBF rejection.

The field has already been tilled by you, it's only one, very easy step for her to stay in that suspended comfort – "can't we just be friends?" And then the cycle repeats. The AFC believes the LJBF is a genuine offer (not a rejection) and then falls back into the Sniper Mentality. He mustn't have been convincing enough to prove his worth to her and therefore returns to further proving himself as the perfect boyfriend until he once again presses his intent of intimacy after another period. All this goes on apace until she becomes intimate with a 'real' boyfriend and/or he acquires a new target after realizing his efforts with the LJBF girl aren't bearing fruit.

The Friend Zone

The problem with a lot of the 'friend-zone' advice women tend to offer is that they cast doubt on whether a LJBF rejection is in fact a rejection and not a genuine offer of friendship. To which I'll say, the only reason the 'friend-zone' is such a common issue among men & women for so long is because it's been repeated so regularly and the outcome so predictable as a rejection.

A woman's behavior is always the only gauge of her intent, and thus when a rejection like LJBF has been so consistently met with the same outcome and behavior (as evidenced by millions of identical stories from men) it's only prudent for a Man to behave in kind.

A man's default response should always be to excuse him from the LJBF situation.

The reason for this is because it serves his best interest whether she is testing him or is rejecting him. If he is confident enough in himself to walk away from the sexually tense environment, he proves himself as decisive enough to put himself above being 'played' like this. Ergo, he leaves her with the impression that he is the **prize**, possibly has contacts with better prospective women and is confident enough to take away his attentions from her and thus passes any shit test she might have implied, while placing the responsibility of a re-connection on her (where it should be anyway).

If she has in fact had a change of heart (her prerogative, remember?) and is using the LJBF as a means to reject him, he still benefits from all of the above and plants the 'seed of doubt' in her about her initial estimation of his acceptability for her intimacy. Even if she is truly not interested in the guy, he walks away on his feet and not his knees, by playing "friend" with her and wasting still more time that could be far better spent with more productive prospects.

It is really one of the few win-win Game situations for a guy to make a wholesale withdrawal of his attentions when he is confronted with an LJBF. Women know all too well how an LJBF places social pressure on a guy to accept what basically amounts to an ultimatum of negative social proof, and that's a hell of a shit test no matter what her real intent is. If the guy turns down her offer of friendship, he's the dickhead, not her. But the guy that can do what common sense and gut instinct points out to him will be the one to succeed, with her, other women and himself.

Confrontation

Human being's natural inclination is to avoid confrontation. When a man makes an approach to intimacy with a woman this becomes confrontational. If she is unsure of a man's sexual acceptability for her intimacy she must resort to psycho-social, learned behaviors to diffuse this confrontation.

Preferably these techniques should be reinforced beforehand and proven to diffuse just such a confrontation, thus the LJBF response is acted out through generations of women across many different cultures – quite simply it works more often than not.

You can also apply this to the **Boyfriend Disclaimer**; women who not-so-nonchalantly weave into their casual conversation that they have a boyfriend in a preemptive effort to diffuse a potential suitor's interests. It's basically a proactive LJBF rejection – she reads your telegraphed intent and prevents your further pressing her for a date.

It's the guy who is unwilling to accept these conventions that makes the most lasting impressions of confidence with women. It goes against what our common human heritage dictates for us – avoid conflict, don't make waves, be her friend, etc. By not accepting a LJBF you emphatically make known that you are good at confrontation, you have an understanding of her motives and you're confident enough in yourself to make it known.

Not only does this impress her with potential for security provisioning it also implies future confidence. The problem for most guys is enacting this and making it a default behavior when our biology would have us move away from conflict rather than engage in an unacceptable social dynamic that is subtly damaging to his own interests.

LETTING GO OF INVISIBLE FRIENDS

LDRs are not relationships.

I'm sorry to break this to you, but there is no such thing as a long distance relationship (LDR).

That's correct, you have no relationship. An LDR simply does not meet the criteria necessary for it to be considered a legitimate relationship. There is no reciprocity of anything more than words passing over a phone line or an instant message text. Understand me here – you have no relationship. You have self-assumed accountability, self-assumed liability and internalized responsibilities to be loyal to this person, this idealization, in your head. You are entertaining a commitment to fidelity with an idealization, and ignoring what everyone outside of your LDR will regularly tell you is insanity.

LDRs are one of the more insidious forms of ONEitis.

LDRs are the most easily identifiable form of ONEitis, and it would be laughable if it weren't so damaging to a guy's life maturation. The LDR man generally sacrifices years of his life in this pitiable effort to pursue his 'soulmate' across the planet or even a hundred miles away.

The very thought of refuting the idea that an LDR can work is equatable to denying his belief this fantasized ONEitis fueled idealization that he's swallowed for the better part of his life. It's easy to criticize an LDR in the terms of questioning either party's earnestness and fidelity in entertaining an LDR and this is usually the tact that most people giving advice on LDRs follow. One or both parties are or will 'cheat' on the other over the course of time, it's true, but LDRs are far more telling of a mentality that results in much more damaging consequences as a result of deeply conditioned self-expectations and fears.

I can't begin to list the number of otherwise intelligent and ambitious men I've known who've drastically altered the course of their lives to follow their ONE. Men who've changed their majors in college, who've selected or switched universities, men who've applied for jobs in states they would never have considered, accepted jobs that are sub-standard to their ambitions or qualifications, men who've renounced former religions and men who've moved across the planet all in an effort to better accommodate an idealized woman with whom they've played pseudo-boyfriend with over the course of an LDR; only to find that she wasn't the person they thought she was and were depressive over the gravity that their decisions played in their lives.

An LDR is akin to a LJBF, but writ large and festering in a man's life. You play surrogate boyfriend, voluntarily accepting and internalizing all of the responsibilities and account-abilities of being a woman's exclusive, monogamous partner with no expectation of reciprocating intimacy or sexuality in the immediate future. However an LDR is worse than a LJBF arrangement since it pervasively locks a man into a success or failure mentality with regards to the relationship actually being legitimate. After all, she's agreed to remain his girlfriend (from miles away) and if he's the one to falter it's his lack of perseverance in this ONEitis ego-investment that dooms them. Once the LDR inevitably ends he's the one left with the self-doubt, he's the one beating himself up over wast-ing time, money and effort and he's the one feeling guilty whether he or she is the true 'cheater'.

Invisible Friends

An LDR is like having an invisible friend with whom you're constantly considering the course of your actions with. Consider the personal, romantic, familial, educational, career, personal maturity and growth opportunities that you've limited yourself from or never had a chance to experience because of this invisible friend. When you finally divorce yourself from this invisible friend, will it have all been worth it?

Guys cling to LDRs because they've yet to learn that **Rejection is better than Regret**.

AFCs will nurse along an LDR for years because it seems the better option when compared with actually going out and meeting new women who represent a potential for real rejection. They think it's better to stick with the 'sure thing', but it's the long term regret that is the inevitable result of an LDR that is life damaging.

Nothing reeks of desperation or verifies a lack of confidence more than a guy who self-righteously proclaims he's in an LDR. Women see you coming a mile off, because you are a guy without options, clinging to his one previously realized option. In fact the only reason a man entertains an LDR is due to a lack of options. If you had more plates spinning an LDR would never look like a good idea.

And finally, it's not uncommon to see the "not in my case" defense offered about how you actually *do* see your invisible friend once every 4 or six months. To this I'll say, again, what opportunities are you censoring yourself from experiencing by playing virtual, long-distance, house with a woman you only see this often? Do you honestly think you're the exception to the rule? The truth is you're molding your lifestyle around what you hope your relationship will be in the future – that's no way to live.

ENTER WHITE KNIGHT

The following was a timely question by a SoSuave forum member:

"Just wanted to find out: who do you talk to about aspects of game with off this site? I'm talking here about "game" in the broadest sense of the term, so pick-up, but also self-esteem, how to keep a relationship healthy, the roles of men and women in society etc."

"My experience with voicing the views advocated in the 'manosphere' in public has nearly always been negative. I have 3 - 4 good male friends who are interested in pick-up, and they love it. But these friends are the exception rather than the rule. My parents (beta dad, controlling mum) think my attitude towards women is sexist and my opinion of ONSs (one night stands) "disgusting." Just about everybody I know subscribes to the Disney / soulmate view of relationships, and some of my contemporaries (I'm 21) are even starting to settle down and get married. God help them. Talking to girls in bed about what they find attractive in a man is interesting, if only to see the extent to which they delude themselves, but ultimately counter-productive, since a woman (tacitly) expects a man to know how to express his sexuality."

"Can we as men ever talk about these things in public? What are your experiences?"

Before I begin, let me say that I think it's encouraging to see such an insightful question posed by so young a Man.

From The Matrix:

MORPHEUS: *The Matrix is a system, Neo. That system is our enemy. But when you're inside, you look around, what do you see? Businessmen, teachers, lawyers, carpenters. The very minds of the people we are trying to save. But until we do, these people are still a part of that system and that makes them our enemy. You have to understand, most of these people are not ready to be unplugged. And many of them are so inured, so hopelessly dependent on the system, that they will fight to protect it.*

Every random chump within earshot of your conversation about Game, about your 'changed' way of seeing inter-gender relations, about your most objective critical observations of how women 'are', etc. – understand, that chump waits *everyday* for an opportunity to "correct" you in as public a way as he's able to muster.

That AFC who's been fed on a steady diet of noble intent, with ambitions of endearing a woman's intimacy through his unique form of chivalry; that guy, he's aching for an opportunity to prove his quality by publicly redressing a "villain" like you for your chauvinism. Even under the conditions of relative anonymity (like the internet), he'll still cling to that want of proving his uniqueness just on the off chance that a woman might read his rebuff and be fatefully attracted to him.

This is the bread and butter of the White Knight Beta.

It's best to assume that most guys who pick up on just your Game vibe, to say nothing of overtly talking about it, are going to side with the feminine imperative by default. For practitioners of Beta Game (which is to say the better part of 90% of guys) this is an organic opportunity to identify with women and engage in the same shaming conventions women use without the fear of having it seem contrived.

Now this is the mechanics of it, but the rabbit hole goes deeper than that. For the Beta Game that our noble white knight is so invested in to work, he depends on an assumed system. He depends upon reaffirming his assumed understanding of how to best achieve a woman's intimacy (sex). He must reaffirm that presumption *by* defending it and looking for opportunities to show he adheres to the feminine imperative (or the version of the imperative he's been taught to believe). His Game, his ego-invested identity is literally dependent upon that system. So not only is he defending his Game and his ego, he's also defending the social architecture that makes his Beta Game even possible.

You see, when an AFC clings to the mental schemas that make up an AFC mindset it requires a constant need for affirmation and reinforcement, particularly in light of his glaring lack of verifiable success with women while clinging to, and behaving in accordance with the mindset.

AFCs are like crabs in a barrel – once one gets to the top to climb out another drags him back in. The AFC needs other AFCs to affirm his blatantly obvious lack of success. He needs other AFCs to tell him, "don't worry just be yourself" or "she's just not a quality woman because she can't see how great a guy you are."

So when an AFC finally does get a second date and then finally does get laid it becomes the ultimate validation for his mindset. "See, you just have to be a patient Nice Guy and the right ONE really does come along." This is when the self-righteous phase begins and he can begin telling his PUA friends that 'his Game' does work, and he's "getting some" now without all the Positive Masculinity claptrap. In actuality he rationalizes away all of the conditions that led up to him getting the girlfriend and the fundamental flaw that he's settling for a woman "who'd fuck him", but this doesn't stop him from claiming a moral high ground. His long wait is over and he's finally hit White Knight pay-dirt.

THE HONOR SYSTEM

The concept of Honor that men began has been made to serve a feminine purpose.

I have no doubt that the principle of honor dates back from as long ago as we can track human civilization, but like so many other social foundation Men have instituted, the feminine will covertly position them to its own purpose.

In the introduction to the *Art of Seduction* author Robert Greene explains why there was an original need for seduction to be developed into an art. For this we can look back to ancient civilizations where women were essentially a commodity. They had no *overt* external power to control their fates, but they excelled (and still do) at *covert* psychological internal power, and this of course finds a parallel in men and women's preferred communication methods. The feminine's primary agency has always been sexuality and manipulating influence by its means.

Much in the same way that each gender communicates, so too is their method of interacting within their own gender. As Men we're respected when we keep our word, sacrifice ourselves for a worthy cause (even to the point of disposability), solve problems rationally, our word is our bond, and a whole host of other qualifiers that make us respectable and worthy of integrity. We must be **overt** and above board; and when we encounter a man who is **covert** in his dealings we call him 'shifty' and think him untrustworthy. Even for the most noble of purposes, practicing the art of misdirection is not something men are respected for – at least not publicly.

It's just this overt masculine interactive nature that women are only too ready to exploit. In combination with their sexual agency and influence they use this overt male social interactive dynamic to position themselves in places where they can use indirect power.

Cleopatra was an excellent example of this – sending armies to war by appealing to powerful men's pride and honor, while reserving her sexuality as a reward. Virtually every Feminine Social Convention is rooted in appealing to, or attacking male social institutions – a dedication to an idealistic sense of honor being chief among them. The obvious example is of course "shaming" and the "do-the-right-thing" social contract.

In fact to be a "Man" has become synonymous with living up to a feminine imperative that's cleverly disguised as masculine Honor. It's not that women created Honor, but rather that they've recreated it to serve their purpose. In the Biblical Ten Commandments we're told not to commit adultery – don't sleep with another man's wife – which probably wasn't too hard to abide by when polygamy was the norm. In fact multiple wives was a sign of affluence, it used to be the conspicuous consumption of the epoch. Why then is polygamy a social perversion now? What changes occurred that made polygamy honorable (even enviable) into a very evil taboo?

Along with language and culture, social conditions evolve. What we think of as Honorable today are the result of centuries molding. It's very easy to romanticize about times when Honor among Men reigned supreme, and then lament the sad state of society today in comparison, but doing so is a fools errand. Honor in and of itself is, and should be, a foundation for Men, but it's only useful when we understand it in the perspective of how it can be used against us.

Man Up or Shut Up – The Male Catch 22

One of the primary way's Honor is used against men is in the feminized perpetuation of traditionally masculine expectations when it's convenient, while simultaneously expecting egalitarian gender parity when it's convenient.

For the past 60 years feminization has built in the perfect Catch 22 social convention for anything masculine; The expectation to assume the responsibilities of being a man (Man Up) while at the same time denigrating asserting masculinity as a positive (Shut Up). What ever aspect of maleness that serves the feminine purpose is a man's masculine responsibility, yet any aspect that disagrees with feminine primacy is labeled Patriarchy, 'Male Privilege' or Misogyny.

Essentially, this convention keeps Beta males in a perpetual state of chasing their own tails. Over the course of a lifetime they're conditioned to believe that they're cursed with masculinity (Patriarchy) yet are still responsible to 'Man Up' when it suits a feminine imperative. So it's therefore unsurprising to see that half the men in western society believe women dominate the world (male powerlessness) while at the same time women complain of a lingering Patriarchy (female powerlessness) or at least sentiments of it.

This is the Catch 22 writ large. The guy who does in fact Man Up is a chauvinist, misogynist, patriarch, but he still needs to man up when it's convenient to meet the needs of a female imperative.

In contemporary society we have a very different understanding of what Honor was, or was intended to be initially. One of the psychological undercurrents I see in most AFCs is a strong, self-righteous dedication to a very distorted conviction of Honor. A main tenet being an unearned, default respect for women; essentially an unearned Honor placed on a woman for no other reason than she's female. We learn this (usually) from the time we're children, "never hit a girl". Naturally, this has only been ferociously encouraged by the feminine since Victorian times because it served a latent purpose right up until on demand (feminine exclusive) birth control was offered, and then prompted the sexual revolution.

Today, we still have women using the anachronism that is male Honor in a manner that serves their interests, but it's contrasted with a sexually emphasized opportunism. A Man's responsibility should be "Honoring" her as 'the fairer sex' while recognizing her 'independence'. The AFC gobbles this stuff up and in an effort to better identify himself with her ideals he begins to convince himself that he's unique in that he better exemplifies this false-virtue, this feminine defined sense of Honor than "other guys".

THE SAVIOR SCHEMA

"Every time a man is being nice to you, he's offering dick. That's all it is.
'Uh, can I get that for ya? How 'bout some dick? Can I help you with that? Can I help you with
some dick? Do you need some dick?'" – Chris Rock

The Savior Schema – the Beta male expectation of reciprocation of intimacy (usually sexual) for female problems solved.

This is a learned/developed behavior that results from men's natural push to deductively search for the most rational solution to a problem. It's really a linear logic:

I need sex + women have sex + I must discover what is required for me to get sex from women + I will perform/embody/identify with said requirements = woman will reciprocate with her sexual intimacy.

Needless to say this is simplistic at best, but as is the root cause for most of men's frustrations with women, men have a tendency to believe that women will respond as rationally as they themselves would in qualifying for her *stated* desires. The manosphere is full of men who can tell you this simply isn't the case for any number of reasons, but sadly they still think that women ought to live up to, and honor, their implied "agreement."

The fundamental flaw of the Savior Schema (a.k.a. "Cap'n Save a Ho") is that it is essentially negotiated intimacy, and negotiated intimacy is never genuine. You can fix a woman's flat tire, help her out of a financial jam, fix her a nice lasagna, give her the perfect shoulder to cry on, babysit her kids and listen to her drone on for hours on the phone, and she'll still go fuck her outlaw biker boyfriend because her intimacy with him is genuine, unnegotiated, unobligated desire. She *wants* to have sex with him, she doesn't owe him sex.

What AFCs fail to understand is that all the financial, emotional, dependable support you could possibly offer a woman is no substitute for raw, unmitigated, chemical desire. Some of the most irresponsible, unreliable, poverty level washouts often get more sex than any dutiful, loyal AFC suffering from a Savior Schema, because there is no obligation.

Reciprocity

In the wild, the law of reciprocity and fair exchange is a fairly obvious one. Most high-order social animals have some innate understanding of exchanging resources. In fact you could argue that pair bonding, family structure and social collectives are for the most part based on this shared exchange arrangement. So it stands to reason that in the course of human evolution we too developed this innate psychological wiring, thus making men prone to deductively seeing it as the shortest distance between what we have and what we want.

The difficulties arise when (perhaps cleverly) women learned to covertly use this innate psychology of exchange within the context of a social framework that gives them a resource advantage for little or no exchange of their own. Thus women modeled a social norm, that mirrors men's natural default position of disposability, and placed their attentions and intimacies as unassailable resources, so valuable that no effort on a man's part can overtly merit it. When a woman is appalled by the notion that she should be obligated to have sex with a man in exchange for a dinner and a movie (even over multiple occasions), this social convention is the root of that insult.

The Protector Dynamic

Of course the flip side to this argument is the Protector Dynamic which is the natural propensity for a man to want to provide protection for his mate.

Over the course of our evolutionary history certain psycho-biological behaviors proved to be beneficial to the survival of our species. Specific hormonal releases prompt different emotions and behavioral reactions as a response to our environments. Women, for instance, produce higher volumes of oxytocin and estrogen thus prompting a natural instinctual feeling of wellbeing and nurturing her children (which also, interestingly enough, is released after female orgasm). The same is true for men. Being generally physically stronger and possessing 12-17 times the testosterone levels of women, men have evolved chemical cocktails of their own and thus feel a natural protection instinct when prompted.

The conflict comes when the AFC confuses this Protector Dynamic with a Savior Schema. The natural feelings derived from his biochemistry only serve to reinforce his Savior mentality and solidify it as part of his personality. Even when a woman's repeated behavior directly contradicts this notion of reciprocating intimacy for help (or his idea of 'protection') the Savior Schema only rationalizes it as being inconsistent with a single, individual woman.

This then is the root of the White Knight schema; exchange protection for intimacy (i.e. sex). And, once again, women cleverly, almost subconsciously so, use this dynamic to arrange a beneficial, but unequal, exchange of resources.

INTERGENDER FRIENDSHIP

Ever since "When Harry Met Sally" was released there's been a constant droning about the validity of intergender friendships. To even suggest that men and women couldn't be strictly platonic, mature friends is to invite reproach from a society that's been steeped in notions of egalitarian equalism. If men and women are fundamentally "the same" there should be no impediment to developing and maintaining a friendship in like terms to a same sex friendship.

While it would be foolish to think intergender friendships aren't possible, it's important to understand that men and women cannot be friends in the way or to the degree that most people perceive same-sex friendship to be.

Now the natural response to this is *"I have lots of female friends"* or *"what are you trying to say, I can't have female friends, they all haffta be enemies?"*

Which of course is the standard binary (black or white, all or nothing) retort and the trained AFC thinks anyone suggesting that men and women's relations as friends could be anything less than equitable and fulfilling is just a Neanderthal chauvinist thinking. However, they are incorrect – not because you wouldn't want to actually be a woman's friend. There are fundamental differences in the ways men and women view friendship within the framework of their own sex and the ways this transfers to the concept of intergender-friendship.

Quite simply there are limitations on the degree to which a friendship can develop between men and women. The easy illustration of this is that at some point your female "friend" *will* become intimately involved with another male; at which point the quality of what you perceived as a legitimate friendship will decay. It must decay for her intimate relationship to mature. For instance, I've been married for 17 years now; were I to entertain a deep friendship with another female (particularly an attractive female) other than my wife, my interest in this woman automatically becomes suspect of infidelity – and of course the same holds true for women with man-friends. This dynamic simply doesn't exist for same sex friendships because the sexual aspect is inconsequential.

I understand how stupidly obvious this seems, but remember we're qualifying the characteristics of intergender friendships in the face of a social undercurrent that wants to convince us that men and women are fundamentally equal. According to this precept, men *should* essentially possess the capacity to repress their sexual impulse to the point that it *should* have no bearing on his rational decision to engage in a platonic friendship. Likewise, a woman should be able to dissociate herself from her hypergamous nature to pursue a completely asexual friendship. And both genders should maturely pursue the friendship for their mutual enrichment, however, reality tells a different story.

Girl-Friends

All of this isn't to say that you cannot have female acquaintances, or that you must necessarily be rude or ignore all women with contempt (that is binary thinking once again), but
it is to say that the degree or quality of friendship that you can experience with women
(as a man) in comparison to same sex friendships will always be limited due to sexual
differences.

Most men will only ever engage in friendships with women that they initially find attractive which then, of course, is colored by their attraction to that woman. I'm sure the "not
in my case" card will get played and attempt to make an anecdotal case for how much
an exception to the rule you are. To which I'll say, even if you legitimately are, it makes
no difference because the very nature of an intergender friendship is *always* going to be
limited by sexual differences. Even if you can legitimately make the case that you aren't
now, or weren't in the past, attracted to your opposite sex friend, your other intimate,
intergender relationships will still modify and/or limit the depth of that friendship.

Even the best, most asexual, platonic, male-female friendships will be subject to mitiga-
tion based on sex. The easy example is; I'm sure you'd be jealous and suspect of your
girlfriend were she to be spending any "quality time" with another 'male-friend'. It's
simply time spent with another male who isn't you and you'll always question her desire
to do so in favor of spending time with you.

Bear in mind that it's also important to consider how women relate with their same-sex
friends as a template for their intergender friendships. Remember each sex uses it's same-
sex model of friendship on which to base their understandings and expectations for an
opposite sex friendship. Very few men have the patience to sort out how women interact
with their women friends, so they opt for the easy answer that equalism gives them –
we're all the same, so your male buddies are the same as women.

Any guy that's been in the circular hell of being a woman's "phone-friend" knows this
isn't true. Girl-friends have a much different dynamic for friendship than do men, but
likewise, and by way of her innate solipsism, she's presuming her intersexual friendships
will follow along a similar template to that of her girl-friends.

And why wouldn't women expect their male friends to conform to their template for
friendship? In a feminine-centric world it makes practical sense for men to realign themselves to women's friendship frame. Men will all too readily tolerate behavior and
attitudes from girl-friends that they'd come to physical blows with their male friends
were they to do the same. Since the prerogative of maintaining that friendship is, by
default, cast in a feminine-centric frame, women (generally) wouldn't even think of
altering their own interpretations of friendship to accommodate a male perspective.

Get it out of your head now that you're even in a so called "friend zone" with any
woman. There is no friend zone – there is only the limbo between you being fooled
that a girl is actually a friend on an equitable level to your same sex friends, and you
understanding that as soon as she becomes intimate with another guy your attentions will

become a liability to any relationship she might want to have with the new sexual interest and she puts you off, or you do the same when you become so involved with another girl.

The Female Wingman

A lot of guys cling to this mistaken notion that they can parlay a female friendship into action with one of her hot friends. You may even have legitimate examples where that might've happened, but for each one, I'll show you a girl who would've fucked you irrespective of whether or not you had a mutual female friend to vouch for you. That friendship may have been a convenient pivot into another hot girl, but it wasn't the prior intergender-friendship that got you laid; it was that the girl who banged you found you attractive enough to fuck.

I'm not denying the utility of 'Social Circle Game', nor am I ignoring that the conspicuous attention of hot women is good social proof – that's not what the friend pivot is about. It's about assuming a girl-friend will endorse you as a preselected, potential sexual partner.

You may think it's great social proof to have some hot friend endorse you as a good lay for her other friends, but women talk. In fact it's all they do most of the time. Your status as a friend gets transferred to her girlfriends. Why?

First, if she was a prior target for you who turned into a LJBF, you already have that as an association of your friendship. Any of her girlfriends that would subsequently date you will know that she was your primary interest initially – not them. Secondly, assuming you even could have a completely innocuous, asexual, platonic beginning to your inter-gender friendship, there will be competition anxiety with the other girlfriends. This will result in a tendency for the original friend to filter your exposure to which of her girlfriends she finds the least threatening. You have to consider the balance between your value to her as another friend / orbiter against her endorsing you as a potential intimate for one of her girlfriends. Just because you have a girl-friend with a social circle of attractive female friends doesn't mean you'll get her endorsement for the one you'd prefer to get with.

To complete the circle here, all of this leads up to understanding that your female friend will *never* be one of your guy friends. This silly notion is founded on the expectation that your female friend will hold the same interests and have the same reactions that your male friends will. Women are never going to be your wingman. One of the great down-falls of men today is too much female influence in their lives, to the point that it's become stigma. Beware the guy with too many or exclusively female friends. This might make for the plot of stupid movies, but most women are wary of guys with so many female friends that they question their being able to relate with and be Men.

Part of being Alpha is your facility with male interactions. If all your friends are women this calls your Alpha cred into question for a woman.

CHAPTER 3

UNPLUGGING

DISPELLING THE MAGIC

Women get the men they deserve.

One point I try to make in my roaming about the blogs dedicated to intergender dynamics is reading articles from many different perspectives. When I have the time, I actively hunt down articles that I know I will disagree with. I think it's far too easy to get locked into the habit of seeking out bloggers, articles and statistics that reaffirm our own particular views. Even within the circles with which we'd be inclined to agree with there will often be a lot of conflicting viewpoints – such as the recent conflict pitting the MRAs (men's rights activists) vs. the PUAs (pickup artists), or Game vs. MGTOW (men going their own way).

I began my own blog with the intent of studying the reasons why intergender social and psychological dynamics evolve, what functions they serve, and develop contingencies or actionable methods of bettering one's life using this information – this is really the core of Game. The problem inherent in this, truly unplugging and becoming aware of your own feminine conditioning in general, is that it often comes with a healthy dose of disillusionment.

Once you strip away the heady fantasies of soul-mates and expectations of 'happily ever afters", and replace it with a more practical understanding based on reasonably reliable, empirical, explanations, what you're left with looks a lot like nihilism. Even for the most staunch realists among the 'community' there's still a desire to want to apply, however slightly, some kind of magical thinking to the process of connecting with another human being. For other Men it may be some esoteric desire to cast their association in terms of honor, integrity or respect – for women it comes as idealization or predestination.

I'm not saying this desire to spiritualize these connections is without merit, but I can't help but see the conflict it has in coexisting with the practicality of what we're learning about ourselves. Just in the last 30 years we've come to understand the biochemical / hormonal natures of our emotions. We know a hormone like oxytocin induces feelings of trust and promotes nurturing. We know that the endorphin / dopamine profile associated with feelings of infatuation, lust and love is chemically similar to that of heroine.

Poof! There goes the magic.

We have an understanding of women's ovulatory cycles and the resulting sexual behavior predispositions that are induced by them. Only the generations of the late 20th and 21st are privy to this information. Evolutionary psychology has only risen to prominence as a field of study in the past 15 years.

Discomfort and Disillusion

All of this makes for some very uncomfortable realizations, particularly when men become aware of the social schema established to keep them in a female-centric reality.

Game is simply the most recent countermeasure developed by men to better adapt to this feminine primacy, but it was only possible through advances in both communication technologies, access to globalized information and new socio-psychological theory. Prior to these advancements, and with the rise of feminization from the late 60s to the late 90s men were clueless as to their social predicament. From the start of the sexual revolution until the beginning of this millennia, western masculinity (and femininity) has been subjected to the greatest deliberate social and psychological restructuring, any generation has ever known. And I shouldn't limit that exclusively to western culture; now we see this effect filtering into Asia, Japan, even traditionally masculine Latin cultures. As westernization spreads, so too does it's feminization.

What have men been left clinging to? The false-guilt we've been taught to be ashamed of as part of our past "patriarchy" to be sure, but more importantly we were left with the legacy of that magical thinking. In the face of a yet undefined hypergamy, we wanted to still believe in the 'Sugar & Spice' myth, the respect her wishes motive, the marriage goal – all of which were (are) still actively reinforced by a feminine imperative that knew its time had come and men were too stupid in their romanticism to know it. That is until Game was conceived.

The great and powerful Oz that was feminization is finally having the curtain pulled back on it. In this new age of communication men can globally "share notes" and come to their own conclusions – and women shriek all the louder as we hit closer to the truth.

Thanks to its relative anonymity, no longer is there any social stigma to fear from even broaching the subject of how best to deal with women. The great wailing we hear and read from women is less about current social implications and more about having the 30 year social program of feminization being exposed for what it truly was and now is. Yet even in the face of men seeing the Empress with no clothes, they still make appeals to the romantic, magical association men have always clung to before they became aware of a hypergamy-enabling feminization. We read cries of "Man-Up!" Accept your previous responsibilities of being a husband and leader, but don't be overbearing and crush our spirits. In the back row a new generation of women, the 22 year olds, scream "where's the party?" as they upload a fresh set of nudes shot in the bathroom mirror from their cell phones.

Women get the men they deserve. For all the crowing and publicity of feminine triumphalism, there's still a wonderment at why men are increasingly less and less motivated to play along in their feminine reality. As tough as it is for men to disabuse themselves of their romanticism, it's even more so for women to accept their own natures in the shadow of the experiment that was 20th century feminization. They're reaping the whirlwind that the Matriarchy of the sexual revolution has sown. It's all the more ironic to read the same mothers who created this generation of men lament how their daughters are unmarried and childless at 35.

IDENTITY CRISIS

Below is a response I gave to a guy I was counseling and I thought it sufficiently insightful to post on the blog in regards to a pretty common topic that comes up. I think you'll agree.

"Rollo, is it possible to identify with women without compromising yourself?"

If it is a conscious effort on the guy's part, no.

You bring up a good topic though, obviously when I refer to 'identifying' with a woman, this could use some explanation. What exactly is 'identifying' with a woman?

The root of this word is 'identity', meaning who you are and what characteristics, traits and interests constitute your individual personality. 'Identity', in a way, is a pretty subjective and esoteric term – kind of like trying to define what art is – it can be argued that 'identity' is what you make of it.

While at university, my field of specialization in behavioral psychology was personality studies, and I can tell you there are a lot of theories and interpretations of what constitutes identity. However, one article that is agreed upon almost universally is that identity and personality are never static and are mailable and changeable due to influencing variables and conditions. A very pronounced illustration of this would be soldiers retuning from combat with post traumatic stress disorder – a very identifiable and verifiable form of psychosis. These men are changed individuals and their identities are altered from the time they were subject to the psychological rigors of warfare to returning back to a normalized life. Some have the resilience to adjust their personalities back to a somewhat normalized state, others sadly do not. Yet in each case the change was influenced by conditions and environment.

Likewise, most young men are subject to their own set of personal conditions and environments, and their personalities and identities reflect this accordingly. The guy who's naturally "lucky with the ladies" is going to reflect this in his identity. The young man who doesn't receive regular female attention for whatever reasons is going to manifest this condition in his identity. The guy who is focused on his own ambitions is going to reflect this in his own personality as well, but for all, when conditions are such that they feel deprived of certain experiences in their own life, this creates a conflict between a former identity and the altering of, or forming of a new one to meet the need for this experience. Couple this with the natural chemical/hormonal desire for sexual experience and you can see how powerful an influence deprivation becomes to a man's identity.

Far too many young men maintain the notion that for them to receive the female intimacy they desire they should necessarily become more *like* the target of their affection in their own personality. In essence, to mold their own identify to better match the girl they think will best satisfy this need. So we see examples of men compromising their self-interests to better accommodate the interests of the woman they desire to facilitate this need for intimacy (i.e. sex).

We all know the old cliché women are all too fond of repeating, "Guys will do anything to get laid" and this is certainly not limited to altering their individual identities and even conditions to better facilitate this. It's all too common an example to see men select a college based on the available women at that college rather than academic merit to fit their own ambitions, or even choose a college to better maintain a pre-existing relationship that a woman has chosen and the young man follows. In order to justify these choices he will alter his identity and personality by creating rationales and new mental schema to validate this 'decision' for himself. It becomes an ego protection mechanism for a decision he, on some level, really knows was made for him.

This is just one glaring example of this identification, but thousands more subtle ones exist that men (and women) pass off as social mores and contrivances. The guy stuck in the 'Friend Zone' who got the LJBF ("lets just be friends") line when he attempted to become intimate with his target, will happily listen to her drone on for hours on the phone in order to find out how better to alter himself to fit her conditions for intimate acceptability.

He will readily "change his mind" about even his own personal beliefs if it will better fit what he perceives is her criteria for compatibility with her. This is the compromise of identity – to fundamentally and voluntarily alter one's own personality to achieve the acceptability of another.

When we are directly and overtly faced with this sort of challenge to our beliefs we naturally recoil – you are your own person and would resist were your employer or your burdensome parents to tell you how you should vote (political belief), but when it comes to personality and sexual/intimacy interests, and done voluntarily, it's surprising to see the limits of what men (and to an extent women) will do.

Men will entertain the idea that a long distance relationship (LDR) is a desirable arrangement even if intimacy has never occurred because the potential of that intimacy is a perceived possibility. These same guys will espouse every reasoning they can conceive as to why *their* "relationship is different" and that they 'believe' that "love conquers all" only to come full circle when he or she 'cheats' or breaks off the relationship and the man comes back to his prior (though he thinks new) understanding that LDRs are in fact a bad prospect. His identity changed and then changed again to accommodate his conditions.

However, it's not that he never truly changed or had the belief in the first place. Were these guys to take a polygraph test at the time they would indeed pass when asked if this was what they actually accepted as truth. Men will do what most deductively solves a problem, and in this he is only following the tenants of deductive pragmatism.

"I need sex + women have the sex I want + I must discover what women want to give me sex + ask women + women want X = I will do X to get sex and alter my own identity in order to better facilitate X."

It should be this easy, but that's rarely the case since more often than not women are unaware of what X really is, or X is subject to constant change depending on her own conditions, her innate hypergamy, etc.

Now, after all of this, is it possible that a man and a woman may in fact share genuine common interests? Of course. You may indeed find a perfectly beautiful woman that enjoys Nascar or Hockey as much as you. You may find a woman you're attracted to who genuinely shares your passion for deep sea fishing. It's not uncommon to share common interests, it's when you alter your interest to better facilitate a connection that you force it.

Making this determination between genuine interests and created interests is the hair that needs splitting. I've personally advised guys who have literally changed careers to be in a better place to proposition a girl they fancied. I know men who've moved thousands of miles to live closer to women who've never reciprocated their interest in them, yet they continued to attempt to identify themselves with her.

I know 65 year old men in 40 year marriages, who even after intimacy was resolved years ago with the woman, are still attempting to identify with their wives because they've internalized this identity compromise as a standard means to getting sex from her. Their wives's expectations of them have become their identity and at 65 this mental schema has become so ego-invested that no amount of shedding light on their condition will ever convince them of anything to the opposite.

The most ironic thing about this 'Identity Crisis' is that the least attractive thing to most women is a man who is willing to compromise any part of his identity to placate to her, much less a wholesale selling-out of it. Women are naturally attracted to that masculine independence as it represents a very strong cue for security and the potential to provide that security to her (and any children she may have).

Women don't want a man who'll "do everything she says" because this sends the message that this man can be bought with even the prospect of a sexual encounter. Why would that indicate anything more than insecurity and a lack of confidence? Women want to be told "No", and constantly test a man's resolve to say this to her (a.k.a. shit testing) in order to affirm that she's made the right choice (even in marriage) of a guy who'll put his sexual impulse (knowing full-well how powerful it is with men) on hold to stick to his own self-interest, beliefs and ambitions.

This covertly communicates to a woman that his goals and determination trump her one real power over him – her sexuality. That is the man who is the **prize**, the 'great catch', the male to be competed for with other women.

DREAMGIRLS AND
CHILDREN WITH DYNAMITE

"Self-love is not so great a sin as self-neglect." - Henry V

Pride is one thing that people get very confused about. It's a healthy thing to have pride of oneself, to be proud of our accomplishments; it's a very real source of self-confidence.

Humility is an admirable quality too, don't get me wrong, but humility is only genuine when you're confident of your own abilities. It takes a humble Man to walk away from a fight that he knows he could win, but chooses not to engage in. Generally humility is only self-gratifying, because only rarely will others appreciate it as humility (those familiar with your abilities) and not view it as cowardice, or at best a lack of confidence.

Pride often appears arrogant because people of lesser accomplishments become envious, and people of better accomplishments think less of them than you do. It's very important not to appear too perfect, but it's equally important not to seem spineless.

It's quite another thing to be "prideful"and this is where the disconnect comes for a lot of AFCs, particularly ones with strong ego-investments in morality, chivalry, honor, etc. My old AFC self used to struggle with this as well. The AFC sublimates himself; he self-deprecates because he believes, erroneously, that this ideology will separate him from the herd and make him,"not-like-*other*-guys". He mistakenly believes that he's unique in this when actually his thinking is the mindset of the majority.

Why? For the answer all you need do is look at the most common responses in the blog/ forum comment threads from guys just recently discovering the community.

I have no doubt that there are some guys who go from zero to PUA and then parlay that into some kind of seducer-hood. I would also argue that they are the rare exceptions. Guys don't search out community forums or blogs like mine because they're getting too much pussy. They search it out on Google because what they've been doing isn't producing the results they want. They've been doing exactly what most plug-ins criticize Game for – they're working from a script.

They like to point out the flaws in autonomously adhering to a script with regards to PUA techniques; you become a social robot, not "yourself"; but from an opposite side, what you're doing now, or have done, as an AFC is equally as scripted. The only difference, and far more insidious, is that they've internalized these AFC "scripts" that society on whole has conditioned into them as personal investments over the course of a lifetime.

After dropping your AFC mindset for a one based on self-interest, what happens? You probably began to see results. You can hook up with women the caliber of which were previously unavailable to you, and all it took was replacing your chump behavior and mentality with one of self-concern and self-priority. You might feel like an asshole, people may say you've changed or accuse you of becoming bitter, or you're being someone you're not, but you couldn't argue with the results.

One of the biggest dangers of the PUA ideal is that it does nothing to address the root problem of AFCism (for lack of a better term). AFCs don't want to stop being AFCs. Largely, they just want their ONEitis (or their "dream girl") to hook up with them long-term and then drift back into a comfortable state of 'just being themselves'. According to *The Game* ,by Neil Strauss even the Godfather of pickup, Mystery, with all his PUA prowess, degenerates into a simpering, borderline suicidal chump when he realizes that his PUA scripts do nothing for him in a monogamous LTR with Katya (his ONEitis). The most notorious PUA in modern history was still an AFC, because he hadn't killed that mentality, that AFC internalization – he hadn't killed his inner AFC.

Another very common occurrence is the "reformed" AFC who makes progress toward becoming more Game savvy, and as a result gets his "dream girl", only to lose her after reverting back to a Beta frame once he's in an LTR with her. I'm not a big fan of PUA founding father Ross Jefferies, but he did say something very profound once, he said "teaching PUA skills to these chumps is like giving dynamite to children." This is probably truer than he realized, because the potential for disaster is much higher. Most guys want that silver bullet, the magic formula that will get them the girl, but it does nothing to prepare them for the idyllic LTR their Beta nature has fantasized about for so very long.

They don't become Men, they become children with dynamite. So are we really surprised when the guy who finally gets his Dream Girl as a result of learning Game becomes despondent and suicidal when he loses the "best thing he'll ever have" when she leaves him? Are we shocked when his ONEitis turns out to be a BPD (borderline personality disorder) girl and his life's ambitions pitch into a death-spiral because he was unprepared to deal with a post-Game LTR?

The problem with just employing PUA skills to get any woman is that sometimes it actually gets you *any* woman. There's no vetting process, no discernment, taught as part of technique. AFCs get so impressed with their new found PUA confidence and getting hotter women, getting their old friend-zone girl interested, or getting women at all, that they have no motivation to think about who they should get involved with. They're unprepared for emotionally manipulative women, and particularly when they're more attractive than anything they'd ever had before. They obsess. They predictably get ONE-itis, but they develop a ONEitis in such an extreme case that they can be suicidal about a woman they'd previously never been able to attain.

Remember this, PUA skills are tools, and valuable ones, but adopting a positive masculine mindset prepares you for more. An AFC needs to divorce himself from deep set social and psychological schema – he needs to unlearn the self-delusions that a lifetime has conditioned him to internalize into his personality. Giving an AFC Game skills before this transition will only condemn him to disappointment and despair in an LTR. The more important lesson is learned in the discarding of that old, Beta, way of thinking, while understanding the tools and techniques to apply your new, confident, positive masculine mindset.

KILL THE BETA

Rational Male blog reader, Paul, sought out my guidance for probably the single most asked for advice I receive:

"I've read through your blog entirely, and my biggest issue is, how do I kill the beta? Every girl I sleep with, or even fool around with, I end up developing feelings for. Even if it was a one night stand or the girl is cheating on a boyfriend with me. It's like I have no self control; like I'm a girl that agonizes over every guy she sleeps with."

I wish I honestly had a definitive answer for Paul. If I could construct some step-by-step program, a universal template, that men could all follow in order to kill their inner Beta, I'd be rich beyond my wildest dreams. Just as I said about the Alpha Buddha (Cory Worthington), if I could find a way to bottle the essence of Alpha I'd be set for life.

The real truth is that there is no simple answer to this, because each man's conditions are unique to him. To be sure there are common roots to their problems, and common mind-sets that form as results of attempting to formulate working sexual strategies (Beta Game) within the feminine Matrix, but undoing these mental schema and re-forming a better functional sexual strategy is unique to the individual.

I feel that this is the major reason Game is not taken as seriously as it should be – it's a lot of work doing your own self-analysis and then creating a strategy to remake yourself. One of the reasons PUA gurus and the Game demigods of the last decade seem so cheap, like snake oil salesmen, is because they fail to take into account the degree of personal-ization necessary to truly kill the inner Beta that guys eventually have to confront. That's an element of internalized Game that the guys doing pickup seminars would rather not address because your degree of success, in truth how you even measure success, is entirely dependent upon you. Hooking up with girls you'd never had access to before may sell pick up DVDs, but changing the inner workings of your personality is a much tougher order. If you ever look through the 'self-help' psychology section of a book store and wonder why there are so many books published in that topic, it's exactly due to this dynamic – effecting a fundamental change in one's life requires an effort that few people have the patience and perseverance for.

So with all of this in mind, let me say right now, I don't have a map for you – anyone telling you they do is selling you something – however, I will attempt to point you in the right direction. I can't say what will work, only you can find that out on your own, but try to bear in mind that changing yourself is a process that takes time.

Even for the guy's who have an easier go of transitioning to an internal Game-state personality, it's still an ongoing process. I'd like to think of myself as at least a lesser Alpha, but that doesn't mean I don't trip up at times.

This is what I mean by the process; you're not going to be bulletproof and pass every shit-test ever thrown at you, but be encouraged in knowing that because of your new awareness you'll learn from what you do wrong and adjust for the next time. There is no grand arrival moment when you know you've got it all down, you're an Alpha, or if you don't like that term, there really is no definitive point at which you've fully internalized Game. You don't get some certificate of Game completion. You can, however, definitively change your thinking – it's always on-going.

Knowing is Half the Battle

If there truly is a first step in internalization then it has to come from educating yourself. This is actually one of the most difficult tasks. If you're a reader of my blog, or are at least peripherally aware of Game as a concept, this is going to seem pretty obvious, but remember that there's an entire world of men who are still plugged-in, still locked in a way of thinking that's been prescribed for them by feminization since before they were born. Only a fraction of them will even be amenable to considering Game and positive masculinity, and fewer still will see its value.

From our perspective it seems like a matter of course. We read the books/blogs, familiarize ourselves with the concepts and terms, we pick what might work, experiment with ideas, evaluate the validity of them and adopt them or toss them. However what's apparent to the unplugged seems like blaspheme to the plugged-in.

Your "education" doesn't stop once you've unplugged. In fact I'd argue that it's even more vital in internalizing a new mindset since you're now putting things into practice. One thing I remind guys who spit the red pill back up is that there is no going back. A lot of frustrated guys who discover Game and fail to apply it because they lack the social skills or they convinced themselves that PUArtistry was their easy magic formula to fuck the girl of their dreams, they tend to want to regress back into the comfortable shell of their former ignorance of intergender social dynamics. Only they find that there is no return. They see the truth in the what they'd been blind to no matter where they turn. The social interactions, the feminization, the raw deal they've been conditioned to accept as normal – all of that subtly reminds them of the truth they're avoiding and they hate it. They become hostile to it.

I add this because it's a very real danger for guys transitioning into internalizing positive masculinity. In the same respect you now have become (or should become) more sensitive to Game truths and the unplugged reality you now find yourself in. There's a point of departure from what you thought was normal to seeing the signs around you.

An easy illustration is really contemplating any gender related issue in popular media. You'll hear a song, watch a sit-com, overhear a conversation in the lunch room, and begin to realize how surrounded you are by basic presumptions of a culture remade by feminine primacy. Understanding what your position in all of this is crucial to internalizing a new mindset or backsliding into your old frame of thinking.

Practicing the Change

It should be self-evident that applying what you've come to see as a new truth for yourself is vital. You need to get off the internet and field test the theories you learn here and elsewhere. Whether that means going to approach women at the clubs, or adopting a new attitude with your wife, or even the women you deal with at work, it's really up to you. The hardest part of practicing change is the initial shock of having the people who know you question the validity of the new you. If you were to move to a new city, completely change your social circle and play the role of an asshole Alpha, no one is the wiser. However, make a radical shift in your personality with those who've known you for years and you'll be a poser who's "trying to be something he's not".

Human beings need predictability – it gives them a sense of control over others. When you alter yourself, or have your personality altered by an outside force, this is a threat to that predictability, so the logical counter is for others to attempt to put us back into our places. Shaming comes as a natural tactic for women, but the push is always to get you back into their frame. That's essentially the threat others interpret; the new you is a frame grab. Do it all at once and people will accuse your personality of being a disingenuous reaction to having been burned. Do it subtly and persistently over a time and people will be more willing to accept the change as genuine. Always insist on change, but never too quickly.

This is important to remember because your friends will be your biggest source of doubt in your transformation. They might mean well, but understand, that intent comes from a desire to see normalcy, not *your* best interest. The first time an old girl-friend you had a thing for calls the new you an "asshole", it's kind of a shock to the system. There's always this stab at the old you who wants to set things rights, but you have to resist this impulse to take offense. It's really hard to say "yeah, I am an asshole" as a point of pride when your whole prior life's learning taught you not to offend others and particularly not girls you'd ever wanted to fuck. It's counterintuitive to the Beta in you. As sadistic as it sounds, you'll be more consistently rewarded for your capacity to indirectly offend the women you want to get with, but the internal conflict this creates between the Beta you and the burgeoning Alpha you is the hardest part to reconcile. This is where most guys fail in transitioning, and this is primarily due to an unpracticed ability to keep their emotions in check.

Aesthetics vs. Social Robots

This will sound counter to anything your feminine conditioning has ever taught you, but men are the True Romantics, women are simply the vehicles for that rarely appreciated romanticism. One of the biggest gripes the post-sexual revolution feminization had with men was some prepackaged notion that men weren't in touch with their feminine sides. We were "out of touch with our feelings". God curse Carl Jung's rotten corpse to hell for ever convincing popular culture that each sex had equal, but unexpressed, measures of feminine and masculine energies. Western culture has been so saturated with Jungian theory that we don't recognize it as such. It's become normalized to believe an idealized goal-state is a genderless, androgynous society.

Rants aside, up until the last 50 years, it has in fact been men who've been the sex with the most self-control regarding emotion. It's been just this reservation that's made Men more endearing to women. Either as enigmatic poets and artists for women to figure out, or as natural stoics who's every measured expression of emotion is an event unto itself, it's been Men's classic reservation of emotional inaccessibility that's made women more interested in Men.

In contemporary society, men are encouraged to express themselves as a primary way of accessing a woman's intimacy – essentially killing any sense of mystery to unravel with full disclosure. Brain function gender differences aside, it would be my guess that men socially evolved a more reserved expression of emotion, not due to some juvenile insecurity, but rather because it so consistently worked in generating interest in women.

Not so in this age. At every instance boys and men are conditioned to think that emotional expression is a means to solving problems. Boys don't cry, was instituted with a purpose. Unguarded easily expressed emotion is an evolved feminine trait. It's not that men should become social robots, deadened to all but the most intense emotion, it's just become normalized to cheapen that expression by overuse. Displays of a Man's emotions should be rarely given divine gifts for women who are generally lacking in true appreciation as it is.

Unlearn What You Have Learned

It's very difficult for a Beta man, conditioned for so long to be emotionally available, to turn these emotions off. The good news is I'm not suggesting you do. What I am suggesting is that you unlearn your reasons for developing emotional sentiments so easily. It's easy to go emotionally cold as a result of being burned, it's a much taller order to tamp that emotionality back into check when you're really feeling good about it. Our emotions make us human and humane. It's important to embrace that as essential to the human experience, but equally important is to see how easily it's used against you. You need to unlearn the reasons why you're so easily emotional. Maybe it's abandonment issues, maybe it's a more deliberate conditioning in your upbringing, but the first part of controlling it is to recognize it..

Remember in high school, in Drivers Ed class, when you were taught to turn into a skid rather than turn with the skid? When we're driving and we find ourselves in a skid our natural impulse is to slam on the breaks and/or, worse still, to turn with the skid. Everything in our self-preservation instinct tells us to do this, but all it does is aggravate an already precarious situation. However, when we're taught, and we practice, not hitting the brakes and not turning with the skid, but into it, often enough we make this our default reaction and we find that the car rights itself, we avoid disaster and continue safely on down the road.

You have to unlearn the old behaviors and condition new ones in order to right your course. This takes practice and repetition – even in the face of conditions that you would impulsively think would need to be reacted to otherwise. There is no substitute for perseverance.

Changing your mind about yourself is the first step. This is actually the most difficult step for guys because most don't want to believe they need to internalize a new way of thinking about themselves. Lethargy, for the most part, can be the primary reason most guys don't want to change. It's far easier to create rationales for oneself as to why they are happy in their present condition than it is to critically confront and initiate real change.

Unfortunately, I can't give you some standardized program to help you magically turn into the Man you hope to be. Only you can determine that course, but I will say this, the Man you wish to become requires you to take action. The goal posts for your own satisfaction will always keep moving away from you, and that's a good thing. This is what inspires us to grow and mature and develop a capacity to overcome challenges. However, all this requires action on your part.

You can pour through all of the advice and sift out the wisdom from this book, my blog and the community at large, but none of it will amount to anything for you if you wont act. I can't begin to recall all of the times I've counseled young guys, giving them all manner of advice and encouraging them to put it into practice, only to have them constantly bemoan that they can't find the motivation. More often than not it takes some traumatic experience or they have to be reduced to having nothing left to lose before they'll really have the fire lit under their asses to become more than they are.

I don't consider myself a motivational speaker, but at some point you have to cross the abyss and change your mind about yourself. You must kill the Beta you, to become something more. You will only get what you've gotten if you keep doing what you have done.

APPRECIATION

I've had a fantastic marriage for over 17 years now, but I'm not going to sugar coat the facts that marriage involves life changing sacrifices for men that no woman will ever fully understand or appreciate. After digging four chapters in here the idea that I may be averse to the institution of marriage would follow. I realize this, and I've dealt with it enough on my blog and more than a few community forums, but for the record, I'm not anti-marriage. I'm anti-uninformed, Pollyanna, shoulda'-saw-it-coming, ONEitis fueled, shame induced, bound for bankruptcy, scarred my children, damaged my life, marriage.

A woman loves you when she takes you for granted. That sounds odd I know, but it's when she's not fawning all over you and you're in your 10th year of marriage and it's just part of everyday conversation. "OK, love you, bye" is at the end of every phone call. You're not thinking about it, because you don't need to.

If you're asking the question "how do you know when she loves you?" You're not in it. It's only when that familiarity and regular comfort is removed that she can appreciate it. Once the commonness of love is established women will only rarely express it overtly – in fact the expression will be what's expected of *you* – so you have to look for it covertly.

All the flowery crap you read in your Hallmark card on Valentines Day or your Anniversary was written by someone else. Though it's nice to have these gestures of appreciation occasionally, it's more important to see the forest for the trees. It's not individual acts of affection or appreciation so much as it is the whole of what you both do on a regular day-to-day basis. It's what you and she are all about after your three hundredth bowl of oatmeal together on a Saturday morning and your kids are fighting for control of the TV remote while you're sitting across the breakfast table discussing which bills need to be paid first this month and how bad the lawn needs mowing that defines love and marriage.

Yes, *precisely* the things you'll never think about when you're sarging her or considering moving her up in your plate spinning line up.

This is what marriage is; not necessarily boring per se (although it certainly can be more often than not), but ordinary. It's normal, common, or becomes so. Think about how many people who've lived, married and died on planet earth who did exactly the same things as you. That's the real test of marriage that no one who hasn't experienced it can really relate in any meaningful sense.

The happy, Oprah-ized idea is that you have to "keep it fresh", but even after a night of freshening it up and the Wal-Mart lingerie is in the clothes hamper, and you pick up the kids from spending the night at her sisters house the morning after, you go back to the day-to-day marriage you've always had.

This is the shit no one tells you about when you're being sold on the Marriage Goal – the "now what?" feeling that comes directly after you've found the ONE you've been conditioned to think you're looking for, or "did the right thing" with and married because she suddenly rediscovered religion *after* you'd had marathon sex with her for 3 months straight and wouldn't abort the pregnancy.

Appreciation

I think what most men uniquely deceive themselves of is that they will ultimately be appreciated by women for their sacrifices.

Learn this now, you wont. You can't be because women fundamentally lack the capacity to fully realize, much less appreciate the sacrifices a man makes to facilitate her reality. Even the most enlightened, appreciative woman you know still operates in a feminine-centric reality.

Men making the personal sacrifices necessary to honor, respect and love her are commonplace. You're *supposed* to do those things. You sacrificed your ambitions and potential to provide her with a better life? You were supposed to. You resisted temptation and didn't cheat on your wife with the hot secretary who was down to fuck and ready to go? You were supposed to. Your responsibilities to maintaining a marriage, a home, your family, etc. are common – they're expected. They are only appreciated in their absence, in their lack and in their failing.

This is the totality of the feminine-centric reality. Men only exist to facilitate the feminine reality, and any man who disputes this (or even analyzes its aspects) is by definition *not* a 'man'. It just *is*. Even the most self-serving, maverick amongst men is still beholden to the feminine imperative in that he's only defined as a rebel because he doesn't comply with the common practices of 'men' in a female defined reality. Ironically it's just this maverick who is appreciated by the feminine above those men who would comply with it (or even promote it) as a matter of course.

The concept of appreciation dovetails into a lot of other aspects of intergender relations, so try to bear this in mind as you continue reading.

For instance, assume for a moment that a 40 year old Man with the options to pursue younger women "does the right thing" and seeks out a relationship with a woman his own age. Would he be appreciated for essentially giving an aged woman a new lease on life or would he be viewed as doing what is to be expected of him?

Would a man who marries a single mother and helps with the parental investment of another man's child be appreciated more for having done so? Would it even factor into a woman's estimation of his character, or would he simply doing what's expected of a man? The question of appreciation is a real quandary for the White Knight.

Relationships aren't work.

Familiarity does in fact breed contempt,..and mediocrity, and routine, and banality, and commonness,.. which is why so many marriages end up in the shit can. Men and women give up on themselves.

The "Relationships are work" meme is a feminine Social Convention.

How often do you hear men say these words? This convention has filtered into popular consciousness even amongst men now. For the LTR men who subscribe to this I'd also speculate that many of them are in relationships where *they* are "doing the work" for the women who are giving them the 'grade' so to speak. And of the single men who subscribe to this mythology, each had to be conditioned to believe this is the case in LTRs by women. This is rooted in the mistaken belief that men's actions and sacrifices can ever be appreciated by women.

What would the best method be to get a man to live up to the idealizations a woman has as her perfect mate (however twisted and convoluted this may have been defined for her)? Women love the 'fixer upper'. "He'd be such a great guy if only he would, ____ " or she'll say "I'm working on him." It's when the conditioning goes from "I'm working on him" to "We're working on our relationship" that he has now internalized her frame control.

This is where the mythology of Relationships-as-Work is derived from. How often is it the woman who needs the 'work' in the relationship? And if it is her, the terminology of the relationship and the associations change. 'Work' implies a man better conforming his identity to her ideal relationship, to better fit the feminine-centric reality. What better way to initiate this than to psychologically condition him to want to embody her ideal – even before he's ever met a woman or been involved in a relationship?

DREAM KILLERS

Women should only ever be a compliment to a man's life, never the focus of it.

How common it is today to be married or getting married before we've realized any of our potential. For all the articles I read moaning and groaning about what a listless gener-ation of "kidult" males we've inherited, that's far removed from the reality of the young men I do consults with. No, what they want is just enough Game knowledge to connect with their Dream Girl and relax into a blissful beta cocoon of monogamy. They want to commit. Their lifetime AFC psychological conditioning makes commitment an urgency.

It never ceases to amaze me when I talk with these young men in their teens and 20s and they try to impress me with their fierce independence in every other realm of their lives, yet they are the same guys who are so ready to limit that independence and ambition in exchange for dependable female intimacy. They're far too eager to slap on the handcuffs of monogamy, rather than develop themselves into men of ambition and passion that women naturally want to be associated with.

The truth however is that the longer you remain uncommitted, the more opportunities will be available to you. It's been stated by wiser Men than I that women are *dream-killers* – and while I agree with this, I'd say this is due more to the man involved, and their own complicity and apathy, than some grand scheme of women.

It's actually in women's best interest that you don't commit to them for a variety of reasons. I realize how counterintuitive that reads, but in your being so readily available you decrease your value as a commodity to them. Scarcity increases value, and particularly when the reason for that scarcity is something that serves another's interest (hers in this example).

The mid-20s Man pursuing his ambition to become an attorney in law school or the pre-med intern spending long hours at the hospital with aspirations of becoming a doctor is hindered and encumbered with the complications that maintaining a monogamous rela-tionship necessitates of him. His time and efforts need to be applied toward achieving his goals to become an even higher value Man – not just in terms of financial success but for his own edification and confidence. Needless to say, the constraints and obligations that maintaining a monogamous relationship require – both in time and emotional investment – make achieving these ambitions far more difficult.

I tend to promote the idea that Men should be sexually, emotionally and relationally non-exclusive until age 30, but this is a minimal suggestion. I think 35 may even serve better for Men. The importance being that as a Man ages and matures in his career, his ambitions and passions, his personality, his ability to better judge character, his overall understanding of behavior and motivations, etc., he becomes more valuable to the most desirable women and therefore enjoys better opportunity in this respect. Women's sexual value decreases as they age and it's at this point the balance tips into the maturing Man's favor. It's the Men who realize this early and understand that bettering themselves in the now will pay off better in the future while still enjoying (and learning from) the opportunities that come from being non-exclusive and non-commital make him a Man that women will compete for in the long term.

In your mid-20s you are at the apex of your potential with regards to the direction you will influence your life to go. I'm not going to make any friends by pointing this out, but what pisses off most "serial monogamists" is the unspoken regret of having assumed the responsibilities, liabilities and accountability of what monogamy demands before they truly understood, much less realized their personal potentials.

If you are single at 35 with a moderate amount of personal success, you are the envy of man-dom because you possess two of the most valuable resources most men your age or older statistically do not - time and the ability to maneuver. I envy you. You are unshackled by the responsibilities, liabilities and accountabilities that most men your age in marriages, LTRs, with children, or recovering from divorce must contend with daily. Without any intention you are in such a position that you can go in any direction of your choosing without considering the impact of your choice for anyone but yourself. Many other men, in the most ideal of LTRs, do not have this luxury.

When you think of all the responsibilities that are required of most men (and women) in modern life today, you have won the lottery! I was once asked what I'd buy if money were no object, to which I answered, time. Power isn't financial resources, status or influence over others; power is the degree over which you control your own life, and right now, if I've just described you, you are powerful. Trust me, this is as good as it gets and this is made all the better because you are old enough to understand and appreciate what is really at work here.

Women are damaged goods for you now? So what? You have the freedom to sample as indiscriminately or as particularly as you choose. Can't find a good LTR? Why would you want to?! Let her find you! You fear you'll end up old and lonely? I'd fear ending up so paralyzed by a fear of loneliness that you'd settle for a lifetime of complacent misery in a passionless marriage.

I'm an adherent of the 'build it and they will come' school of thought in this regard. Women should only ever be a compliment to a man's life – never the focus of it.

Is it better to choose the path of least resistance to get to an idealized, prefabricated intimacy or self-develop and get the same intimacy? True, both instances put women as the focus of a Man's life, and this is a position that most women will find endearing at first, but suffocating in the end.

Women want to 'want' their men. Women want a Man who other men want to be, and other women want to fuck. She doesn't want a slave to her intimacy since this puts her in the masculine role. Rather, she wants a decisive mature man who has the confidence to put her off, to tell her 'No', in favor of his ambition and passions as this serves two purposes.

First, it sets his frame and his direction as the one of authority, and his development as the primary; the results of which she and her potential children will benefit from. Secondly, it puts her into a position of chasing after him – essentially his legitimate ambitions and passions become the 'other woman' with which she must compete for his attention.

Note that I stated 'legitimate' ambitions here. A woman involved with a law student or an intern who have the *potential* to become lawyers and doctors are fairly solid bets for future security. An artist or musician, no matter how talented or committed to their passions will only be viewed as beneficial if they can prove their case to select women. However this can be offset by single-minded determination, once again, with select women with a capacity to appreciate this drive. This said, think about the fellow who's chosen to be a plumber or a mechanic as his calling. The best plumber in the world is only going so far unless he has dreams to own his own business.

All of this is limited by a man's attitude towards the opposite sex. Women are dream killers. Not because they have an agenda to be so, but because men will all too willingly sacrifice their ambitions for a steady supply of pussy and the responsibilities that women attach to this.

So yes it is better to develop yourself rather than take the path of least resistance. That's not to say don't sarge until you're out of college, in your 30s and have your career in order. It is to say don't consider monogamy until you are mature enough to understand it's limiting effects and you've achieved a degree of success to your own satisfaction according to your ambitions and passions. It is also to say that women should compliment and support *your* plans for your own life.

Our great danger in this life is not that we aim too high and fail, but that we aim too low and succeed.

HAVE A LOOK

One of the hardest things to drive home for a freshly unplugged guy is their tendency towards absolutism. You can't really blame a guy who's been desperate for intimacy for so long to want to follow some prescribed program that will *only* solve his most immediate problem.

"OK, what do I haffta do to get girls? Wear this? Say this? Act like so?,.."

It's exactly this type of literalistic, binary bent that makes most Plug-ins skeptical of the proponents of Game, and thus the veracity of Game itself.

Understanding the difference between Peacocking and having *a* style is one of these major entanglements.

"Wear a funny top hat? Black nail polish? Get the fuck outta here!,.."

Most guys new to Game tend to conflate the more extreme aspects of Peacocking with having a style or as Adam Carola puts it, having **A** look. This is a very awkward progression for 'regular' guys to make because for so long they've been told to *Just Be Themselves*. They find comfort in saying things like "I don't want to be with a girl who doesn't like me for who I am" yet wonder why they're dateless virgins who've never kissed a girl at 29.

A Look

It's important to have A Look. The basis of physical attraction is going to be conditional for any individual girl, but always bear in mind that A look is contextual. The archetypal "douchebag" with tats and an MMA appeal is a Look. Guyliner, black nail polish and Emo skinny jeans is a Look. The guy in a 3 piece Armani has a Look, and there are dozens more, but the point is that women are in fact like casting agents looking for the right character to fill a role.

But, does "A" look really imply "any" look? Some of these men look so bizarre that it's hard to imagine them conforming to an interesting character sought by a particular group of women. Can freakishness itself be a strong pivot in attracting women?

"Freakishness" to some is mundane to others. Everyone is playing a role by order of degrees on any given day and in any given circumstance. Where I work I'm free to wear jeans and a t-shirt if I so desire, but I opt to dress much sharper than that, why? Because it commands a certain respect, even if it's not necessarily legitimate. When I'm at a club, say, doing a new product launch, my persona and dress changes to match the environ-ment.

A flamboyant PUA like Mystery doesn't go around wearing elevator boots and top hats to the 7-11 to buy a big gulp. He still peacocks for sure, but it takes far less now because guys like him have distilled the principle down to what draws attention in various situations.

Club hopping in full Gene Simmons stage attire isn't impressing anyone, but that's what a lot of guys without A Look like to poke fun at – the extremes. An extreme douchebag, an extreme Emo, an extreme Orange County Chopper style, etc. make for easy targets, but that's not the point of having A look.

Peacocking

Peacocking is not a style, it is a functional PUA skill (use of props actually). It takes a sense of style to know how to pull it off effectively, but peacocking as a skill is more about use-of-instance than it is about your overall look.

When PUA studies were in their infancy, the idea of peacocking was pretty much a no-brainer. In fact it was a concept that libertines throughout history have always known. It's not too hard a concept to follow since most socially intelligent people (and even low order animals) will want to set themselves apart from the mating herd. Everyone peacocks to some degree. Just selecting a tie or a pair of shoes for an occasion may seem innocuous enough, but subconsciously you make choices and develop preferences for certain items in certain situations because you think they improve your appearance, and thus your odds for drawing attention to yourself.

The intent behind peacocking is more about having a subtle difference, or a conversation piece that draws a woman into your frame. Oddly enough (or not) I've found that nice expensive shoes seem to be a natural pull for some girls. This isn't surprising considering most women's obsession with shoes. One thing that's important to remember is women's sensitivity to covert subcommunication, body language, appearance, non-verbal cues, etc. In the briefest glance they'll size one another up and come to operative conclusions about a woman's status in their girl-hierarchy. It follows that they use the same tools with the Men they find attractive.

Most newly Game-aware men who are comfortable enough to venture using Peacocking don't realize that a little goes a long way. Your Game isn't peacocking, it's just the flashy lure to get the fish to strike. It's up to you to play the fish once it's hooked.

THE 5 STAGES OF UNPLUGGING

I once read an article about the 5 stages of grief (confronting death) and how they apply to coming into acceptance of a previously rejected truth. Yes, I know, there's no end to the ridiculous interpretations of this played-out pop-psych list, but I was curious about how this might apply to an AFC coming to grips with unplugging from the Matrix, so I did a bit of searching and what did I find on my blog roll search but this:

1. Denial – Still Plugged -In: "These game guys are a bunch of clowns, there's no way this works on women. Women aren't stupid. What a bunch of misogynists."

2. Anger – Post-Red Pill Awareness: "This is ridiculous! Why should I have to jump through all these hoops for women? I just want to be myself. Why couldn't I have been a Natural Alpha®? I blame my parents/siblings/teachers/God/liberals/feminists/media/ society, maybe those famous pussy-starved mass murderers weren't so crazy after all."

3. Bargaining – Unplugged: "Well maybe it does have some good points…but, forget the hot girls, they're way outta my league. I'll give it a try if it can help me get around the bases with a Plain Jane. Do I have to wear the fuzzy hat and black nail polish?"

4. Depression – Bitter Taste of the Red Pill: "Wow, women really respond to this puffed-up act? And guys spend big bucks on it and wind up with more ass than a toilet seat? And I just joined up for this? The world is sad and so am I…"

5. Acceptance – Game Awareness: "Maybe this *is* the way things really work. I guess I should give up the gender relations mythology I've been holding onto…hey, what do you think of these negs I came up with?"

6. Jaded* – MGTOW Permutations: "Fuck learning all these rules. Sex isn't worth it and women aren't that fun anyway. The last thing I want to do is learn routines or the 5 stages of pickup. There's too many websites, too much to read, I can't remember it all much less sort it all out. Who has all that time to go out and chat up women anyway? It's not like I see any women under 40 at work at my engineering job to practice on. Video games and porn are more fun and more available. I just haffta look good and let the women come to me"

I get a ton of private messages from forum members, and read threads about guys with friends or relatives in, or just getting over, horrible relationships and how they've tried to unplug them only to run into stiff resistance. Looking at this process to acceptance it's no wonder why.

* This is a late addition to the list, hardly original and arguably relevant, but I added it for precautionary measures since it's a common aftereffect of unplugging.

THE BITTER TASTE
OF THE RED PILL

I'm going to finish this chapter with one of the most important Rational Male essays I've written according to my readers. I saved this for last because it's the most important precaution to keep in mind when your eyes are being opened and you, or people you know, are worried about your *transformation* into becoming Game / Red Pill aware.

A lot gets made of the Dark Triad or the Dark Side of Game where a skillful player can sadistically use his newly learned red-pill super powers for evil instead of for the greater benefit of both himself and mankind. Game-aware women – the ones who have been forcibly exhausted of all pretense of maintaining the illusion that Game is a lie – will feel as though it's owed to them, in their concession of Game's reality, that Men should use Game to women's primary benefit. Even to the last effort women still cling to the tools of a feminized acculturation:

*"Yeah, OK, you got us, Game is really what women want, hypergamy is the law of womankind, but now it's **your responsibility** that you use it for the better benefit of society by molding a new breed of improved Game savvy Beta men to accommodate a feminine-centric monogamy. You owe us our security for having admitted to the grand illusion that's kept you in thrall for so long."*

It's an indictment of Game-aware women, and sympathizing men, that they should feel a need to delineate some aspects of Game into good camps (pro woman, pro feminized monogamy) and bad camps (manipulative, polygynous, male-centered). Even in the admission of the truth that Game has enlightened Men of, the feminine imperative still seeks to categorize the application of Game to serve its own end. That Men might have some means of access to their own sexual strategy is too terrible a threat; Game must be colored good or bad as it concerns the imperatives of women and a fem-centric societal norm.

As the default, socially correct and virtuous concern, women have an easier time of this.

As Game becomes increasingly more difficult to deny or misdirect for the feminine, the natural next step in accepting it becomes qualifying its acceptable uses. While hypergamy is an ugly truth about women, the characterization of it becomes "just how women are" –an unfortunate legacy of their evolution. However for Men, the characterizations of the harsher aspects of Game in its rawest form (contingencies for hypergamy) are dubbed "the dark arts" by those who have an interest in maintaining feminine primacy.

Myth of the Dark Arts

According to common definition, the Dark Triad is a group of three personality traits: narcissism, Machiavellianism and psychopathy, all of which are interpersonally aversive.

Depending upon context, that may be a convenient assessment of a sociopathic personality, but it is hardly an accurate assessment of Game as a whole. In its desperation to come to terms with a more widespread acceptance of Game, the feminine imperative had to make some effort to dissuade the common man (see Beta) from embracing the means to his release from the feminine Matrix. Associating Game with Dark Triad personality traits makes this qualification process much easier, since the feminine imperative owns the messaging and the defining authority of what is social and what is anti-social.

The problem then becomes one of defining what acceptable use of Game *is* social and anti-social. Predictably Game-accepting women will want to cast Game into terms that suit them individually and accommodates for their own personal conditions as well as the priorities of their particular phase of life. However, because of such diverse conditions, consequently there is a lot of disagreement amongst Game-accepting women about what should constitute appropriate use, thus a pick-and-pull form of rationalization about aspects of Game gets thrown about in their internal debates.

For feminized men this is a very confusing debate. It's difficult enough for them to accept that women love Jerks (despite being told the contrary for half their lives by women), but for the Game-accepting women they still think are 'quality' it's a bitter pill to swallow when these women debate the aspects of acceptable, lovable Jerk-like qualities and the evil, user, manipulative, 'dark art' Jerk that only contextually misaligns with their present conditions and priorities. For both the plugged-in and the freshly unplugged this is an incongruity that they have a tough time reconciling against the ideals of moralism that a fem-centric society has unwittingly convinced them of.

While a broader understanding of hypergamy and Game make for useful tools for enlightened single men, the Game-accepting Beta plug-in will still see it strictly as a means to satisfying the female imperative – long-term provisional monogamy. Any deviation from this narrative, any guy using Game for personal gain, personal pleasure or to enact his own sexual strategy is guilty of crimes against (feminized) society. Since the societal Greater Good has been defined by the feminine imperative, anything counter to it is definitively evil, counterproductive, anti-social and manipulative sociopathy.

The Bitter Taste of the Red Pill

The truth will set you free, but it doesn't make truth hurt any less, nor does it make truth any prettier, and it certainly doesn't absolve you of the responsibilities that truth requires.

One of the biggest obstacles guys face in unplugging is accepting the hard truths that Game and a new awareness of gender relations forces upon them. Among these is bearing the burden of realizing what you've been conditioned to believe for so long were comfortable ideals and loving expectations are really liabilities. Call them lies if you want, but often there comes a certain sense of hopeless nihilism that accompanies what amounts to a system that you are now cut away from. It is not that you're hopeless, it's that you lack the insight at this point to see that you can create hope in a new system – one in which you have more direct control over.

There are no "Dark Arts", this is simply one last desperate effort of the feminine imperative to drag you back into the Matrix. There is only Game and the degree to which you accept it and are comfortable in using it in the context that *you* define.

If you choose the context of a mutually beneficial, mutually loving, mutually respecting LTR monogamy of *your* own choosing, know that it's the fundamentals of Game that are at the root of its success or failure. If that context is in terms of spinning multiple plates, liberating the affections of women from other men, and enjoying a love life based on your personal satisfactions, also understand that it lives and dies based on your understanding the fundamentals of Game.

Just as Alpha is not inherently noble or deplorable, Game is neither inherently good nor evil – the Devil is in the details and whomever's defined context in which you use it. In the introduction section of the *48 Laws of Power*, author Robert Greene explains the same about power. Power is neither good nor evil, it simply *is*, and your capacity to use power, your comfort in using it, doesn't invalidate the principles of power. Likewise, your discomfort or inability to accept those principles does not excuse you from the consequence of having that power used upon you.

The unwritten, 49th Law of Power, is denying the utility of power itself, or demonizing its use both moralistically and socially. With the wide dispersion of Game theory this has been the reactionary tact of the feminine imperative; appeal to the deeply conditioned moral, ethical, honorable, virtuous ideals and feminine-specific obligations engrammatically planted in men by a fem-centric society, while redefining the acceptable use of the same Game the feminine imperative demonizes for its own purposes.

CHAPTER 4

GAME

THE EVOLUTION OF GAME

If you ever need a reminder as to how you came to a particular belief or set of beliefs, the best way to consider (or reconsider) that process is to write a book about it. The book you now hold in your hands is the compilation of the past twelve years of my involvement in the so-called *manosphere*. It wasn't even known as the 'manosphere' back then.

For the men (and women) who've read my ideas since the inception of the SoSuave Forum almost 12 years ago, I expect they'll find this section kind of remedial – like going back over old classics they'd internalized and take for granted now. If I make a reference to Hypergamy or the Feminine Imperative, for most, there's a standard level of pre-understanding about the elements associated to each of these and many other concepts.

However, a problem of familiarity arises when I, or anyone else familiar with *red-pill* awareness makes an attempt to educate the unfamiliar. The Red Pill reddit community makes a good effort of this, but after going through 2 revisions of this book it became evident to myself and my editor that familiarizing the uninitiated is a major obstacle to reaching the men who'll benefit most from *unplugging* (yet another manosphere term).

Familiarity

The majority of the requests I've received over the years for a comprehensive book of Rational Male ideology has come from readers expressing the desire for a condensed version in book form which they can give to family and friends (mostly male) in the hopes that they'll better understand their need for emancipation from their fem-centric mental models. Of course that's always been my goal from day one, but it presumes that a large part of those reading will be unfamiliar with common terms and concepts I, or familiar readers, will already have a grasp of.

Another issue I often run into is the presumption that readers new to my blog or commenters on other blogs have a familiarity with my work. I often find myself having to link back to articles where I covered a specific topic that a critic or an inquisitive reader might want to take me to task about. For the most part I make a conscious effort not to repeat something I've addressed, sometimes years before, but that's simply a part of the medium of blogging.

It's a difficult enough proposal to unplug men from their blue pill conditioning, but leading them to an understanding of principles they mentally have a resistance or aversion to is a particular challenge. For example, my editor is only peripherally familiar with these principles which is kind of a blessing and a curse. In one sense it requires me to revise old posts and concepts to be more 'noob friendly', but it also challenges me to review how those concepts evolved over the years to be what I and other 'red pillers' now consider common foundations. For instance, while I might rigorously debate the concept of the Feminine Imperative with those familiar with it on Dalrock's blog, I had to spend over an hour defining it further with my editor after he'd read my seminal posts about it. More on this later.

Game

Of these concepts the one I return to the most frequently is that of Game. "Just what is Game?" Throughout my blog, and virtually every major manosphere writer's blog, there's a constant presumption that readers will know exactly what Game is when it's referred to. Game has been lifted up to an almost mythical state; like some cure-all for the common guy struggling with attracting women's attentions and intimacy. It's gotten to the point where familiarity with Game has become a flippant aside for manosphere bloggers – we have varieties of Game: we have internalized Game, we have 'natural' Game, direct Game, Beta Game etc., but defining the term 'Game' for someone unfamiliar with the very involved intricacies, behaviors and the underlying psychological principles on which Game is founded is really tough for the uninitiated to wrap their heads around in the beginning.

For the unfamiliar, just the word 'Game' seems to infer deception or manipulation. You're not being real if you're playing a *Game*, so from the outset we're starting off from a disadvantage of perception. This is further compounded when attempting to explain Game concepts to a guy who's only ever been conditioned to 'just be himself' with women and how women allegedly hate guys "who play games" with them. As bad as that sounds, it's really in the explanation of how Game is more than the common perception that prompts the discussion for the new reader to have it explained for them.

At its root level Game is a series of behavioral modifications to life skills based on psychological and sociological principles to facilitate intersexual relations between genders.

Early Game

In its humble beginnings, Game was a set of behaviors, learned, adapted and modified with the express purpose of bettering a guy's prospective sexual 'success' with the women he had only limited (if any) access to. Game was defined as a series of behavioral skills and techniques observationally experimented with, and developed by the burgeoning pickup artist (PUA) culture of the early 2000's. While there was a peripheral acknowledgment given to the psychology that made these behavior sets effective, the purpose was more about the result and less about the head-mechanics that made the result possible.

This introduction was many of the current manosphere's first contact with 'formalized' Game. The quality of the *art* in pick up artistry was (and still is) really left up to the practitioner's capacity to understand the basics of behavioral psychology (with regards to women) and refining a deft ability to adapt and react to his target's changing behavioral cues in a given environment and/or context..

If this were the only extent of Game it would understandably be very short sighted and limited in scope. In the beginning Game had a utility in that it helped a majority of men lacking the social intelligence to approach and develop a real, intimate rapport with women they fundamentally lacked. The problem was that beyond Game's "in-field" uses it wasn't really developed past the point of 'getting the girl', and left even the most socially adept PUAs unprepared to deal with the real psychology motivating women on a greater whole. It was just this feminine meta-psychology that drove men, unaccustomed to enjoying, and then losing, the affections of women formerly "out of their league", to depression and possibly suicide.

Game was a wondrous tool set of skills, but without the insight and foresight to deal with what these tools could build, it was potentially like giving children dynamite.

Evolving Game

From the earliest inception Game was more or less viewed as a solution to a problem. Game has been described as the logical social reaction to the women that the past 60+ years of feminism, social feminization and feminine primacy has created for the men of today. Courtesy of modern connectivity, the internet and collectivized social media, evolving Game or some variation of it was inevitable for men. Despite the public social stigma, ridicule and outright hostility attached to men attempting to understand the psychologies of women, privately the internet facilitated a global consortium of men comparing experiences, relating observations and testing theories.

The behavioral psychology that led to Game which prompted the desired reactions in women began to take on more importance for men. Sure, the now classic Game techniques like being Cocky & Funny, Amused Mastery, Agree & Amplify, Neg Hits, Peacocking, etc. were effective in their own artfully used contexts, but the latent psychology that made those behavior sets work prompted the questions of *why* they worked.

The psychological aspects of effective (and ineffective) Game began to take on a new importance. Through this broader exploration of the role biological, psychological and sociological factors affected Game sprang new ideas, theories and experimentative models leading to new Game behavioral sets and the abandonment of less effective ones.

As connectivity grew, so did the knowledge base of the Game community. No longer was Game exclusive to the PUA pioneers; Game was expanding to accommodate the interests and influences of men who'd never heard of the earlier version of Game, or would've rejected it outright just years before due to their feminine conditioning.

Married men wondered if aspects of Game could reignite the sexual interests of their frigid or overbearing wives. Divorced men embraced the Game they ridiculed when married to improve their potential for new sexual interests, but also to relate their experiences and contribute to that Game knowledge base. Men, not just in western culture, but from a globalizing interest began to awaken with each new contribution not only about how women were, but *why* women were. Game was making the unknowable woman knowable. The enigmatic feminine mystique began unraveling with each new contribution to the Game knowledge-base.

Game was becoming something more. Men were now seeing the code in the Matrix: we knew the medium was the message, we began to see the feminine social conventions used to control us, we began to see the overarching reach of the feminine imperative and fem-centrism, and we came to realize the insidious, but naturalistic, influence feminine Hypergamy had wrought in both men and women. Game was prompting Men to push back the iron veil of feminine primacy and see what made her tick.

Predictably, fem-centric society sought to cast the rise, and expansion of Game as a modern version of the ridiculous macho archetypes of the 50's-70's. The threat of an evolving, more intellectually valid form of Game had to be ridiculed and shamed like anything else masculine, so the association with its infamous PUA forerunners was the obvious choice for the feminine imperative. The feminine standard appeal to the Masculine Catch 22 was the first recourse: any man who desired to learn Game was less than a man for that desire, but also less of a man for not already knowing Game (as approved by the feminine imperative). Any guy actually paying for, or personally invested in, Game was associated with the PUA culture that was characterized as a throw back to the 'Leisure Suit Larrys' of the 70's.

Contemporary Game

For all its marginalization efforts to shame Game back into obscurity, the feminine imperative found that the Game movement wasn't being cowed as easily as it might have been in the mid 1990's. The imperative was falling back on the reliable tropes and social conventions that had always pushed the masculine back into compliance. At the apex of fem-centrism in the 90's these social constructs worked well on an isolated, shamed and ignorant masculine imperative, but with the evolution of the internet, by the late 2000's Game was snowballing into a threat that required new feminine operative conventions to contain it.

Game evolved beyond the behavioral sets, and beyond the psychological and sociological mechanics that underlined women's psyches and larger socializations. While still encompassing all that prior evolution, Game was becoming aware of the larger social meta-scale of the feminine imperative. Game began to move beyond the questions of *why* women are the way they are, and into piecing together *how* the intergender acculturations we experience today are what they are. Game asked *how* did we come to this?

Game branched into specific areas of interest in its scope to answer these broader questions and solve more expansive problems. While we still have all of the prior iterations of Game, we have expanded into Christianized Game, married Game, divorced Game, socialized Game, high school Game, etc.

However, underpinning all of these areas of specialization was still the need to internalize and personalize Game in a Man's life. Game was the path to male re-empowerment; an empowerment that even women today still feel men should Man-*back*-Up to.

Game required a reinterpretation of masculinity towards something positive, beneficial and competent – something entirely apart from the negative, shameful and ridiculous archetypes 60 years of feminization had convinced women and men of. Call it Alpha, call it Positive Masculinity, but Game necessitates the re-imagining of the importance of the masculine imperative. Game needs Men to change their minds about themselves.

Needless to say, even in its most positive of contexts, the male re-empowerment that Game led to was a threat too great for the feminine imperative to allow. Controlling the intrinsic insecurities that the feminine imperative is founded upon has alway depended on men's ignorance of their true personal value, and true necessity to women. Men have to remain necessitous to women in order for their insecurity to be insured against, and the feminine imperative's control to be ensured of.

The well of knowledge and awareness that Game represented had to be poisoned.

The social conventions the feminine imperative had relied on for decades were no longer as effective as they were in a pre-internet era. The continued expansion of Game into the social, psychological, evolutionary and biological realms was evidence that Game was something those old convention couldn't contain, so the imperative evolved new tacts while reinventing old ones.

Shaming and ridicule were (and still are) the rudimentary tactics that the less intellectual of the feminine imperative would resort to, but the expansiveness of Game needed something more distorting. Proponents of the feminine imperative began to concede *certain* universal points that Game had long asserted about the feminine nature (and the feminine imperative had long rejected) in an effort to co-opt the social momentum Game had taken over a decade to develop.

The Feminine Imperative couldn't argue with the extensive, provable validity of the tenets of Game, so it sought (seeks) to re-engineer Game from within and modify it to its own purpose. The Feminine Imperative wants just enough male empowerment to return men to an improved (really an older) state of usefulness to its own ends, but not so much that true male emancipation from the imperative would threaten its dominance. In co-opting Game and conceding to the truths it finds less threatening, the imperative hopes to build better Betas – men who believe they are empowered by Game, but are still beholden to the Feminine Imperative.

True emancipation from the imperative threatens its dominance, so Men with the vision to see past this are labeled Dark, Sociopathic and Deviant by the imperative. It wasn't enough just to infiltrate Game and sanitize it for its benefit, the Feminine Imperative had to categorize Game for itself – Evil vs. Good Game. The good, of course, being charac-teristic of whatever aspects benefited the imperative, and the bad being whatever 'selfishly' benefited the masculine. The Feminine Imperative doesn't care about the various branchings of Game – natural, internalized, marriage, etc. – it only concerns itself with what aspects of those branches that can be distorted to its advantage and what aspects cannot.

This brings us to Game as we know it today. Game is still evolving, and had I the prescience to see where it will go next, I would venture that it will come to men's real emancipation with the Feminine Imperative. Not an emancipation from women, but an emancipation from their imperative's conditioning and purpose. Not a 'men going their own way' negligence of women in the hope that they'll come around to behaving as men would like after being given no other choice, but a true Game driven emancipation from the control that fem-centrism has maintained for so long.

Make no mistake, the Feminine Imperative needs men to be necessitous of it, and it will always be hostile to the Men attempting to free other men from that necessity. In this respect, any Game, even the co-opted Game the imperative will use itself, is by definition sexist. Anything that may benefit Men, even when it associatively benefits women, is sexist. Freeing men from the Matrix, breaking their conditioning and encouraging them to re-imagine themselves and their personalities for their own betterment is, by feminine definition, sexist.

In girl-world, encouraging men to be better Men is sexist.

REWRITING THE RULES

Women would rather share a successful Man than be attached to a faithful loser.

— Pook

One of the most common things I'm asked on the SoSuave forum is "how do you keep a marriage fresh Rollo?" Among my responses to this is usually how, contrary to the advice column Oprah-standard answer, a good relationship should be effortless. All of this "marriage is a constant work" is bullshit meant to keep a husband in a constant state of qualifying for his wife's intimacy intended for her long term frame retention. Women in marriage and LTRs want to push past that nagging hypergamic competition anxiety; they want security, not just financial, but emotional, and the security that comes from a locked in commitment in knowing they are the only source of sex & intimacy for their spouse/partner.

Pre-Commitment to Commitment

One of the reasons sexual frequency declines for women after a romantic commitment is that the urgency of sex that was necessary prior to the commitment is replaced with the agency of sex being a reward / reinforcer within that LTR. In single, uncommitted, non-exclusive life, sex, while being very enjoyable, becomes a proving ground for most women. In essence, it's the free samples before the buy, and its urgency is fueled not only by (hopefully) genuine attraction and arousal, but also at least the subconscious knowledge that she is in a sexual marketplace of competition. It's one of the few times in life when a woman must qualify for a man's approval. Admittedly, most men are so sex deprived or so inexperienced early on in life that the sell is usually not a tough one for her. However, on some level of consciousness, even when the sell is virtually assured, she is aware that she could be replaced by a better competitor. Hypergamy drives women to sustain a prospective man's interest.

This then is the contrast for committed sexual interaction. The dynamic now shifts from qualification sex to utility sex. Now before anyone jumps to conclusions, yes, sex is still enjoyable, it can still be passionate, and she can definitely want it, but the impetus shifts. Sex is now a tool. In her uncommitted sex life it was a tool for qualification; in her LTR life it's a tool for compliance. This is pretty obvious, and it may be more or less extreme depending upon the woman's disposition or how important a particular issue is to her, but make no mistake, there isn't a woman on the planet who doesn't take her sexual agency into account when dealing with her LTR / husband. That agency may be more or less valuable – dependent upon her looks, demeanor, sexual availability, etc. – in comparison to the sexual market value of the man she's paired with.

And this is where the *Cardinal Rule of Relationships* plays in. This is the constant interplay of vying for who is more dependent upon the other. Women have for the past 50+ years made a concerted effort, and using social conventions, to establish their sexuality as the end-all for men in power. Vagina = Authority and this is what all too many men parrot back to others and self-reinforce. "Change, do it, sublimate your desires, or there wont be any nookie for you tonight mister!" On the surface it seems intuitive to 'keep the peace' and finish all the things on her honey-do list in the hopes that she'll recover even a fraction of the desire she had when you were single, childless and getting blow jobs in the car after a date because she couldn't wait to get home to fuck you.

The Upper Hand

Well LTR gentlemen, I'm here to tell you that, yes, you do in fact have an intrinsic upper hand in this regard if you're fearless and willing to exercise your power. What I described in the last paragraph is simply the male deductive problem solving we use for so many other things in life. It's the most intuitive solution – do what she says = get sex.

So it should come as no shock that the answer to this is counterintuitive. You must find ways to, subtly, return back to the state of competition anxiety she had in the beginning. I emphasize subtly, because, as with most everything else female, doing so overtly will be met with hostility, resentment and at best, obligated compliance.

To get more (any?) sex, to retain the frame, to inspire more respect in her, you must disengage from her. That doesn't mean becoming arrogantly aloof, or sulking like a child, or becoming an instant asshole; those are *overt* signs and methods. What is needed is incremental reassertion of yourself as the primary AND that her sexual agency, while still welcomed, is not a motivator for your own decisions.

I'm fond of saying no vagina is worth years of regret, yet this is exactly where most men find themselves, because they are either unwilling or unable to rock the vagina boat. They fail to understand that a woman's imagination is the most powerful tool in the Don Juan toolbox.

The deductive and obvious way of stimulating that imagination would be to blurt out and say "look bitch, your pussy's not made of gold and there are plenty of other girls ready to polish my nob if you don't straighten up, see?" And this of course is met with either resistance or shame from her. What serves a Man better is to make incremental changes in himself that she will perceive as attractive to other women.

Women want to be with Men who other women want to fuck, and other men want to be.

This cuts both ways. The more empowered he becomes, the better physical shape he attains, the more professional achievements he gathers, the more social proof and status he accrues, the more valuable he makes himself, the more anxiety is produce – and this is the same old familiar competition anxiety a woman's hindbrain can't argue with.

One of the first things I tell men trapped in a 'her-frame' relationship is to get to the gym, train hard, look better. This has two effects; first it makes her physical interest in fucking increase, and second it fires up that imagination.

"Why is he doing this? He's really looking better these days, I see it, other women must see it too. Maybe I need to start working out? Gosh those girls at the gym look really good."

She can't argue with a healthy desire to look better, feel better, and be concerned with your health. Getting in better shape is the easiest, most immediate change you can effect. You may have little influence in getting a promotion at work, but you *can* change your body habitus right now. Women, being the calculating gender, know all too well to hit the gym months prior to a break up – she's not getting in shape for you, she's getting ready to hit the ground running with the next guy she'll be fucking. They know this, so your manifesting the same behavior 'caffeinates the hamster' since it hits home for them.

Vagina is Not Authority

Don't accept that her sexuality is the authority of the relationship. The better you make yourself the more authority you command, the more you abdicate to her the less authority (and respect) you command.

Women need to be told "NO", in fact they want you to tell them "NO", especially in light of the 800 pound gorilla in the room – her sexual agency. When a woman controls the LTR frame with her vagina, it's always going to color your dealings with her. This is no way to go through life. It becomes this ever-present, unspoken understanding that she can ultimately play the pussy card and you'll comply.

While this may gratify her in the short term, you will lose her respect in the long term. She wants to be told "NO" in spite of you knowing she's going to hold out on you. This is the ultimate repudiation of her sexual agency – "if he says "NO" with the foreknowledge that he knows he wont be getting any, my sexual powers are devalued." If her sexual agency is called into question it leaves room for doubt and opens the door once again for competition anxiety to creep back in.

As I've said before, marriage is no insulation against the sexual marketplace, and no one knows this better than women who can rely on a society that rewards them for recognizing it. Use that to *your* benefit now.

Nothing is as simultaneously fear inspiring and arousing for women as a Man she suspects is self-aware of his own value.

This is precisely why a feminized culture must continually confuse him, continually inspire doubt and humiliate him; feminization can't afford men knowing their true value and potential.

In the end, who cares if you don't get laid for a week? It's well worth the price for increasing her respect for you as a commodity, and increasingly, an authority. If you want to maintain that anxiety, you must perpetuate yourself as being a commodity women will compete for, even (especially) in the confines of committed monogamy.

FINAL EXAM – NAVIGATING THE
SEXUAL MARKETPLACE

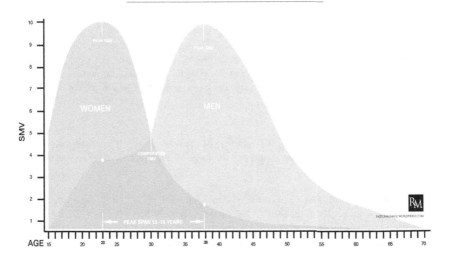

You know, there's really no substitute for graphs, and charts, and data plot maps. Human beings, as essentially a visually oriented species, see a graphic heads-up display, a God's eye view as it were, as essential to seeing the forest for the trees. You may not like being on a budget at home, but show a guy a graph of where all his money goes in a month and he'll feel better about not pissing it away for a peck on the cheek over the course of a couple weekends.

So it was with this in mind that I took it upon myself to plot out a chronology of the little known and far too under-appreciated sexual marketplace (SMP) we presently find ourselves experiencing (at least since the sexual revolution). Bloggers in the manosphere often use the SMP in a context which presumes that readers are already familiar with their mental model of it, and understand the dynamics of the modern SMP. Personally I think this presumption is fraught with individual bias, both intended and unintended. Make no mistake, I'm about to define the SMP and sexual market values (SMV) from my own perception, but I fully recognize the want for defining these dynamics in a clear, understandable format, so I'll beg my reader's forgiveness for this indulgence.

Can I Graduate?

At the time of this writing it was about graduation time for many high school seniors, and with that comes a lot of pontification from 'adults' who want to impart some grand words of wisdom to the next generation as they launch headlong into a future of student debt and/or dismal employment prospects. This is a special time for parents and childless adults alike to reflect upon their own lives and ask themselves "what would I tell my younger self to do differently?" and hope against hope that the 18 year old they feel compelled to cast in the role of their younger selves will tear themselves away from texting their friends about who's going to get whom to buy their prom night liquor long enough for it to sink in. So you'll have to forgive me for playing the professor here for a moment while I make the same vain attempt.

Not long ago I had a commenter tell me,..

"Rollo, I just wanted to say that your stuff has been truly groundbreaking for me. This material should be a graduation requirement for all high school seniors."

Well, far be it from Dr. Rollo J. Tomassi, Professor Emeritus, to be so remiss in his sacred charge of educating the next generation about the perils of the sexual marketplace they would otherwise so blindly stagger into. Challenge accepted.

So please gather round the podium, turn off all your cellular devices (prom night liquor's easy to come by), take a sheet of notebook paper from your Pee Chee folder and prepare to take notes on,..

Navigating the SMP

Now class, if you'll direct your attention to the display above I'll explain the parameters of this graph.

In the vertical column we have Sexual Market Value (SMV) based on the ubiquitous ten scale. Professor Roissy emeritus at The Chateau Heartiste did us all the good service of elaborating upon individuated sexual market valuations for both men and women long ago, however for our purposes today it is important to note that the valuations I'm illustrating here are meant to encompass an overall sexual value based on both long and short term breeding prospects, relational desirability, male provisioning capacity, female fertility, sexual desirability and availability, etc. et. al.. Your mileage may vary, but suffice it to say the ten scale is meant to reflect an overall value as individuated for one sex by the *other*. Outliers will always be an element of any study, but the intent is to represent general averages here.

On the horizontal metric we have a time line based on the age of the respective sex. I've broken this down into stages of five year increments, but with notable ages represented for significant life-to-valuation phase for each sex to be detailed later in our lecture.

As an aside here you may notice I began the SMV age range at 15. This is intentional as it is the baseline starting point for the average girl's midrange desirability value as evaluated by the average high school boy of the same age. Also of note will be the age range between 23 and 36 which represents the peak span years between the sexes, also to be detailed later.

Lastly, I've delineated each gender's respective SMV range bell curve and indicated their crossover phases accordingly.

Women's SMV

In various contexts, women's SMV is without doubt the most discussed topic in the manosphere. Try as we may, convincing a woman that her sexual peak lay actually between 18 and 25 is always an effort in debating denial. For all the self-convincing attempts to redefine sexual valuation to the contrary, SMV for women is ultimately decided by Men, not by women. Thus this bell curve is intended to represent the sexual value of women based on *men's* metrics, not as women (by way of ceaseless social engineering) would like to define desirability.

As we continue along you can see that the peak years for women's SMV tops out at around 23 years. Fertility, desirability, sexual availability and really overall potential for male arousal and attention reach an apex between 22 to 24 year of age. Remember this approximation isn't an estimate of personal worth, fidelity, intellect, character, or any metric beyond a baseline of desirability invoked in men. Ladies, on average, this is your best year. I don't think I'm relating anything the cold truth of your hindbrain hasn't woke you up at night over.

At no other phase in a woman's life will she enjoy more affirmation or legitimate male attention, more zealously applied for her sexual approval than this brief stretch. Once past the apex, every effort she spends on generating male arousal cues will be in an attempt to recapture the experiences of this phase. Every post-apex, pre-Wall (24 to 30) calorie women burn will be motivated by the memories of her SMV peak.

By the age of 27 women's SMV decline has begun in earnest. That isn't to say that women can't remain stunningly attractive and vivacious in their post-peak years, but comparative to the next crop of 22-23 year olds, the decline progressively becomes more evident. Competition for hypergamously suitable mates becomes more intensified with each passing year. The age's between 27 and 30 are subliminally the most stressful for women as the realization sinks in that they must trade their 'party years' short term mating protocol for a long term provisioning strategy.

It's at this point that rationalizations of 'living a new life' or 'getting right with herself' begin to formulate; not as a result of guilt or conviction per se, but rather as a function of relieving the anxieties associated with the new reality that she will eventually no longer be able to compete effectively in the SMP. The writing's on the Wall; either she must establish her own security and provisioning, or settle for as acceptable a provider as her present looks, personal desirability and sexual agency will permit to secure a man's long term provisioning.

Men

It may seem dismally pessimistic to begin boys SMV at so low a starting point at 15, but recall that we're looking at overall averages. A 15 year old girl will look at an 18-20 year old man's sexual approval as more valuable than that of her same age peers. It's not that notable boys' attentions are worthless, but they are far more mundane to a mid teens girl, thus the evaluation starts much lower.

As men age you can see that their SMV tends to level off during their 20's with a gradual rise up to age 30. This represents men's slow build SMV as they become more valuable by metrics of physical prowess, social gravity, status, maturity, affluence, influence, and, hopefully, dominance. It's a slow process and, unfortunately, of a man's significant maturing to his SMV, most of it occurs while women are reaching their own SMV peak. At age 23, while a girl is enjoying her prime SMP value, a man is just beginning to make his own gradual ascent.

By age 36, the average man has reached his own relative SMV apex. It's at this phase that his sexual / social / professional appeal has reached maturity. Assuming he's maximized as much of his potential as possible, it's at this stage that women's hypergamous directives will find him the most acceptable for her long-term investment. He's young enough to retain his physique in better part, but old enough to have attained social and professional maturity.

Comparative SMV and the Peak Span Years

One important note here is to compare men and women's SMV decline. Women's SMV being primarily based on the physical, has a much more precipitous decline than that of men's. who's decline is graduated upon a declining capacity to maintain his status as well as his health / looks. Since a man's SMV is primarily rooted in his personal accomplishments, his SMV degradation has much more potential for preservation. Women's SMV burns hot and short, but men's burns slow and long.

Now class, please address your attention to the critical 15-16 year span between a woman's peak SMV and that of men's. It should come as no surprise that this span is generally the most socially tumultuous between the sexes. The majority of first marriages take place here, single-motherhood takes place here, advanced degrees, career establishments, hitting the Wall, and many other significant life events occur in this life stage. So it is with a profound sense of importance that we understand the SMV context, and the SMP's influence as prescribed to each sexes' experience during this period.

At age 30 men are just beginning to manifest some proto-awareness of their inherent sexual value, while simultaneously women are becoming painfully aware of their marked inability to compete with their sexual competitors indefinitely. This is the point of comparative SMV: when both sexes are situationally at about the same level of valuation (5). The conflict in this is that men are just beginning to realize their potential while women must struggle with the declination of their own.

This is the primary phase during which women must cash in their biological chips in the hope that the best men they can invest their hypergamy with will not be so aware of their innate SMV potential that they would choose a younger woman (22-24) during her peak phase over her. I write about this later in *The Threat*:

Nothing is more threatening yet simultaneously attractive to a woman than a man who is aware of his own value to women.

The confluence between both sexes' comparative SMV is perhaps the most critical stage of life for feminine hypergamy. She must be able to keep him ignorant of his SMV potential long enough to optimize her hypergamy. The entirety of feminine social influence revolves around optimizing this hypergamy for as long as she is desirable enough to effect it.

In men's case, his imperative is to awaken to his SMV (or his potential of it) before he has made life-altering decisions based on a lack understanding his potential and remaining apart from women's pluralistic sexual strategies to make those life-decisions based on his own best interests.

Every man who I've ever known to tell me how he wished he'd known of the manosphere or read my writing before getting married or 'accidentally' knocking up his girlfriend has his regret rooted in not making this SMV awareness connection before she had consolidated (legally and emotionally) on her own sexual imperatives. They tended to value women more greatly than their own personal potential for a later realized SMV peak – or they never realized that peak due to not making this awareness connection.

Well, I'm afraid that's all I have space for today class. I hope this brief intensive has given you some food for thought as you enter a feminized world legally and socially dedicated to the benefit of optimizing hypergamy. Just remember, as you see your illustrious manosphere instructors gazing proudly from the gallery in our professorial caps and gowns, an ounce of prevention is worth a pound of cure.

Class dismissed. We are who we say we are.

JUST BE YOURSELF

We are who we say we are.

Is the woman who applies make up everyday 'being herself'?

How about the woman with implants, is she 'being herself'? What about the woman wearing high heels because it boosts her height 4 inches? Is the girl you see in nothing but party pics on FaceBook being herself?

Lets turn it the other way, what of the woman wearing a business suit that emphasizes her shoulders with pads in the jacket is she 'being herself'? If she colors her hair does this make her less genuine?

If *being ourselves* is an idealized state then I should reasonably be able to expect a like-minded fitness model to be attracted to me even if my greatest passion is to sit on my couch, eat a large pizza and wash it down with a 6 pack of Michelob while watching Monday Night Football, right? After all, I am just being myself – it's who I am.

Believe and so you shall become

The hardest distinction the uninitiated have with the JBY (just be yourself) dynamic is that personality is malleable. Personality is always in flux. The person you are today isn't who you were 2 years ago, nor the person you'll be 2 years from now. There are traits and characteristics we may carry with us for a lifetime, but even these are subject to change depending upon circumstance. You define what being yourself is at any given moment and it's relative to your personal conditions and environment.

So where do you draw the line? When does a genuine change of character become legitimate rather than being 'shallow' or 'superficial' or "someone you're not?" Those are just catch terms that women (and too many chumps) have used with success over the centuries and men have internalized as being states of perception that women think are undesirable, yet they never accurately define. Rather, they stay intentionally ambiguous and, usually, relative to an individual woman's interpretation, while their behaviors indicate their own motivations.

You are who you believe you are, and you are who she perceives you to be.

One of the hardest things for anyone, male or female, to hear is that they need to change their lifestyle. It implies that their just 'being themselves' is in some way at fault for their present conditions. It's analogous to telling someone they're not living their lives 'correctly' or that they're raising their kids wrong.

If I have a friend that is shooting heroin and I actively encourage him to stop and make an effort to help him 'clean up', society calls me a hero or a savior. When I encourage my friend to quit smoking before she gets cancer, I'm a concerned good-friend helping my friend with a health risk behavior. But when I tell a friend he needs to change his approach to women and this is a reason for his unhappiness and he needs to change his outlook on, and approach with women, look better and feel better, then I'm a 'shallow' prick and insensitive to his 'problem'. Worse still is even attempting to offer constructive criticism, in as positive a light possible, that a person can improve themselves by changing their outlook and modifying their behavior.

Personality is not only malleable, but it can change dramatically under specific conditions.

An easy example of this is veterans with post traumatic stress disorder. These men were exposed to traumatic environments that fundamentally altered their personalities. While this is an extreme illustration it shows that becoming a 'different person' is a matter of conditions. If my conditions are such that I enjoy sitting at home eating a whole pizza, washing it down with a six pack of Budweiser and watching Anime on a Friday evening, can I realistically expect that hot fitness instructor at the gym to come on over and genuinely want to fuck my brains out?

And why not? After all I'm only being myself and she should "love me for who I am", right? If this were my case, the conditions that define my personality are incongruous with attracting and/or maintaining a relationship with someone whose conditions are not my own.

JBY is an operative social convention that aids hypergamy.

Women are only too happy to endorse and reinforce JBY for the conscious reasoning that it 'sounds like the right thing to say'.

It's an unassailable position; who wouldn't want you to be you? If what counts is all on the inside then anyone telling you to change *must* be manipulating you for their own selfish reasons. This dovetails nicely into the popularized fat-acceptance self-acceptance mantra most women will fall back on when the impact of the Wall begins to manifest itself in their physiques and they want to be loved for "who they are" rather than what they used to look like.

However, on a subconscious level, the latent purpose of fostering the JBY social convention in men is yet another sexual selection filtering mechanism. Actually it's more of a filtering failsafe in that by socially mandating a genuineness in the general populace of men, women are more secure in the accuracy of their sexual assessment of men. If all men are *Just Being Themselves* and are encouraged to be the person they 'truly are', this then aids a woman in determining which man will best satisfy her hypergamy.

As I've stated in many a prior post, women claim to want honesty from men, but no woman wants full disclosure. In a general sense I advise this because it serves to sustain a Man's aura of mystery, only to be progressively discovered by women with the appropriate levels of interest and responsiveness to men. However, another reason to remain deliberately ambiguous is to defuse the JBY dynamic that women assume would be a man's default psychology.

An integral part of maintaining the feminine imperative as the societal imperative involves keeping women as the primary sexual selectors. What this means is that a woman's sexual strategy necessitates that she be in as optimized a condition as her capacity (attractiveness) allows for her to choose from the best males available to satisfy that strategy.

JBY is a tool in maintaining the feminine imperative as the social imperative. Furthermore JBY serves in optimizing hypergamy in aiding a woman's sense of security about assessing which man will best suit her hypergamy. Ironically, the JBY dynamic gets upended once a monogamous relationship is established by a woman's anxiety over 'fixing' her partner once in that relationship. What was once the pseudo-genuineness of just him being himself is replace by "I'm working on him" in order for him to become the ideal man to meet with her hypergamic approval – thus exposing the calculated nonsense JBY really is to begin with.

We are who we say we are

We can alter our own personalities and have them altered by our conditions or any combination of the two, but to suggest that personality is static is a falsehood.

The trap is to think that altering personality is in anyway disingenuous – there are certainly terrific 'actors' or 'poseurs', and the like, that when we are confronted with them we sense (or even know) that they are pushing an envelope that they may not be entirely comfortable with, but there is merit to a 'fake it till you make it' doctrine.

We only perceive it as being 'false', 'superficial' or as "trying to be something your not" when we have a concept or knowledge of a previous set of personality behaviors. If you met a likable cocky-funny guy at a club this weekend, how are you to know whether he's the real deal or stretching the limits of his personality if you've never met him before?

From *The 48 Laws of Power*:

Law 25: Re-Create Yourself
Do not accept the roles that society foists on you. Re-create yourself by forging a new identity, one that commands attention and never bores the audience. Be the master of your own image rather than letting others define it for you. Incorporate dramatic devices into your public gestures and actions— your power will be enhanced and your character will seem larger than life.

THE NICE GUY - JERK SPECTRUM

I know, I know, Nice Guy vs. Jerk has been done into the ground many times.

I think one of the easiest targets for Game hate is the terminology. It's far too easy to apply subjective definitions to archetypes like 'Nice Guy' or 'Jerk'. The standard binary response is usually,

"So, I gotta be a complete asshole all the time or girls wont be attracted to me? Screw that man, I'm not into game playin'."

You can sift back through any number of forum pages of advice I've offered and read me over and over again telling young men to "get in touch with their inner asshole." However, in any of my posts, never do I state to in fact become an asshole.

The two most common questions I get asked advice for is "Why do girls love Jerks so much?" and the "How do I get out of the friend-zone?" line. Both of these illustrate different ends of a spectrum.

Try to think of it this way – on one end of the spectrum you have the consummate Jerk, he's obnoxious, an asshole, borders on abusiveness, but women flock to the guy in droves.
On the opposite end of the scale we have the ultimate Nice Guy who does and embodies everything any girl has ever told him he needs to become in order to achieve their intimacy and has internalized this doormat conditioning into his own personality. This is the guy who'll spend countless hours on the phone being 'friends' with a girl or spend fortunes on gifts for her in order to buy her approval.

I think it's important to look at the roots of the terms "Jerk" and "Nice Guy." Lets not forget these characterizations exist because women gave them these names and classifications based on their own common evaluations. Women defined these terms – guys simply made the association with them. We tend to see these as parodies or caricatures now; abusive wife-beating Jerk or doormat Nice Guy. These are two extreme ends of the spectrum and when considering them after candid assessments, the mistake becomes falling into a binary all-or-nothing interpretation.

"So I haffta be more of a Jerk then,..well, I'm just not like that." says the AFC frustrated at what seems like women's duplicity of words and actions, but this misses the point.

The problem is that if you think of a center point between that Jerk and Nice Guy spectrum, most guys lean towards (if not half way over to) the Nice Guy. That's the "get in touch with your feminine side, believe women's words instead of actions" default for the vast majority of men. This is what women are used to because it is so common, and women only encourage it because it suits their gender's imperative best. The real extreme Jerk is as rare as the real extreme Nice Guy, so it's necessary to look at things in order of degrees in this respect.

Most men are Betas, or overwhelmingly invest themselves in a Beta male identity. They opt for the nice, accommodating, supplicating side of this spectrum - for the majority, they've been socially conditioned to suppress any natural masculine impulse in favor of accommodating and identifying with women's imperatives (or at least what they're led to understand as their imperatives) at the risk of intimate rejection. It's exactly this mindset, this Beta male default to the 'nice' end of the spectrum that 85% of guys subscribe to, that makes the guy who leans into the 'jerk' end of the spectrum attractive.

Yes, confidence and indifference are Alpha traits, but in a world awash in nice guys ready to buy a hot girl a drink, it's the guy who 'couldn't give a shit' who she marks as a sexual potential. It's just this conditioning over the last 50+ or so years that makes the nice side of the spectrum the default. That doesn't mean all Nice Guys are pathetic symps without a spine and groveling at the feet of any ONEitis they happen to attach themselves to. It is to say that, by comparison, and because the overwhelming tendency to "go nice" is the standard, the guy who leans even marginally to the Jerk side of the spectrum becomes at least notable, and at best attractive, simply by dissociation from the masses of nice guys.

He's attractive on two levels, the first being the rudimentary Alpha, biological level for a guy who's decisive, in control, confident and has an attitude of caring less about a woman, since he realizes (to some degree) his value as a commodity comes from his having the options to have such an attitude.

The second is that the Jerk-leaning guy is a Purple Cow in a field of bland, colorless Nice Cows. He's notable, and this too, makes him a male worthy of female competition, which then reinforces his sense of having options. He's not an abuser, he's not a manipulator per se, but he tends to put himself before and above (sometimes innocently, sometimes callously) the women who are attracted to him.

Now the irony of all this is that the AFC thinks that this situation is in reverse. He believes that Nice Guys are the anomaly in a sea of Jerks. Of course he believes this because it's all his female-friends talk about – their "Jerk BFs", and how Nice they are for being good listeners. So his self-image gets validated and he believes he's unique and valuable for being "not-like-other-guys" and his patience and sensitivity will eventually pay off – which it very well could once the object of his obsession has had her fun (and possibly bred) with the Bad Boy.

A New World Jerk Order.

Another criticism leveled at Game is a fear that nominally Nice Guys will take this lesson to heart and become a new social wave of intolerable assholes. The fear is a new generation of arrogant pricks 'not being themselves' all in order to hook up. I understand the fear of a mass of men radically leaning their personalities towards the Jerk end of the spectrum as prompted by the PUA or MRA (men's rights activists) communities. Let me be the first to say those fears are unfounded. Guys don't search out the community, blogs or forums because they're getting too much pussy from being archetypal 'nice'. In fact the observation that more, shall we say, "self-centered" Men seem to be getting laid most consistently is so prevalent that there's an entire section dedicated to it on the main SoSuave web-page. This leads me to believe that a sudden paradigm shift to Jerk-ness isn't remotely the threat that anyone should fear. Nice Guys, by definition, have a real tough time effectively pulling off acting like a Jerk, much less genuinely converting their personality's to that of a Jerk.

Most men *would* prefer to inch towards the jerk end of the spectrum, if at all, and assuming they come to believing things aren't as they previously believed. The more common mindset for Beta males is to expect that women should appreciate them for being the 'nice', dependable, self-sacrificing guy that every woman since his mother has told him he should be.

It's far easier to believe that the world should change for you than to accept the truth that you need to improve yourself to get the things you want. It's the lazy man's path to disqualify or cheapen things that he desperately wants, but lacks the motivation to change himself to get. So the hot, 'quality' girl he wanted before, becomes the 'trashy club slut' after she rejects him. The real quality girl should love/desire him unconditionally, "for who he is" rather than force him into improving himself, which in this instance means he ought to become the caricatured Jerk archetype he's been taught to hate. Most people resist becoming what they hate, even if it's a change for the better.

We ought to worry less about social implications of converting nice guys into jerks than making them self-aware to begin with. The risk of creating a bona fide Jerk in such an effort is a decent trade off.

BETA GAME

Before I launch into this proper, let me define a few terms in the fashion that I interpret them. With the popularity of the manosphere and a few notable blogs, there's been a new push with regards to using the terms Alpha and Beta (and sometimes Omega) when describing certain classifications of males in modern culture.

Allow me to go on record as viewing these ideas as mindsets whereas terms such as being an AFC or Alpha are really states of being. For instance, a contextual Alpha can be the master of his professional realm and still be an AFC with regards to women. A Beta male can still be as wealthy and astute in status as his conditions and fortune have placed him in (often by circumstance).

Some states necessitate certain mindsets – a positive masculine state requires an Alpha mindset – others do not. Also, don't make the mistake of associating success (personal and career) with an Alpha mindset. There are plenty of Alphas on hotchickswithdouche-bags.com, however that doesn't necessarily make them well rounded individuals. I tend to think of the ideas Alpha and Beta as subconscious states or attitudes that manifest themselves in our thoughts, beliefs and actions.

Beta Game

With this in mind I'd like to propose the idea of Beta Game. Since we're using the Alpha and Beta terminology here, it's important to grasp where it comes from. Anyone with even a cursory understanding about animal social hierarchies knows the principal of Alpha and Beta individuals within a social collective. Alphas tend to be the males who exhibit the best genetic characteristics and behavioral skills that put them at the top of the potential breeding pool. In fact Betas are rarely mentioned as such in scientific studies; there are Alphas and there is the rest of the pack or collective. The Beta term, in PUA lingo is really something of a novelty. Relating these terms to human social interactions, while at times a subjective stretch, isn't too hard to understand the basic representative concepts. We can see the similarity, and the applications in long term and short term breeding methodologies in the wild that mirror our own.

Like any other Beta animal, alternate methodologies had to be developed in order to facilitate human breeding under the harsh conditions of Alpha competition. In essence, and as found in the wild, Beta males have developed (evolved) methods which attempt to 'poach' potential females from an Alpha's harem, or at least in this case his perceived, potential harem.

Identification

Beta male Game focuses primarily on Betas identifying and assimilating themselves to be more like the women they hope to connect with, but it goes beyond this.

The methodology dictates that the Beta be perceived as being unique (or at least set apart) from the more "common" Alpha males whom his desired women naturally prefer. This is the beginning of the "not-like-other-guys" mental schema he hopes to evoke in his idealized woman.

Due to his inability to compete with an Alpha competitor in the physical, he must fight an uphill psychological battle on his own terms. This involves convincing his target that her best parental investment should be with him (as per her stated requirements) as he more closely embodies her long term prerequisites. The Beta likens himself to her and self-models himself in accord with feminine imperatives in an effort to maximize his compatibility and familiarity with her and the feminine.

This identification process is further reinforced through the feminine social conventions he subscribes to. Feminine society (both Beta men and women) indirectly reward him for more closely assimilating to its ideal – be more like an archetypal woman; sensitive, empathic, emotional, security-seeking, etc.. Not only this, but take de facto feminine offense when presented with anything to the contrary of a female-positive perspective. Lift women up, become less so they become more, and in reciprocation she's more apt to breed with the Beta.

That's the principle, not necessarily the reality. In some ways it's a Cap'n Save a Ho mentality written on a grand scale. The fallacy in this of course is the presumption that like should attract like. Beta men fail to understand that opposites attract, and barring the notable exceptions, most women don't want to marry other women, least of all a carbon copy of themselves.

Disqualification

When presented with a competitor of superior status, both sex's innate, subconscious reaction is to disqualify that competitor from breeding in as expedient a method as possible. For animals this usually involves some kind of courtship performance or out-right competitive hostility. While the same could be said for human beings, our natural social impulse requires we take a bit more tact.

"Look at that girl, she must be a slut to wear / act like that", or "Yeah, he's pretty good looking, but guys like that are usually fags" are an example of the standard social weapons people use to disqualify their respective sex. Disqualify the competitor on the most base level – question their sexuality. Literally cast doubt on a competitor's sexual fitness to breed with potential mates.

While most men (Alpha or Beta) will make similar attempts to disqualify, the Beta's methodology ties back into his need for feminine identification in his disqualifying a competitor. Essentially he relies on feminine ways of disqualification by drawing upon his likeness to the women he hopes to emulate – thus, he believes, furthering potential attraction through an opportunity to prove how well he identifies with the feminine. The competitor may not be gay, but he must be cast as inferior to the Beta himself due to his competitor's inability (or lessened ability) to identify and empathize with his desired female as well as he does.

With Alpha competitors, the field has already been plowed for him by feminine social conventions, all he need do is plant the seeds. The fact that the Alpha tends to embody the masculine opposite of what he's embraced also feeds this drive. His belief is that women aren't attracted to the macho tough guy, they want a man who's kind and thoughtful; a good listener. So the natural recourse is to amplify this disparity – "the Alpha is a 1950's Neanderthal throwback, he's "bitter", he's a misogynist, he's a child in a man's body with a fragile ego only interested in fucking women and moving on." He's unlike anything on women's collective, stated, list of prerequisites for an acceptable male. He must be ridiculed – as all women ridicule – for his selfish, overt, hyper-masculinity.

Furthermore, the Beta needs to make the Alpha seem common, while making himself seem unique. In order to effectively disqualify an Alpha, the Beta has to display his empathy for the feminine, and she must *appreciate* it or it's been all for nothing (which it usually is). Not only is this an ego preservation mechanism, but it's also perceived as a tool for achieving the desired sexual reciprocation / appreciation he desires.

Interpretation

All of this really just scratches the surface of how Beat Game has evolved. I will add that all of these methods come back to a common root; the need to breed under the duress of competition. Most of what I've gone into here, and primarily the feminine identity association, become ego-invested and internalized over the course of a lifetime. It gets to the point that under the auspices of relative anonymity (like the internet) that the Beta will still cling to his mental model, even in the face of very rational, empirical evidence that contradicts the effectiveness of his Game, for no other reason than that a woman, a potential mate with whom he could identify, might read his post and may become attracted to him. The Game is never dropped for him, even in light of proving his errors.

Beta game is like the boy who decides to play on the girls team when a boys vs. girls kick ball game is started. He thinks it will endear himself to them, when all it really does is make him another girlfriend to giggle with.

Everyone has a Game in some respect. The validity of that Game may be more or less effective, but at some point a man is going to adapt to a methodology of seduction as per his conditions and environment warrant. Even master PUAs still need to adapt their Game for differing environments – different clubs, types of women, socio-economic levels, countries, etc. – there needs to be adaptation and improvisation.

The same applies for Betas, but the disparity is that the Beta tends to think of a one size fits all approach. For all the complaints of worry about the Game community turning into scripted 'social robots', it's actually the Beta who adopts a far more embedded script and is less likely to variate from it. Betas tend to stick with what worked for them, what was reinforced for them, in the past.

THE PHEROMONAL BETA

You choke the chicken before any big date, don't you?

Anyone who's seen the movie *Something About Mary* is pretty familiar with the now classic 'Hair Gel' incident.

Dom: *"You choke the chicken before any big date, don't you? Tell me you spank the monkey before any big date. Oh my God, he doesn't flog the dolphin before a big date. Are you crazy? That's like going out there with a loaded gun! Of course that's why you're nervous. Oh my dear friend, please sit, please. Look, um, after you've had sex with a girl, and you're lying in bed with her, are you nervous? No, you're not, why?"*

Ted: *"Cause I'm tired..."*

Dom: *"Wrong! It's 'cause you ain't got the baby batter on the brain anymore! Jesus, that stuff will fuck you're head up! Look, the most honest moment in a man's life are the few minutes after he's blown his load – now that is a medical fact. And the reason for it is that you're no longer trying to get laid, you're actually... you're thinking like a girl, and girls love that."*

Even if you've never seen the film, it's likely you're at least peripherally aware of the Beta Game principle Dom is explaining here. Can you spot the inconsistency?

".. you're thinking like a girl, and girls love that."

No, they don't. Sorry Dom, they want a loaded gun.

De-sexualization as Game is one of the primary mistakes Betas make. This is the *'Something About Mary'* effect; the presumption that your biological impulse to desire sex is a hindrance to getting sex. From a rational standpoint this is ridiculous, but betas eat this idea up because it dovetails nicely into their misguided sexual conditioning that assumes like attracts like – identify more with the feminine to be more attractive to the feminine. Watching this movie is like an effort in deconstructing all the Beta Game tenets of the past 40 years.

I apologize for not having the sources to site for this, but I can remember reading case studies on the biochemical effect of human sexual interaction doing grad work in college. I believe they were done by Dr. Martie Hasselton, but they outlined the chemical endorphin and hormonal profiles present in healthy adults bloodstream's while in various phases of attraction, arousal, pre-sex and post-sex interaction between couples. The most dramatic one to look up is the similarities in the chemical properties of dopamine and heroin for people experiencing "love" or "infatuation."

Even more fascinating is the effects hormones play on portions of men's brains when assessing sexual cues in a potential sex partner. Healthy testosterone levels literally causes men to perceive women as sexual objects; stimulating the same portions of our brains used for cognitive problem solving and manipulating tools.

However, testosterone is mitigated by oxytocin, the hormone secreted just post orgasm. While testosterone is responsible for sex drive and aggressive impulses (not to mention muscular development, deepening of voice and hair growth), oxytocin is linked to feelings of nurturing, trust, and comfort. Oxytocin is believed to be a primary influence in post-sex, and post pregnancy, emotional attachment in women who produce the hormone in much higher amounts than men. Postpartum depression is speculated to be a withdrawal symptom triggered by the decrease in oxytocin (and progesterone) in post-birth women. The effect of post-orgasm oxytocin in men is similar to women, however in men it is also serves as a buffering agent to heightened dopamine and testosterone levels.

Oxytocin plays a critical part in regulating a man's testosterone levels. Just post-orgasm, the human body flushes oxytocin into the bloodstream to balance out the endorphin and dopamine high of sexual arousal. While this hormone promotes feelings of trust and comfort in men, it also serves to 'calm the guy down' sexually. Oxytocin is a testosterone buffer in men, thus resulting in you going limp for a while after busting a nut.

From an evolutionary perspective this makes sense in that it ensures the sperm deposited stays in a woman's vagina, thus increasing fertility odds, instead of being shoveled out by a still erect penis. Not only that, but oxytocin serves to promote 'pair bonding' in that it fosters feelings of protective trust in men. Oxytocin discharge in humans is also triggered by pheromonal and environmental prompts (touch or kino for instance).

In addition to all of this, there's the role that pheromones play in regard to sexual attraction and arousal. You can google these, but there are several pheromonal studies that indicate that men with differing scents from those of women tend to attract opposite scents in women.

From an evolutionary perspective the conclusion drawn is one that people of similar genus or genotype (i.e. blood related family members) will be less aroused sexually by persons of the their own genotype, thus ensuring biodiversity (nature's prevention plan against inbreeding). However in the same "sweaty t-shirt" studies, the perspiration of men with higher testosterone levels were deemed more sexually viable or arousing by women than men with lower T levels – and particularly so for women in the proliferative phase of their menstrual cycles.

You can attribute whatever legitimacy you want to studies like this, but the evidence points to higher testosterone levels as playing an influential part in sexual attraction. Also bear in mind that pheromones influence women living in close proximity to each other to synchronize their menstrual cycles – another evolutionary mechanism believed to ensure fertility and communal support for social animals.

The Pheromonal Beta

From a biomechanical perspective, the indication is that men who consistently masturbate are essentially broadcasting their status as Pheromonal Betas – and women's biochemical mechanics subconsciously registers this about them. Higher testosterone males manifest their sexual viability in both sexual assertiveness and scent.

If you are chronically depleted of testosterone, and/or subjected to the calming effects of oxytocin your sexual viability is at a disadvantage. In fact, from an evolutionary standpoint, the Beta males of our feral hunter-gatherer beginnings would be more prone to masturbation as a sexual release since, theoretically, they would've had less access to breeding opportunities than Alpha males. It would then follow that definitive, subconscious behavioral and chemical cues would evolve to aid females in selecting the best mate for parental investment.

So, for as much as Beta guys would like to have you believe that snapping your radish before a date will improve your chances of fucking the girl, odds are you're shooting yourself in the foot. This stupid belief is rooted in the "Something about Mary" myth that women don't want an overly sexualized man, but the biological truth is far from that. The myth is one that women need to be comfortable with a guy in order to sleep with him, so men will actively de-sexualize themselves in order to comply. However, all indications point to a need for sexual anxiety and tension in arousal to prompt sexual intercourse.

Comfort and trust are post-orgasm conditions; anxiety, arousal and sexual urgency are pre-orgasm conditions – and both have their own unique hormonal signatures.

Disclaimer

And now for the disclaimer; I'm not a endocrinologist, biochemist or physician. I'll admit this is a work in conjecture, but it's plausible conjecture. For the record, it's not about 'less' desirable pheromones, it's about a lower incidence of any sex-cue pheromones due to depletion and the behaviors that depletion prompts. It stands to reason that women would be more attracted to men motivated to being sexual with them, manifesting this in chemistry and behavior, than sexually unmotivated men manifesting signs of disinterest.

I used to think that the primary issue with beating off was this feminine double standard – women masturbating is sexy, arousing and, nowadays, socially empowering. For men, masturbation is a perversion. It implies an inability to be 'man enough' to fuck a real woman; whacking off is failure for a man, but empowerment for a woman. Why would this social conditions exist, and what is it's latent function?

I still see the double standard in all that, and while I think it's valid, it kind of only brushes the surface of self-pleasure from a social convention perspective. Sigmund Freud once said, "all energy is sexual", meaning that subliminally we will redirect our motivation for ungratified sexual impulse to other endeavors. Thus it's men, being the sex with the highest amount of libido inducing testosterone, who must look for far more outlets to transfer this motivation to than women.

So is it any real surprise that it's historically Men who've primarily been the empire builders, the conquerors, the creators, and destroyers who've (for better or worse) moved humanity the most significantly?

Masturbation defuses this impulse. It kills that drive, or at least sublimates it. So wouldn't it stand to reason that a global social convention that shames men for masturbation would be beneficial to a society interested in expanding? Thus the cultural meme becomes men who jack off are losers, and Men who don't thereby prove their sexual viability (because if they're not beating off they *must* be fucking women semi-regularly for sexual release) *and* become motivated to redirect that impulse to the betterment of themselves and/or society.

DREAD GAMES

The original huff amongst women in the manosphere about dread came in the wake of a post about instilling a sense of dread in a woman in order to help maintain a consistent frame control in a relationship. Naturally, women's unconditioned response to this overt assertion of control was to demonize the whole idea of dread. When you think about it dread, as proposed, is really a sense of conceptualizing the potential outcome of losing the intimacy of a partner and the resulting fallout (emotional, financial, familial, personal, etc.) from that loss. Such an overt declaration for promoting a sense of dread conjures melodramatic images of fiendish men blackmailing their women into emotional enslavement to their possessive and insecure whims.

I think what's lost amongst all this sensationalism about dread – a very weak term for the concept – is the applicability dread has in a much broader scope (and particularly for women) than the overly dramatic characterization of it when men openly discuss using it themselves.

Faces of Dread

I have a good friend, John, who's just this side of 37. I love the guy, but John's not much to look at. At around 30 he essentially gave up on himself. He got married far too young on the business end of a do-the-right-thing 'accidental' pregnancy, and from a personal standpoint that was the end of his window of opportunity to explore any other options he may have had. His wife let herself go just after the second pregnancy, ballooned into a beach ball, and he followed suit. In actuality it wouldn't take much for him to get back on top of his game, but he has no desire to.

Now, after detailing John's situation you might think he'd be the last candidate to participate in anything resembling a manipulation of dread in a relationship, and you'd be right, but he, and guys like him are often the unwitting participants in their wives' or girlfriend's own dread-games.

Although John isn't going to spontaneously attract women with either his looks or due to his complete obliviousness to Game, he is an exceptional provider for his family. He regularly busts his ass as a programmer and is the sole breadwinner of the family – singlehandedly funding his wife's schooling. In addition he's a very attentive father, husband and is somewhat of a handyman around the house.

In spite of all this his wife tends to be a bit of a shrew, browbeating him on a regular basis, which has been passed onto the personalities of his teenage daughters who engage in the same heavy handedness their mother does.

Yet for all the passive-aggressive derision, John's wife is easily one of the most possessive women I've ever known. He literally lives in a constant state of surveillance as to his whereabouts. She calls to verify he is where he says he is, and continually suspects him of running off to a strip club (which to my knowledge he's never set foot inside one) or engaging in anyway with another woman. It's gotten to the point that it's comical to think that she'd have any worry that he'd be snatched away by a better woman, but there it is, the dreaded competition anxiety prompting unease in an, albeit low self-esteem, woman with no realistic possibility of it ever occurring.

"I can't compete with that,.."

Some of the most neurotically possessive women I've ever known have been the girlfriends and wives of amateur circuit bodybuilders. Most of these girls, even the fitness competitors, had to either be very self-assured or they resorted to controlling tactics and possessiveness due to the constant reminder of how desired their Men were by other women. Even when that was explicitly not the case, the perception of their desirability was enough to bring this out in them. They had the love and desire of very physically elite Men, but this still wasn't enough to pacify that innate sense of dread.

Manosphere blogger Dalrock has blogged ad infinitum about the feminized notion of how a man's viewing "using" porn is conflated with adultery by wives. To say nothing about the constant push to pathologize the male sexual response, this is an easy out for women following the Eat, Pray, Love script wanting to exit a marriage with cash and prizes. However, the fundamental point in that conflation is a woman's, often overstated, inability to *compete* with the "porn star ideal of physical perfection and sexual acrobatics that no *normal* woman could ever be comfortable with." Considering the sheer variety of men's sexual appetites this is ludicrous on the surface of it, but it is illustrative of the predominance dread plays in women's psyches. It doesn't matter what the particulars of his sexual appetites are, she feels inadequate in that competition and fears a loss of intimacy.

Dread Games

I catch a lot of hostility from the femosphere for even suggesting a Man directly foster competition anxiety in his LTR, but the underlying reason for this venom is a preexisting condition of dread in women that can barely be tolerated when it's under the surface, much less when it's exposed.

Dread, in this context, is an innate fear of loss of security that intensifies as a woman progresses further beyond the Wall and with her diminishing capacity to reestablish that provisioning security with a new partner. In fact it's exactly this dread that is the root source of the gynocentric laws that award women cash & prizes in a divorce settlement. So powerful is this fear that legal assurances needed to be instituted to account for a woman's lessened ability to secure long-term provisioning after a failed marriage, after the Wall, after pregnancies, etc.

Dread, for lack of a better term, is a female condition.

Although I've suggested casually returning flirtations with other women as a means to amplifying desire and illustrating social proof, this is hardly the only, or best, means of fostering competition anxiety. Overt flirtations are a blunt means of stoking this anxiety, but often all it takes is a nuanced shift in a predictable routine to trigger that imagination. The idea isn't to instill and sustain a constant terror from fear of loss, but rather to covertly, subtly, demonstrate higher value; particularly when a woman's attention is straying into comfortable, routine familiarity and she begins seeking indignation and drama from other sources.

Sometimes all that's necessary to provoke that imagination is to get to the gym, dress better, get a raise, travel for work, change your routine, adopt a Game mentality, hang out with a new (or old) friend, be cocky & funny with her – risk to offend her sensibilities.

Most women believe that their pussies are sufficient to hold their men in thrall for a lifetime, but as a woman's SMV declines and a Man's appreciates their confidence in this form of leverage falls off, thus forcing them to adopt new schema for controlling the fear of loss. When you head off to Las Vegas for that trade show and your wife fucks the ever-lovin' shit out of you the night before you go, you're experiencing one of those new schema. It doesn't take much, most times the lightest touch will do. Good dread game doesn't even have to be initiated by you. Often enough, women will do it themselves, or discover sources of social proof that reaffirms your desirability.

In light of this ambient fear of loss women seek to avoid, one might be tempted to use a more sympathetic approach in order to allay a woman's fears. This is hardly worth mentioning here since this is generally the tact that most men intuitively use in their LTRs anyway – a constant reassurance of love and devotion to settle her fears. Guy's like my friend John will follow a perpetual strategy of appeasement in spite of themselves.

Lets be clear, the vast majority of women are secure enough not to allow this condition to get the better of them, and it's in the extreme cases I've used above that real neuroticism flourishes. Contrary to popular belief I'm not an advocate of the Dark Triad method-ologies of Game. Not because I think they're ineffective, but rather because, with the right art of Game they're not even needed. Only in extreme cases are the dark arts to be employed, and if a situation necessitates their use it's important for a guy to understand that a line has been crossed with a woman who necessitated their use.

So yes, you should be seeking to reassure an LTR of your love and devotion, but know that due to women's intrinsic fear of security loss and the competition anxiety that comes from a declining capacity to compete with her sisters' attentions, you will never achieve an ideal state of contentment of it, and certainly not by relying solely on comfort and familiarity. She wants you to rock the boat, it's what makes her feel alive.

THE META-GAME

In the starting of my blog I'd been contemplating the last 10 or so years I've spent on SoSuave. Every time I consider the things I've written for the 'community' I always need to put them into the perspective of where I've come from and what I've learned in that time. I reviewed a 'single-mommy' story in another forum thread, one that I learned from almost 20 years prior. I also go into how things were before the advent of the internet occasionally.

I think it's really hard for a generation of young Men to fully appreciate the progress that guys in their mid-30s, mid-40s and even 50s have made in their respective times. It's hard for mid 20s and teenage guys to relate to a time before the level of communication we take for granted today. There was no term for an AFC, Beta or "herb" in 1995. I didn't own a cell phone until 2002 and never texted anyone regularly until 2005.

When guys in their 30s and 40s now were learning the lessons I relate in this book and on my blog, there were no forums, no PUAs (formally anyway), and the phenomenon we call feminization and the 'Matrix' was at the peak of its influence by virtue alone of no one questioning, let alone being aware of, its influence. We lacked the male-to-male social communication, certainly the global communication, to really bring common experiences together and form ideas from those observations. We were in the dark.

Remember, no internet, and the "how to pick up girls" books were what losers ordered by mail from an ad they saw in the back of a Hustler magazine. In fact porn was only accessible by renting it from the back room of a VHS rental store, by magazine or pirating the Spice channel from cable. Good times.

Now lets flash forward to 2013. I can't go a day without having Viagra or porn solicited to me in my email. Porn is now part of the utilities; it's like hot and cold running water, but moreover, so is the collected experience of literally a world of men considering the same nagging questions. Thanks to globalized, instant communications, a new generation of Men can collectively consider experiences and observations that were previously left unsaid. Where before there was a stigma of "not being man enough" just in asking questions and seeking relevant advice about women, now it's been replaced by the 'community'.

The internet is to Men what the sexual revolution was for women.

The genie is now out of the bottle, and for better or worse the information is liberating.

This is the Meta-Game. Lets consider it for a moment: Just last week I added my voice to a chorus of other men from around the world to help out a young man struggling with his

AFC problems. I joined guys from Britain, Australia, Spain, Canada, New York, Los Angeles, and anywhere in between. A global collective of Men advised this kid. That's pretty powerful stuff. This is a world of men advising a young man about his situation with a girl acculturated in a world that's been influenced by women's interests for over five decades.

This is the Meta-Masculine pushing back against the Meta-Feminized. We're now aware that this Feminine Matrix is everywhere, and I think we can appreciate how encompassing and pervasive it is. I know the Jezebel.coms of the world are largely the antithesis of the Meta-Masculine. I didn't say the mountain looked easy to climb. However, just the collectivity of the global community gives me hope. Every time we unplug a guy from the Matrix it's a group effort. We are the collective fathers these sons never had.

Yes, there's differences of opinion. The community advocates, Game gurus, and theorists of the world are going to lock horns over priorities and details, but the bigger pictures is making Men aware. The global collective waking them up is the first and best benefit. It is dirty, filthy, work unplugging Men from the Matrix, but that's the start.

If I'm optimistic about anything it's in the hope that the next generation of men will at least have the opportunity to be made aware of the "code" in the Matrix – that simply didn't exist when I was struggling to unplug myself. By that I mean that a younger generation of men will develop at least a capacity, or at least a sensitivity to acknowledge that certain feminine social conventions exist, and were the gender roles reversed they'd be accused of sexism. I've always felt that making these comparisons is the first real step in understanding what the Matrix is. I am far more attentive to the veiled, socially excusable, feminine sexism that we casually pass off in common culture today because I realize the latent function those conventions serve. Like G.I. Joe says, knowing is half the battle.

The main obstacle for the positive-masculine Meta Game is that a majority of the same men it would serve are the unwitting (or at least willfully ignorant) pawns of the feminized Meta Game. I think its wrong to think of these men – the Betas, the AFCs, the plugged-in Alphas – as "recruits" for the feminine imperative. I come to that because it takes an entire feminized society to condition a young man over the course of a lifetime to psychologically ego-invest himself in the feminine Meta Game as a means to achieving his best interests. They need to be raised and trained before the ego-investment becomes self-propagating, at which point only extremely traumatic experiences will open his eyes to that conditioning.

I used the example of a typical rAFC (recovering AFC) or 'seeking' young man asking for advice from the collective. Almost universally the problems they want to solve are themes so tired and so thoroughly covered by the collective of men in the community that we'll defer them to well-worn advice or rephrase old posts on the same topic. I do this myself, but think about the profundity of that for a moment; here we have a questioning guy dealing with a problem I dealt with, sometimes, over 20 years ago, and men my senior dealt with 30 or even 40 years ago.

The memes haven't changed much in the past 60 years. I think a common missive is to think that the only reason guys seek out the community is to "get laid more" or "find the secret to getting their dream girl". While that's a definite motivator, so many more want solutions to relational problems that have existed in their current form for over half a century now:

How do I get her back? Why did I just get LJBFed? Why does she fuck the Jerk, but tell me I'm a such a great guy? Do looks matter? How do I get my LTR to bang me now that we moved in together?

There are countless others. Our Meta Game does a great disservice to 'seekers' when we dismiss them as just wanting to get their lay count up. Of course that's only the recognizable motivator, but what they're really searching for, what they're unaware they're searching for, is a real, positive, confidence in a masculinity that can rise above the chatter of the invectives of feminized Meta Game.

When I see five pages of advice on the SoSuave forum explaining to a noob the reasons he's in the situation he finds himself in, and instructing him how best to deal with it based on collective experiences while opening his perspective up to consider the greater landscape he's in, *that* is the masculine Meta Game pushing back.

Think of that; a poor, isolated kid, frustrated by how to approach, how to deal with a LJBF, how to "man-up", etc. pits the influence of a world-wide collective of men's experience against the behaviors and mindset of an individual girl who's been socialized and acculturated by the feminized imperative. That is the Meta Game.

COMMUNICATION

THE MEDIUM IS THE MESSAGE

I hate the term 'Mixed Signals' or 'Mixed Messages'. More often than not there's nothing 'Mixed' being communicated and rather it's a failure (willful or not) to read what a woman is communicating to a man. The average guy tends to 'get' exactly what a woman has implied with her words, but it takes practice to read her behavior and then more practice in self-control to apply it to his own interpretation.

When a woman goes from hot to cold and back again, *this* IS the message – she's got buyers remorse, you're not her first priority, she's deliberating between you and what she perceives is a better prospect, you were better looking when she was drunk, etc. – the message isn't the 'what ifs', the message IS her own hesitation and how her behavior manifests it. Ten dates before sex? This IS the message. Canceling dates? Flaking? Strong interest to weak interest? This IS the message.

Women with high interest level (IL) wont confuse you.

When a woman wants to fuck you she'll find a way to fuck you. If she's fluctuating between being into you and then not, put her away for a while and spin other plates. If she sorts it out for herself and pursues you, then you are still playing in your frame and you maintain the value of your attention to her. It's when you patiently wile away your time wondering what the magic formula is that'll bring her around, that's when you lean over into her frame. You need her more than she needs you and she will dictate the terms of her attentions.

What most guys think are 'mixed messages' or confusing behavior coming from a woman is simply due to their inability (for whatever reason) to make an accurate interpretation of why she's behaving in such a manner. Usually this boils down to a guy getting so wrapped up in a single, solitary girl that he'd rather make concessions for her behavior than see it for what it really is. In other words, it's far easier to call it 'mixed messages' or fall back on the old chestnut of how fickle and random women are, when in fact it's simply a rationale to keep themselves on the hook, so to speak, because they lack any real, viable, options with other women in their lives.

A woman that has a high IL in a guy has no need (and less motivation) to engage in behaviors that would in any way compromise her status with him. Women of all ILs will shit test men, and men will pass or fail accordingly, but a test is more easily recognizable when you consider the context in which they're delivered.

More often than not women tell the complete truth with their actions, they just communicate it in a fashion that men can't or wont understand. As a behaviorist, I'm a firm believer in the psychological principal that the only way to determine genuine motivation and/or intent is to observe the behavior of an individual. All one need do is compare behavior and the results of it to correlate intent. A woman will communicate vast wealths of information and truths to a man if he's only willing to accept her behavior, not exclusively her words, as the benchmark for what she's relating. He must also understand that the truth she betrays in her behavior is often not what he wants to accept.

We get frustrated because women communicate differently than we do. Women communicate *covertly*, men communicate *overtly*. Men convey information, women convey feeling. In relating information, men prioritize *content*, women prioritize *context*.

One of the great obfuscations fostered by feminization in the last quarter-century is this expectation that women are every bit as rational and inclined to analytical problem solving as men. This is the result of an equalist mentality that misguides men into believing that women communicate no differently than men. That's not to discount women as proficient problem solvers in their own right, but it flies in the face how women set about a specifically feminine form of communication.

Scientific study after study illustrating the natural capacity women have for exceptionally complex forms of communication (to the point of proving their neural pathways are wired differently) are flags proudly waved by a feminized media as proof of women's innate merits, yet as men, we're expected to accept that she "means what she says, and she says what she means." While more than a few women like to wear this as a badge of some kind of superiority, it doesn't necessarily mean that *what* they communicate is more important, or *how* they communicate it is more efficient – just that they have a greater capacity to understand nuances of communication than do men.

One of the easiest illustrations of this generational gender switch is to observe the communication methods of the "strong" women the media portray in popular fiction today. How do we know she's a strong woman? The first cue is she communicates in an overt, information centered, masculine manner. She communicates like a man.

You don't need to be psychic to understand women's covert communication, you need to be observant. This often requires a patience that most men simply don't have, so they write women off as duplicitous, fickle or conniving if the name fits. Even to the Men that are observant enough, and take the needed mental notes to really see it going on around them, it seems very inefficient and irrational.

And why wouldn't it? We're Men. Our communications are (generally) information based, deductive and rational, that's Men's overt communication. Blunt, to the point, solve the problem and move on to the next. Feminine communication seems insane; it is a highly dysfunctional form of communication…,to be more specific, it's a childish form of communication. This is what children do! They say one thing and do another. They throw temper tantrums. They react emotionally to everything.

Yes, they do. And more often than not, they get what they're really after – attention. Women are crazy, but it's a calculated crazy. Covert communication frustrates us every bit as much as overt communication frustrates women. Our language has no art to it for them, that's why we seem dumb or simple at best to women. We filter for information to work from, not the subtle details that make communication enjoyable for women.

This is the same reason we think of feminine communication as being obfuscating, confusing, random, even when it seems they are making earnest attempts to clearly relate their intent. The difference is that our confusion and frustration is put to their ultimate use. So long as women remain unknowable, random, irrational creatures that men can't hope to understand (but can always excuse), they can operate unhindered towards their goals.

"Silly boy, you'll never understand women, just give up" is exactly the MO. Once you accept this, she's earned a lifetime of get-out-of-jail-free cards. The myth of the 'Feminine Mystique' and a woman's prerogative (to change her mind) is entirely dependent upon how adept she is in using this covert communication.

Now as Men we'll say, "Evil, immoral, manipulative woman! Shape up and do the right thing, saying one thing then doing another makes you a hypocrite!" and of course this is our rational nature overtly making itself heard in exposing a woman's covert communication. An appeal to morality, that'll get her, but,..it doesn't. This is because women instinctively know that their sexuality is their first, best agency, and covert communication is the best method to utilize it.

Appeals to morality only work in her favor, because all she need do is agree with a Man's overt assessment of her and suddenly he thinks he's 'getting through to her'. As Men, we have become so conditioned by the Feminine Mystique to expect a woman to be duplicitous with us that when she suddenly leans into masculine communication forms and resorts to our own, overt communication method and agrees with us, it seems she's had an epiphany, or a moment of clarity. "Wow, this one's really special, 'high quality', and seems to get it." That is so long as it suits her conditions to do so. When it doesn't, the Feminine Mystique is there to explain it all away.

Have you ever been in a social setting, maybe a party or something, with a girlfriend or even a woman you may be dating and seemingly out of the blue she says to you privately, "ooh, did you see the dirty look that bitch just gave me?!"

You were right there in her physical presence, saw the girl she was talking about, yet didn't register a thing. Women's natural preference for covert communication is recognizable by as early as five years of age. Women prefer to fight in the psychological, whereas boys fight in the physical.

Within their own peer group, little girls fight for dominance with the threat of ostracization from the group. "I wont be your friend anymore if,.." is just as much a threat to a girl as "I'm gonna punch you in the face if,.." is to a boy. This dynamic becomes much more complex as girls enter puberty, adolescence and adulthood, yet they still use the same psychological mode of combat.

Their covert way of communicating this using innuendo, body language, appearance, subcommunications, gestures, etc. conveys far more information than our overt, all on the table, way of communicating does. It may seem more efficient to us as Men, but our method doesn't satisfy the same purpose.

Women enjoy the communication more than the information being transferred. It's not a problem to be solved, it's the communication that's primary. When a chump supplies her with everything all at once we think, yeah, the mystery is gone, he's not a challenge anymore, why would she be interested? This is true, but the reason that intrigue is gone is because there's no more potential for stimulating that need for communication or her imagination.

Lastly I should add that women are not above using overt communication when it serves their purposes. When a woman comes out and says something in a fashion so as to leave no margin for misinterpretation, you can bet she's been pushed to that point out of either fear or sheer exasperation when her covert methods wont work.

"Can't we just be friends?" is a covert rejection, "Get away from me you creep!!" is an overt rejection. When a woman opts for the overt, rest assured, she's out of covert ideas. This is an easy example of this, but when a woman cries on you, screams at you, or issues an ultimatum to you she is powerless to the point of having to come over to your way of communicating her frustration.

Likewise, men can and do master the art of covert communications as well. Great politicians, military leaders, businessmen, salesmen to be sure, and of course master PUAs all use covert communications to achieve their goals. It's incorrect to think of covert communication as dishonest or amoral, or even in a moral context. It's a means to an end, just as overt communication is a means to an end, and that end whether decided by men or women is what's ethical or unethical.

JUST GET IT

To be sure, relationship Game (or married Game) varies widely in application compared to the Game used in single-man-sex-life, but the foundational principles are essentially the same – as are the pitfalls – only the risks are higher and the rewards negligible by comparison.

Having experienced the ups and downs of single-man-sex-life as well as married-man-sex-life, I can honestly say that I've never found Game more necessary than when it's within the context of marriage. I've also written volumes about the all-risk proposition of marriage for men, and women's utter inability to appreciate the all-risk sacrifices men assume in committing to marriage. So it should be obvious that under such conditions if a man chooses to entertain a lifestyle of marriage the only acceptable condition is that it be within his frame and his terms. And this, gentlemen, requires not only an internalized commitment to Game itself, but an understanding of, and an internalization of a much tighter Game than would be necessary in single-man-sex-life.

Higher risks mean less margin for error.

In your single-man-sex-life Game, you have the leisure to Spin Plates, drop the ones which don't produce dividends, and non-exclusively enjoy the ones who do. Though it may pain you to lose a particular girl as the result of fumbled Game, or to miss the opportunity of experiencing a woman due to a failed approach or consolidation, it pales in comparison to the risks inherent in lacking the long-term Game necessary to contend with women's hypergamy in the context of marriage.

Dumping a girl (or getting dumped) when single may be an emotional ordeal for some guys, but the decay of a marriage and the financial, familial and emotional consequences for lacking Game in marriage is a punishment that will make a single man's break up tears seem like a blessing. Tight relationship Game means much more than just getting your wife to fuck you more regularly after the honeymoon.

A lot of men will respond that marriage is just not worth all that contextualization of Game, and they'd be right. It's all risk with negligible reward / appreciation and the liabilities are too steep. Furthermore, there's a contingent of men who'll say that it's impossible to perpetuate the solid Game necessary to assuage female hypergamy indefinitely – and they'd be right too, if all Game was is a constant act for them that they felt they had to keep up forever.

Some guys get mad at just the suggestion that they'd need to Game their potential wives. "She should just love me for who I am!" They expect to be able to drop the Game, relax and be who they are, only to have their wives progressively convert them into their imagined ideal which really isn't the guy who tingles their vaginas. Then they find out that their wives loved them for who they *were*.

Crossover

When the lines of communication are broken between you and your wife or girlfriend, you aren't going to get a message that the lines of communication are broken. That's what the lines of communication being broken means. When she checks out of the relationship, she doesn't tell you *because* she's checked out of the relationship. That's what being checked out of the relationship means.

I usually have to control my laughter whenever I overhear an AFC in the crab barrel parrot back the Matrix-speak about how "good relationships are all about communication with your girlfriend/wife." When this is coming from a single guy I can at least partially excuse him for lack of any practicable experience, but when it comes from a married Plug-In it's just evidence of the totality of his conditioning. Most guys who tell you this are repeating what their girl-friends always told them was the most important key to a good relationship, but as with everything femme there's always a latent purpose underneath the veneer of aphoristic truth they sell themselves.

I was once at a liquor event with my usual 'pour girls' and during our conversations one tells me about her 'guy problems' with a "clingy boyfriend" obviously on the down end of an SMV imbalance.

"It's so frustrating Rollo, why can't guy's just get it?"

With a practiced, but cute, little wrinkle of her nose, and the huff of her $5,000 tits, my girl had just indirectly revealed one of the most vexing complexities of intergender communication – women want men to "just get it."

Just Get It

The guy with the capacity to call a woman's bluff with a confidence that implies she is to be worthy of him rather than the other way around is the Man to be competed for. Essentially the 'chick speak', 'chick advice' phenomenon is a shit test writ large on a social scale. And even your own mother and sisters are in on it, expecting you to 'get it'; to get the message and see the challenge for what it really is, without overtly telling you.

She wants you to 'get it' on your own, without having to be told how. That initiative, and the experience needed to have had developed it, makes you a Man worth competing for. Women despise a man who needs to be told to be dominant, told to be confident, told to be anything they have on their list of prerequisites for their intimacy. Overtly relating this to a guy entirely defeats his credibility as a genuinely dominant male. The guy she wants to fuck is dominant because that's 'the way he is' instead of who she had to tell him to be.

Observing the process will change it. This is the root function of every shit test ever devised by a woman.

If masculinity has to be explained to a man, he's not the man for her.

In my Pour Girl's example we see this 'get it' paradox from the single-man-sex-life perspective, but due the risks and punishments inherent to marriage, it is even more important in the married-man (or LTR) -sex-life perspective. Many men will complain that they hate the presumption that they need to be a mind reader and ideally women ought to just communicate overtly and directly – just as a reason-based man would communicate. The problem is that in doing so it changes the dynamic for hypergamy. As I've stated so often, women say they want the truth, but they *never* want full disclosure. Hypergamy will not be pandered to, and will not be negotiated with.

This is why the "communication is everything" meme has been responsible for the demise of more relationships than anyone will ever admit. It's not *that* you communicate, it's *what* you're communicating and *how* you communicate it. I've counseled more men than I care to recount who've sobbed from the depths of their souls, "IF SHE'D JUST TELL ME WHAT I HAVE TO DO TO MAKE HER LOVE ME I'D DO IT!" not realizing that their very verbalization of that, and a belief in open, rational communication, is the very thing that's killing (or killed) their woman's desire for him.

A cardinal truth of the universe is that genuine desire cannot be negotiated. The moment you tell your wife, your girlfriend, that you will exchange a behavior or attitude or belief or any other compromise for her desire you fundamentally change her organic desire into obligation.

What she wants, what her hypergamy wants confirmation of, can never be explicated, it can only be demonstrated. If her desire is for you to be more dominant, her telling you to be so negates the genuineness and the validity of your becoming so. Again, observing a process will change it – on a limbic level of consciousness her innate hypergamy is aware of that truth.

She wants a man who *knows* he needs to be dominant with her, that is the confirmation of hypergamy.

DIJO SIN HABLAR

Dijo sin hablar – Told without speaking.

Communicate with your behavior. Never overtly tell a woman anything. Allow her to come to the conclusions you intend. Her imagination is the best tool in your Game toolbox. Learn how to use it.

This is the single greatest failing of average frustrated chumps: they vomit out everything about themselves, divulging the full truth of themselves to women in the mistaken belief that women desire that truth as a basis for qualifying for their intimacy or enduring commitment. Learn this now:

Women NEVER want full disclosure.

Nothing is more self-satisfying for a woman than to think she's figured a Man out based solely on her mythical feminine intuition (i.e. imagination).

When you blurt out your 'feelings' or overtly make known your optionless status, regardless of the context or the nobility of your intent, all you do is deny her this satisfaction. And like an easily distracted child she discards you for another, more entertaining, toy that holds some kind of mystery or puzzle for her figure out.

Always remember, women care less about the content of what's being communicated and more about the context (the how) of what's being communicated. Never buy the lie that good communication is the key to a good relationship with out considering *how* and *what* you communicate. Women are naturally solipsistic. Your 'feelings' aren't important to her until you make them important for her.

Despite what any pop-psychologist has ingrained into you, communication is *not* the key to success in an LTR. It's what and how it's communicated that is. It seems counterintuitive to deliberately withhold information that you think would solve whatever problem you have. Since socially instituted feminization has taken root, every touchy-feely therapist will tell you to open up and express yourself, but all that leads to is the negotiation of desire and the disingenuous obligations based on those terms.

You cannot 'tell' women anything, they must be led to your conclusion and be made to think that they are the ones coming to it with their own devices – preferably by way of her imagined feminine intuition. How you effect this is subject to your own situation with your LTR or your prospective woman, but understand that internalizing the idea that she can be made to understand your perspective *indirectly* is the first step in 'real' communication. Indirect communication is the foundation of effective Game.

You want to be a guy who 'Just gets it'?

Speak without speaking. Women would rather be objectified than idealized.

THE HORSE'S MOUTH

One of the best litmus tests for how unplugged a guy truly is how he reacts to the words of his idealized woman. I briefly covered this idea in the Self-Righteous AFC:

You see, when an AFC clings to the mental schema that make up an AFC mindset it requires a constant need for affirmation and reinforcement, particularly in light of their glaring lack of verifiable success with women while clinging to, and behaving in accordance with the mindset. AFCs are crabs in a barrel – once one get to the top to climb out another drags him back in. The AFC needs other AFCs to affirm his blatantly obvious lack of success. He needs other AFCs to tell him, "don't worry just be yourself" or "she's just not a quality woman because she can't see how great a guy you are."

So when an AFC finally does get a second date and then finally does get laid it becomes the ultimate validation for his mindset. "See, you just have to be a nice guy and the right ONE really does come along." This is when the self-righteous phase begins and he can begin telling his Game / PUA friends that he's "getting some" now without all the Positive Masculinity claptrap. In actuality he rationalizes away all of the conditions that lead up to him getting the girlfriend and the fundamental flaw that he's settling for a woman "who'd fuck him", but this doesn't stop him from claiming a moral high ground. His long wait is over and he's finally hit pay-dirt.

This need for validation of a Beta Game mindset is very strong for guys – particularly when you consider a lifetime of being steeped in fem-centric conditioning. When you grow up in girl-world you want to believe the idealizations of women are actually attainable. This is what makes the 'red pill' so hard to swallow; men truly want the fantasy, the romanticism and love, in the context girl-world presents it to them for so long, to really exist for them. This is what makes believing women's individualized words, rather than their globalized behaviors, so seductive for men – even for Men who've become self-aware in the feminine Matrix.

Straight from the Horse's Mouth

When a woman (or a man impersonating a woman) posts some self-description or personalized experience about how they conform more to this idealization than to the "silly caricatures of bitter misogynists" online, this triggers an internal conflict for men.

Men want to believe that the exception to the rule *could* exist for them since it agrees with his initial social conditioning, but the learned, unplugged, conditioning he's applying to see the forest for the trees, and factoring in women's generalized, observable behaviors, fights against this. Becoming Game-aware teaches Men that the medium is the message, but to varying degrees Men still want to believe that women are completely self-honest, rational agents, and completely cognizant of their internal motivations. Eventually applied behaviorism puts the truth to this deception, but it's very hard to let go of that want for an easier answer.

In our 'plugged in' years, men rely on the same deductive pragmatism with women that we use to solve most other problems. Our problem solving natures predispose us to identifying the elements of a problem to arrive at a solution. Even our neural wiring is designed to achieve this end, so it's literally a 'no-brainer' to want reliable, rational data on which to base our plan to solve a problem – in this case getting laid and receiving intimate approval from a woman. Thus our next question is "what do women want?"

What Women Want

I can remember asking this very question uncounted times in my plugged-in teenage years. Hindsight being what it is, I can only laugh now when I read teenage guys still asking the same thing four generations later. It seems so intuitive and considerate of a woman's sensibilities; guys think it presents the countenance that a man cares enough to create himself in her idealized image.

Women and girls naturally love to answer this question because it gives them a default authority, while at the same time feeds their attention needs. It's such a popular topic that even rom-com movies are based on the question and the zany misunderstandings that result from men's ridiculous attempts to understand the oh-so unknowable, mysterious natures of women's true desires. Silly, silly men.

The truth is much simpler. Women either lack the awareness and self-honesty to acknowledge what it is about men that women in general (not just individualized to themselves) want, or they deliberately misdirect and evade men's efforts to make deductive sense of their motivations because, in truth, they want a guy who 'gets it' on his own without having to be told.

In either case, whether due to ignorance or duplicity, the secret of the ugly, cruel truth of female hypergamy is to be protected and obfuscated as women's first priority. So important is keeping this truth from men that the feminine imperative must socialize it into women's collective psyches. One of the great threats that Game theory represents to feminine primacy is revealing the truth, and the atrocities that result from feminine hypergamy.

What do women want? Maximized hypergamy with a man blissfully unaware of hypergamy. The perfect union of emotional investment, parental investment and provisional investment with her hypergamous nature.

However, men still want to believe that women earnestly want to communicate their intimate desires in an effort to make better men. We believe that women, the emotional, erratic, dramatic, mysterious and romantic creatures of story are also consistent, well-grounded pragmatists that rival men themselves and are only waiting for the man unique enough to listen to her. The more her story agrees with our mental construct of what women *should* want, the more we want to believe she exists. If she's convinced of the story this is all the validation most men ever need – he got it from the source, a woman who confirmed the fantasy.

QUALITIES OF THE PRINCE

You know, I'm not quite sure if my readership is aware of this, but I'm a Prince.

No really, I'm a Prince (stop laughing), or at least that's the expectation I've come to have others recognize in me after sifting through women's online profiles on such fantastical dating resources such as Plenty of ~~Whales~~ Fish and OK ~~U-Bid~~ Cupid. But don't think I'm such a rare bird, because amazingly enough, if you're reading this book (or my blog), you're probably a Prince too! And you didn't even realize it did you?

You see, virtually all the women you encounter on these online dating resources are simply undiscovered, under-appreciated jewels in the rough. They're Princesses, and goddammit they deserve to be treated as such. Just reading through each profile is like going on safari and encountering a virtual cornucopia of rare and exotic animals (kind of like a zoo), each meticulously described in encyclopedic detail of their uniqueness and rarity of finding. What mere mortal man could possibly deserve to touch such feminine refinery?

A few years ago the denizens of the SoSuave forum accidentally conducted one of the most humorous social experiments ever performed. A member by the handle of *Bonhomme* was a frequenter of Plenty of Fish and noticed an interesting trend in women's profiles. Though most of the women using online dating run the gamut from hopelessly fat to 2-drink fuckability, the one thing most had in common was an entirely overblown sense of self-worth to compliment their grossly overrated self-impression of their sexual market value (SMV for those of you playing the home game). This is nothing shocking for unplugged Men; the 'community' has long held that social media and online Buffers work in tandem to convince a woman she's 1 to 2 degrees higher on her SMV scale.

What hadn't been studied up to then was the descriptors and qualifications that online women used in both their "list of demands" and their own self-evaluations, or "the brochure of value added features" any man with common sense (see fem-centric conditioning) would ever be considered a 'Man' for appreciating in a woman.

The following is an actual example pulled from a typical profile:

"Here is a well thought out idea of what kind of guy I am interested in… 5'10" or taller, lives near by, compassionate, intelligent, giving, VERY Attractive (someone other than your mother or sister has said so, lol) and in shape, prefer self employed, FAMILY orientated, open to new spontaneous things, likes to camp, likes to golf, wants children, would be a good father and faithful husband, a gentleman, gives me my space when I need it, not a nerd or too sarcastic, can take a hint, social, calls for no reason, remembers sending a note or a nominal gift IS romantic and necessary, respectful, sense of humor, and thinks the world of me. I am not interested in anyone older than 41 and anyone who makes less money than me since I do not plan on changing the lifestyle I have grown

accustom to and hope to one day be a stay at home mom and furthermore... my children will never want for ANYTHING (but of course will not be spoiled brats either lol). You should also love animals I am not attracted to red heads at all lol sorry.

Wow! A rare find indeed. Thank heaven for the internet in providing men such a valuable resource that we might encounter so rational and strong a woman as this. This is one common example, but by far the most common self-references women made involved the word "Princess" – *"I'm a Princess waiting for my Prince"* or *"I'll admit it, I'm a Princess, I just need to find a man who can appreciate that and treat me right."*

Well, far be it from Rollo J. Tomassi to deny these undiscovered royals their due!

Quickly I began to craft a cunning profile of my own; one which these pouting Princesses would surely recognize as that of none other than the Crown Prince of Man-dom. Using their own profile's jingoisms and idioms as a template, I established an idealized persona, one that any woman worth her equalist "common sense" salt would instantly be irresistible to,...

"Here is a well thought out idea of what kind of gal I am interested in...5' 5" or taller, but not over 6 feet (because while I don't mind being eye to eye with you, I won't ever be looking up to you), lives close enough to be at my house within 10 minutes after I make the call, genuinely passionate, intelligent enough to be good company, sexually available (preferably insatiable) and VERY attractive – we're talking Jessica Alba, Keyra Augustina attractive – women with a body-fat percentage higher than 8% need not apply. Must be employed but not so well as you'll interfere with our sexual activities, FAMILY oriented, but only after you've hit 30-33, open to spontaneous sex (you know, like outdoor stuff or a surprise 3 way with one of your hot girlfriends after our 2nd martini), likes to camp (in the nude), knows not to complain when I go play golf with the clients from work.

She must want children after 33 years of age if at all, and only after she's proven to be a good mother and faithful wife, must be a lady with class and know when the right time is to speak and not to speak, not a prude or bitch, can take the first hint, sociable, unexpectedly texts me pictures of her wearing something new from Fredericks of Hollywood, understands that the best gift she can give me is expressing her desire to fuck me like a wild animal, and also understands that gifts for her are treats or rewards for desired behavior.

Must be respectful of my decisions being final, can't take herself too seriously and thinks the world of me. I'm not interested in anyone over 31 (since this is most women's expiration date anyway), she cannot have exorbitant spending habits or a credit debt load in excess of $1,000 since I do not plan on changing the lifestyle I have grown accustomed to and hope to one day be able to send my own children to college (rather than pay for your student debt), and furthermore... my children will be taught to reasonably earn their achievements on their own and respect the decisions of their Father and mother (and absolutely will not be spoiled brats either). I'm very attracted to redheads, blonds, brunettes, Caucasians, Latinas, Asians, African-Americans, Pacific Islanders, etc., pretty much any woman that meets my physical requirements. I am not attracted at all to even slightly fat women no matter how much "inner beauty" you think you may possess. Hope to meet you soon, your Prince."

There! What woman could possible fail to appreciate all of the qualities of a Prince based upon their very own template? Insidious, clever and witty. All I had to do was await what could only be a landslide of returned affection and positive responses. I contemplated how I would gently let down the poor cast off Princesses who failed to meet my humble criteria as the first response came in,...

"I read your profile, and is any of it serious?????"

A bit perturbed I reply,

"Why do you think it's not serious? Am I not allowed to be a bit specific?"

"Sorry not about to put up with your kind of shit."

Strange and yet strange again. Here I'd learned that self-confidence and assertiveness were traits women admired in the land of gender-equalism. Ah, perhaps this Princess was a bit jaded by such a dearth of qualified Princes at her disposal. I waited a bit more and was rewarded by a Princess called *'Lil Sweet Heart'* who'd randomly read my glowing self-description,..

*"what a profile
see iam a strong willed person!!
i speak when i want to say what i want and when i want and the way ur profile sounds i dont we;d be a match and the part about raising a spoiled brat thats a hard one to over come depends what u see as spoiled sure my boys r a bit spoiled well a lot but thats the way i was raised and it did me no wrong my kids know that they have to work to earn their spending and treats but no reason why a parent cant buy something just because so maybe ur profile can off wrong but my feeling is not some one id wanna meet hmmmmm"*

Egads! I respond,

"Honestly, I really tried to read your message to me, but all of the bastardized English and the run-on sentences made it virtually impossible to understand what you were trying to say."

I do say. Whomever this royal child's *au pair* was is deserving of a public flogging! The thought of so ill-preparing a Princess for courtly discourse with the Man who will one day be her King is inexcusable. Bah, the blazes with this one, I'll be patient on another,..

"uh, yeah, i don't think so. maybe your profile's a joke (which would make it less sad), but i don't find it amusing, not my sense of humour at all.and the fact that i'm even bothering to reply to say no, rather than just ignore you, should tell you how distasteful it is.happy hunting. (though you'd have better luck if you went back in time 100 years or so, have fun finding chics like that today)"

"After checking out your profile, you are one of the rudest people i've even encountered. In your dreams..."

Hmm, I was beginning to see a flaw in my profile design.

You see I had simply reworded the profile of my original Princess' profile and changed the gender specific terms to the masculine, while adding a bit of my own desires to the outline of the ideal Princess I'd like to meet. After all, they all want to be treated like Princesses, I'm just asking to be treated like a Prince. But,..perhaps I'd been remiss in my waiting for the Princesses to respond to me. How unmanning of me! I would seek out my prize and pursue her. This profile caught my eye,...

"I am friendly, outgoing, generous, loyal, honest and adventurous. I work in a hospital. I also drive and have my own car.
I love to get my nails done every two weeks. I love fashion and style. I care about pop culture and social issues.
I have an IQ of 146. I am extremely intelligent and educated.

First Date: I dont want to meet Cheaters, users, players, haters, crumb bumbs, guys who want booty calls or fuk buddies... ya'll dont let the door hit cha on the way out... I guess Im looking to meet someone around my own age, who is taller than me preferably caucasian, attractive, who likes to work out, has a unique, ghetto and sarcastic sense of humor like me."

Well,..not the ideal prize I'd been seeking, but perhaps this was another jewel in the rough that just needed a bit of spit and polish. I respond in the affirmative to her brassy, assertive equalist nature. After reading my profile, she responds,..

"i mak emy own moneya nd pay for own 5hit.. and for someone with such high stan-dards take a good look in the mirror becuz these girls aka jessica alba are way out of ur league... if u want someone who is hot at least BE hot urself!"

I found this confusing since I had no picture on my profile at this point. I'd have to address that, but strange that the assumption was that my physical stature would necessarily be inadequate for her. I respond,..

"Dear woman, for someone with such a high opinion of her intelligence your grammar, punctuation and syntax are far from reflecting this. You type like shite."

What I'd found most entertaining about this whole affair is that these women somehow felt compelled to respond to the profile. As if it were so personal an affront to their sensibilities that it should need their attention to correct, rather than simply move on to the next profile with indifference. Judging from the frequency and intensity of the responses, how many men do you suppose responded to the original woman's profile with the same fervor?

One of the best ways to illustrate how insaturated feminization has become in society is to flip the gender script on certain gender-specific dynamics.

As funny as all this was, it serves to show that women live and operate in gender assumptions that they simply take as normalized conditions. Were a Man to publicly expect the terms and demands for his own provisioning and intimate access that women demand without an afterthought, he'd be instantly accused of misogyny at worst, comedy at best. There are many more dynamics that illustrate this fem-centric normalization. My critics get fits of hysteria when I describe the acculturated, feminine-centric undercurrent operating in society. Girl-world is the only world for them, so pulling back the iron-veil of the feminine reality like this is usually a hard revelation. Ironically it's the vitriol engendered in the responses to my reworded profile that prove the point.

SOCIAL CONVENTIONS

OPERATIVE SOCIAL CONVENTIONS

Often I'll be in the middle of some socio-psychological tear on a particular topic when I'll come to a dead halt because I play my own devil's advocate while I'm typing and reasoning aloud, and have to review and edit the paragraphs I've spent the last two hours constructing because I'd failed to consider how others might interpret my intent. Other times it may be I'd overlooked some element and had to go back and address that issue, or at the very least have a source ready to cite for the most predictable rebuttals.

Needless to say it's an arduous process, however I've found that starting blog topics, in regards to certain theories and ideas, bearing in mind that I have to see what their intent will be read as helps me greatly. So with this in mind I'm presenting a particular section of my work here to see what the consensus is on what I've come to call Operative Social Conventions. I had originally titled the section Feminine Operative Social Conventions, and I may still go back to that, but after you read this you'll see how these conventions (or contrivances) need Men to play along with them for them to exist in the first place, or so I've reasoned.

Operative Social Conventions

In the 'community' we've become all too familiar with a standard set of problems that are commonly asked of us for advice – *"Should I date younger/older women with/without children?" "what about women with money/career?"* etc. for example. So often are we petitioned for our take on these dilemmas that we have a tendency to repeat back a standard reply for them.

I count myself among those who do this as well. I'm very prone to see the forest for the trees so to speak and fire back with my stand by reply of Spin More Plates, or NEXT. While these response are novel to those reading them for the first time (and hopefully having their eyes opened for the first time too), I'd come to realize that I was guilty of not seeing the forest with regards to why certain topics are more frequently reoccurring problems for the Beta-AFC and the aspiring Game student alike.

For the most part, Plate Theory covers a multitude of AFC sins, but my concern was with understanding *why* these dilemmas come up so often and what their root cause is. To this effect I've attempted to 'distill' down the symptoms (i.e. the commonly related problems) to the motivation behind them (i.e. the disease rather than the symptoms). This led me to a new theory of Operative Social Conventions.

I've posted on my blog and in more forum threads than I care to recall about these conventions before, but never really explored the idea in depth. Essentially all of the symptoms of these conventions are manifested as the frequent problems guys come up with, but the disease is the latent purpose of these conventions. For every guy asking if it's a good idea to date a single mother or an older woman, there's a single mother or older woman perpetuating the pro side of that convention in order to best ensure her capacity to secure a man capable of provisioning for her. I wont ramble off into the bio-psychological aspect of why this is such an all important drive for women (and men in some cases), instead I'll focus on certain conventions, the way they operate and their latent operative function.

Shame

Perhaps the easiest and most recognizable form of social convention is shame. Not only this, but it is also the most easily employable and the most widely accepted – not just by women of all ages and descriptions, but also by popular culture and the media.

Examples:
"Men should date women their own age."
"Men shouldn't be so 'shallow' as to put off single mothers as viable long term mates."
"Men have 'fragile egos' that need constant affirmation in an almost infantile respect."
"Men feel threatened by 'successful' women."

As well as being popularized myths, all of these are subtle (and not so subtle) manipulations of shame. Each is an operative social convention that places a man into a position of having to live up to an idealized standard that simultaneously raises the standard for a woman, thus placing her into a better position of sexual selection and in some instances, leveling the perceived playing-field with regard to the feminine competition dynamic (i.e. single moms, older and professional women *ought* to be just as sexually marketable as the younger women men biologically prefer).

The 'Shallow' effect – The useful myth of superficiality.

I'm mentioning this as an aside to the Shame methodology since it appears to me to be the root of the Shame operative. In all of the above examples (or symptoms) the burden of expectation that is placed on a man comes with the threat of being perceived as "Shallow" or superficial. In other words, the very questioning of whether or not a man ought to date a single mother comes with the veiled threat of having women (mothers or not) tar the questioning man with being 'superficial'. This 'Shallow' effect is so pervasive in so many AFCs, young and old, I've counseled that it becomes an automatic default defense. Even under conditions of complete anonymity, the Shallow Effect becomes so ego-invested in their personality that just the potential of being perceived as "shallow" is subconsciously avoided.

This is a major obstacle in transitioning from AFC to positive masculinity. AFCs all initially laugh at PUA technique (Cocky & Funny, Peacocking, Neg Hits, etc.) because they carry the potential of being perceived as 'shallow'. The truth of the matter is that individually we are only as superficial as our own self-perceptions allow, but the Shallow Effect is a useful convention so long as it keeps men doubting their ingenuousness and self-validity in exchange for women's intimacy.

Selection Position Insurance

Examples:
*Women are 'allowed' to understand men, but women must necessarily **always** be a mystery to men.*

Getting "lucky" with a woman when referring to sex.

Selection position insuring methodologies revolve around fomenting the Scarcity Mentality in men. If the value can be inflated, the value can be increased, thus ensuring a controlling frame. This convention holds fast to the Feminine Mystique or Female Intuition mythology. So long as women remain 'unknowable' there becomes less motivation to *try* to understand them. In fact this convention actively discourages any attempt to understand the feminine to the point that men have adopted it and parrot it back without being cognizant of it.

This is exactly the reason why guys will ridicule men seeking an applicable understanding of women when they search it out in "how to get girls" books, DVDs, PUA seminars or on the internet. It's also why men who profess to '*know*' how women operate are ridiculed; it's a perfect paradox – to attempt to understand the feminine *or* to profess to know the feminine is not only laughable, but it places a man into the Shallow Effect in either case.

Social Escape Clauses – A Woman's Prerogative

Examples:
Women always have the prerogative to change their minds. Men must be resolute.

Proactive and Reactive Pseudo-Friendship Rejections:
LJBF rejections – "I already have a boyfriend" (boyfriend disclaimers) or "I'm not interested in a relationship right now" rejections.

Default female victimhood

Escape clause conventions always offer an *out* to a woman and absolve her of, or dramatically reduce her responsibility of personal accountability by means of social reinforcement. A stripper can complain of her self-degradation by men, but be completely blameless for her decisions to strip by virtue of her social conditions, that are, again, the perceived result of a male controlled society.

The Feminine Prerogative has been an accepted social norm since the early Renaissance and the advent of 'courtly love'. Like the Position Insurance convention, this serves to ensure that the 'mysterious woman' is validated in her ambiguity by socially plausible reinforcement. The opposite of this convention is enforced for men, they must be resolute while accepting that a woman "has the right to change her mind."

This, and the cart-carrot of a woman's intimacy reward, is exactly why it is socially acceptable for a man to wait hours for a woman to prepare/show for a date and the kiss of death for a man to be more than 5-10 minutes late. He must be punctual, she is afforded leniency.

I don't think I need to go into too much detail regarding the LJBF ("lets just be friends") escape clause, but I will add that the LJBF escape is perhaps the single most useful convention ever conceived by women. The LJBF rejection has classically ensured that a woman can reject a man yet still maintain his previous attention. It also puts the responsibility for the rejection back on his shoulders since, should he decline the 'offer of friendship', he is then responsible for entertaining this friendship. Of course this has the potential to backfire on women these days since the standard AFC will accept an LJBF rejection in the mistaken hopes of 'proving' himself worthy of her intimacy by being the perfect 'surrogate boyfriend' – fulfilling all her attention and loyalty prerequisites with no expectation of reciprocating her own intimacy.

Sexual Competition Sabotage

Examples:
"She's a 'slut' – he's a 'fag'" and the sub-communications in the terminology.

Catty remarks, gossip, feminine communication methodologies

This convention is the reputation destroyer and it's easy to observe this in the field. Since it also serves a woman attention needs, it is among the most socially acceptable and widely flaunted, however the foundations and latent purpose of this convention takes some consideration to understand. When women employ gossip it comes natural since it is an emotional form of communication (men have a far lower tendency to use gossip), but the purpose of it is meant to disqualify a potential sexual competitor.

In terms of female to female gossip this satisfies the attention need, but when men are brought into the salaciousness it becomes a qualification tool. By saying a woman is a "slut", the sub-communication is, "she sleeps with a lot of guys and should therefore be ineligible as a candidate deserving of a man's long term provisioning capacity, due to her obvious inability to remain loyal to any one, individual male." This then becomes the ultimate weapon in influencing a man's (long term) sexual selection.

I'll also add that this breeding sabotage isn't limited to just women. What's the first thing most men are apt to say about another, anonymous, extremely attractive male? *"He's probably a fag."*

Men have learned this convention from women, they sexually disqualify a man in he most complete way possible; "this guy might be as attractive as a GQ model, but he would never breed with a woman and is therefore disqualified as a suitor for your intimacy."

Gender Role Redefinition

Examples:
Masculinity is ridiculous and/or negative with the potential for violent extremes.

"Men should get in touch with their feminine sides." – Identification as false attraction.

Although there are more operative conventions to outline, I'll finish with this, the most obvious and most discussed convention. There's no shortage of articles dedicated to this convention, so I wont rehash what's been stated. Instead, I should point out the latent purpose behind the popularity and mass cultural acceptance of this, the most damaging convention. The function behind this convention could be promoting androgyny as an idealized state, or a power struggle to redefine masculine and feminine attributes, or even to ensure women as the primary selectors in mating. All of those can be argued and are valid, especially considering how prone to accepting and perpetuating this convention is among men today, but I think the deeper purpose, the real latent function is a sexual selection process.

It's the man who remains in touch with his masculine side, the guy who, despite all of pop-culture denigrating and ridiculing his gender and the very aspects that make it a necessary, positive strength of human society, will endure and steadfastly resist the influences that want to turn it into something it was never intended; it's this guy and his confidence that women all over the world find irresistible.

He embodies the masculine arousal that their feminine has been seeking and they can't explain it. This is the ultimate meta-shit test in sexual selection – to discover or learn what it is to be positively masculine and remain so in a world that constantly berates his gender, that tells him he's poisoned by his testosterone while confirming the same masculine attributes as a positive for women.

It's the guy who understands that it's gender differences, not androgynous similarities, that make us strong. It's the Man who can see that the sexes were meant to be complimentary, not adversarial, who passes this shit test. Gender redefinition, as a social convention, serves as an Alpha filtering mechanism.

AFC SOCIAL CONVENTIONS

After detailing the Qualities of the AFC, I feel it's necessary to illustrate that social conventions aren't the exclusive realm of the feminine imperative . AFCs have their own set of social conventions – those which are commonly practiced and self-reinforced by the Beta mindset. I realize that more than a few of these conventions are going to get under the skin of some readers, however, as you read this, please try to do so objectively. I'm writing this as an observation; it's not intended to be a personal affront to anyone.

You could simply call AFC Social Conventions AFC 'rationalizations', but I think this ignores the socially reinforcing element of these conventions. When I wrote the Qualities of the AFC I outlined the characteristic traits, behaviors and core mental schema of what are commonly believed to be AFC qualities. This was a brief list to sum up a few root elements in identifying and dealing with a Beta mindset and aid in unplugging an AFC. Social conventions are different in that they are socially reinforced (usually by both genders) rationalizations for behavior. Technically some of the AFC qualities I outlined previously could be considered social conventions as well, but I was attempting to address the symptoms rather than the disease.

I'm going to define a few more examples of what I'm most commonly noticing as AFC mental schema that are reinforced socially. A strong part of the internalization process of these conventions is that the reason they are socially reinforced is because they're socially unassailable (or at the very least foolish to do so). In other words the common response to them would be to reinforce them more, rather than challenge them, and this then becomes an integral part of the internalization process.

The Myth of the "Quality" Woman

It seems like all I read about in the manosphere is the never ending quest for a "Quality Woman." There's always been plenty of articles and comment threads asking for clear definitions of what constitutes a "Quality" woman and most conveniently set women up into 2 camps – "Quality Women" and Whores, as if there could be no middle ground or grey area. How easy it becomes to qualify a woman based on her indiscretions (as heinous as they're perceived to be) for either of these categories. This is binary thinking at its best – on or off, black or white, Quality woman or Whore.

I think the term 'Quality' woman is a misnomer. Guys tend to apply this term at their leisure not so much to define what they'd like in a woman (which is actually an idealization), but rather to exclude women with whom they'd really had no chance with in the first place, or mistakenly applied too much effort and too much focus only to be rebuffed. This isn't to say that there aren't women who will behave maliciously or indiscriminately, nor am I implying that they ought to be excused out of hand for such. What I am saying is that it's a very AFC predilection to hold women up to preconceived idealizations and conveniently discount them as being less than "Quality" when you're unable to predict, much less control their behaviors.

The dangers inherent in this convention is that the AFC (or the even the 'enlightened man' subscribing to the convention) then limits himself to only what he perceives is a Quality woman, based on a sour-grapes conditioning. Thus, they'll end up with a "Quality" woman by default because she's the only candidate who would accept him for her intimacy. It becomes a self-fulfilling prophecy by process of elimination. Taken to its logical conclusion, they shoot the arrow, paint the target around it and call it a bullseye, and after which they feel good for having held on to a (misguided) conviction.

So why is this a social convention then? Because it is socially unassailable. Since this convention is rooted to a binary premise, no one would likely challenge it. It would be foolish for me to say "Yes Mr. Chump I think you ought to avoid what you think of as Quality women." Not only this, but we all get a certain satisfaction from the affirmation that comes from other men confirming our assessment of what category a woman should fit into. Thus it becomes socially reinforced.

Beware of making your necessity a virtue in making a Quality woman your substitute for a ONEitis idealization.

The Myth of the Dodged Bullet

In my lifetime I've had sex with over 40 women and I never once caught a venereal disease, nor did I get anyone pregnant. I can also point to men I know who contracted Herpes from the only women they'd ever had sex with. The fact of the matter is that you can equally be a rock star and tap hundreds of women without any consequence and you can be a virgin saint and contract a disease on your wedding night.

The myth of the dodged bullet is a social convention that's rooted in the rationalization that monogamy serves the purpose for controlling sexually transmitted diseases and thus fewer partners are more desirable than many. From a statistical standpoint this may seem logical on the surface. Fewer opportunities for sexual intercourse would indeed decrease the risk from a single individual, but unfortunately this isn't a practical estimate. You'll also have to base the numbers not only on how many sex partners you and your monogamous partner have had, but also how many prior partners they've had and how many those partners had as well and so on exponentially. Despite all this, the odds that you'll die from a form of cancer, heart disease, smoking or obesity related diseases, or even an alcohol related traffic fatality far outweigh any risk of dying from a venereal disease in western society. The mortality rate for contracting gonorrhea, syphilis, chlamydia, herpes and even HIV pale in comparison to many – in some cases more easily preventable – diseases.

Of course, since this is a social convention, I would be grossly negligent and severely lambasted by the public at large for even implying that I'm condoning, much less advocating, that a man explore his options and open his experience up to having sex with multiple partners. Again, this social convention is unassailable. It sounds like it makes good sense, "boy, am I sure glad I got married/shacked up/stayed with the only girl I've ever had the opportunity to bang and didn't catch a disease, pffew!" It sounds like conviction, when in fact it's a rationalization for a lack of other realistic options with women or an inability to deal with a fear of rejection from multiple sources. Again, necessity becomes virtue.

Location, Location, Location

Another common contrivance is the presumption that less than desirable (low quality) women will necessarily be found in bars & clubs (or other places of "ill repute"). Thus the chump will only too eagerly avoid these places. This is, yet again, another example of the binary logic of an AFC and completely ignores that A.) women with whom they might make a successful connection with do in fact frequent clubs and B.) less than desirable women can also be met in "alternative" meeting places too (coffee house, university campus, library, Bible study or any number of other "safe places"). However, making approaches in a club are difficult for the inexperienced Game adherent and AFC alike. There's a lot of competition and a lot of potential for 'real time' rejection for the unprepared. By masking this deficit in Game with condemning such places, the AFC thinks he's killing two birds with one stone – he's protecting his ego from very real rejection and he's lauded by "proper" society (see people who go to clubs anyway) for being an upstanding individual for avoid those "dens of iniquity."

The Myth of 'Other Guys'

This is perhaps the most dangerous AFC social convention.

We'd all like to think we're unique and special individuals. It's a comforting thought, but our uniqueness means nothing if it isn't appreciated. We'd all like to be beautiful, talented, intelligent and extraordinary in some way to some degree and have others notice these qualities unequivocally.

This is the root for the **Not Like Other Guys** convention. The idea is that the AFC can and will be appreciated in a greater degree for his personal convictions and/or his greater ability to identify with women's stated prerequisites of a man by comparing himself to the nebulous *Other Guys* who are perceived not to abide by her stated conditions for intimacy. The intent is to, in essence, self-generate social proof for attraction while substituting a real social element with social evidence.

The fallacy in this schema is that it's always better to demonstrate social proof than to explicate it, but this is lost on the AFC subscribing to this convention. This only becomes more compounded by the reinforcement he receives from other AFCs (and really society at large) sharing his desire to outshine the phantom *Other Guys*. He's patted on the back and praised by men and women alike for voluntarily molding his personality to better fit a woman's perceived ideal and told in so many words "oh AFC,..I'm so glad you're not like *Other Guys.*" You can't fault the guy. He genuinely believes his Nice Guy personal conviction and everyone applauds him for it.

I'd argue that 95% of men aren't even aware that they're repeating / reinforcing a social convention at all because the convention is so embedded into our social fabric that it's taken for granted. The most effective social conventions are ones in which the subject willingly sublimates his own interests, discourages questioning it, and predisposes that person to encourage and reinforce the convention with others. This is the essence of the Matrix; anything can become normal.

I encounter AFC mentalities all day long in my line of work, and I don't encounter them strictly from men either. More often than not I find myself in some social/work environment where it's women fomenting an AFC attitude and it's men who jokingly play along with them in an attempt to identify with these women in order to qualify for female intimacy. It's this pop-culture 'agreeability' factor that is taken as an unquestioned norm. It's expected that female-centric social conventions should simply be a matter of fact without any need for critical thought.

For a positively masculine Man there is no better opportunity to set yourself apart and start to plant the seeds of critical thought into AFCs than when you're presented with these social situation. I think most men lack the balls to be a fire starter at the risk of being perceived as some caveman, but it's a good opportunity to truly set yourself apart from *'other guys'* when you do.

THE PARADOX OF COMMITMENT

The concept of commitment is a fantastic utility for women. Men can be simultaneously shamed for not sticking to a commitment that benefits them and still be shamed for steadfastly adhering to a commitment that doesn't. The social convention is so developed there's even a cute term for it – "commitment-phobic" or "commit-o-phobe".

There's an interesting control of the message here; the principle of commitment is cast in feminine-centric perfection. The idea is that commitment should only have meaning in a feminine defined reality. Ironically, it's Men who commit far more readily to ideals, family, military, business ventures or partnerships, and servitude than women have the capacity to appreciate, because recognizing this doesn't serve their imperative. In other words, a commitment to anything that doesn't directly benefit the feminine isn't commitment; answer? Redefine commitment to uniquely reflect feminine interests.

Whenever I get into these debates about infidelity (albeit usually from the male perspective), and it becomes an immoral / amoral / moralist menage à trois, I wonder, what is the greater "moral" imperative; to remain faithful to your morally obligated commitment with your spouse in spite of a loveless, passionless, sexless partner, or to break that commitment in order to pursue the obligation and commitment you owe yourself as a "superior" Man deserving of a better "quality" partner?

What has moral priority, a commitment to yourself or a commitment to marriage? You see it's easy to wave the flag of self-righteousness when the issue is a right vs. wrong issue. It's much more difficult when the question is right vs. right. I have no doubt that all the answers to this will be entirely circumstantial, rationalized twisting in the wind, and maybe that's what decides for you, but think about it for a moment in the terms of what one must sacrifice for the other.

Whatever you cannot say 'No' to is your master and makes you it's slave.

This is a favorite go-to trope for moral arguments where there's a clearly defined right and wrong, however, by this definition then, does not commitment make you a 'slave' by default? If by the circumstances of a commitment you cannot, figuratively, say "no" to the that (or due to that) commitment, are you not then a slave?

You can even take marriage out of the equation; if I'm in a committed LTR with a girlfriend and over the course of that relationship I realize that she's not what I'm looking for (for any number of reasons, not just sex), even though she's 100% faithfully committed to me and the LTR, should I then break that commitment? If I do, am I then being unethical for having broken that commitment irrespective of how I break it? Should the commitment to my own personal well being and future happiness be compromised by another commitment?

What's my obligation; neglect myself in favor of a bad commitment or to the principle of commitment itself?

It's my take that commitment 'should' be a function of genuine desire. Ideally, commitment should be to something one is so passionate about that the limiting of one's own future opportunities that come from that commitment is an equitable, and mutually appreciated exchange. This is unfortunately rarely the case for most people in any form of commitment because people, circumstance, opportunity and conditions are always in flux. A commitment that had been seen as an equitable sacrifice at one time can become debilitating five years after it depending upon circumstance.

So what I'm getting at is where do you draw the line? People go all kinds of crazy when I suggest a guy NEXT some girl that's obviously showing all of the indications that she's using him (or has proven so) and then two comments down suggest that it's Men's obligation to vet women by "walking away." If I have one life to live and one precious lifetime to do it in, what is more important; a commitment to oneself in learning and securing the best options for a lifetime or being committed to the principle of self-sacrificing commitment?

In the 'community' we brazenly tell freshmen chumps to dedicate themselves to self-improvement; to seek out and accomplish what's best for them – in other words, to uncompromisingly commit themselves to their own cause in as positive a manner as possible.

I'd argue that genuine desire is a necessary precursor to this, but in advocating this self-concerned improvement, are we not then doing them a disservice if their duty ought to be focused on the principle of commitment, even when that commitment is (or becomes) deleterious to their commitment to a positive self?

What holds more water, being a martyr to chivalrous commitment, or a steadfast dedication to ourselves? Should we not then hold AFCs in the highest respect when they selflessly sacrifice their futures due to their devoted commitment to a ONEitis girl who'll never reciprocate on, much less appreciate, that commitment? We'd call them chumps, but in contrast to their devotion to the principle of commitment, maybe they've got it right? You can't doubt their (albeit misguided) dedication to their convictions.

BITTER MISOGYNISTS

When men can be convinced to participate in women's
social conventions half their work is done for them.

One of the surest indicators of an AFC-beta mindset is the automatic presumption that anything remotely critical a man would say about women, or the feminine, is by default, equated with misogyny.

All a man need do is open his mouth, in the most objective way he can muster, about anything critical of the feminine and he's instantly suspect of sour grapes. He must've been burned, or is bitter and on the verge of desperation just for even a passing mention of some critical observation of women's incongruent intents and behaviors.

What an amazingly potent social convention that is – when a man will censor himself because of it on his own. The most successful social conventions are ones in which the subject willingly sublimates his own interests, discourages questioning it, and predisposes that person to encourage others to participate in it.

"You're just bitter because you got burned by some bitch in the past and your misogynist ideology is just your way of lashing out."

I hear this a lot from both men and women. It's an easy response to parrot and it's very useful. It foists the responsibility of confronting one's critical ideas back on the man, all while shaming him for forming an ideology based on what he (and now a community of many other men) confirms by observations. It's like a JBY (just be yourself) response; it sounds right, everyone uses it to the point of cliché, and it misdirects and discourages any further critical analysis.

This is a feminine social convention that's in the same vein as shame. Any guy that has a point about the feminine, no matter how valid, can always have his argument poisoned because he's a guy, most guys are frustrated that they aren't getting laid, and this is his petty way of venting. When men can be convinced to participate in women's social conventions half their work is done for them. In presuming a default state of male misogyny, it implicitly denotes a default state of 'correctness' or blamelessness of the female. In other words, you're guilty by association and must prove innocence.

The Protector Dynamic

The protector dynamic has evolved into a beta breeding methodology. It's like a Darwinist version of Cap'n Save A Ho – so at the slightest critical word about a woman or the feminine in general it's, "See how quickly I come to a woman's defense? What girl wouldn't want a great protector like me? I'm unique. I'm not like those bitter 'other guys' so your best emotional/sexual/parental investment would be coupling with me as evidenced by my example." Of course that isn't their conscious, cognitively recognized reaction, but it is the subroutine that's running in their unconscious. When this psychological schema is a practiced breeding methodology it becomes second nature; so much so that when *any* opportunity arises to display it (even under the conditions of anonymity), the guy snaps to attention. It's really a Beta attempt to DHV (display higher value), and in and of itself it's not necessarily a bad impulse, it just that it's used to further a feminized social convention.

Whiners and Losers.

"Game Blogs, PUAs, MRA guys, they're all a bunch of whiners who'd rather kvetch about feminism and real or imagined wrongs than just get up and get along."

The problem I think most people have with the tone of what Game has, or is evolving into, is that essentially Game is a masculine response to what feminism (really feminization) has evolved into. While I can empathize with the feeling that Game can assume a plaintive tone at some blogs – particularly MRA oriented ones – contemporary Game is really a countermeasure to the social conditions feminist ideology has embedded in our culture for the past 50+ years. However, the social framework has been established as such that even my pointing this out makes me suspect of complaining or "bitter". See how that works? My belief is still, 'don't wish it were easier, wish you were better', but it's been built into feminization that to even analyze and have critical opinion of it makes you a whiner.

There is no going back.

One dynamic I encounter from guys who've experienced the 'community' in varying degrees is a desire to go back to their previously comfortable, ignorant bliss. The reality they become exposed to is too much to bear and they spit the red pill back up. They want to plug themselves back into the Matrix.

No person both frightens and disgusts me more than one who understands truth, but willfully opts for denial. It's not the desire to do so that disgusts me, I understand the desire, it's that there is no going back.

Even if you never read another post or blog and regressed back to your old ways, you'll still make the associations, see the signs of what others have analyzed in your own periphery, in women's and the world's behaviors and motivations, and you'll be reminded (even if subconsciously) of that truth, or at least the uncomfortable push to get at the truth. You will only get what you've gotten if you keep doing what you've done. There is no going back now. Don't wish it were easier. Wish you were better.

There comes a point of conflict (or revulsion if you want) after a guy has been unplugged from the Matrix long enough where he begins to doubt himself and what he's seeing go on around him. All of the gender dynamics and the complex, but discreet, interplay between the sexes that's been such a mystery for so long starts to become apparent to him. The Neg Hit PUA techniques he never would've dreamed of attempting in his AFC days become so predictably reliable at sparking interest that it becomes depressing. A backhanded compliment shouldn't work; it goes against everything any girl has ever told him will endear him to a woman, but once he musters up the courage to experiment, he finds that they do work.

What's depressing isn't that a well delivered neg, or being Cocky & Funny, or harnessing the attractive Alpha Asshole energy could actually generate sexual interest in women, it's the principle behind them – the *reason* why they work – that prompts the internal conflict.

Are women, generally, more like this than not? So a guy experiments a little more, and tests other theories, and discovers that with some minor variations, yes, for the most part the principles are valid if not predictable. This then becomes a real tough pill to swallow, especially when you consider ideas like the ruthlessness of feminine hypergamy. It's very despairing, almost nihilistic, to a man fed on a steady diet of the flowery tropes of feminization for the better part of a lifetime. It's very hard to measure oneself up and adjust to a new understanding of how women think and behave. He can't reconcile what he'd been told and conditioned to believe before (the soul mate myth, pedestalize her, just be yourself, etc.) with this new paradigm. So either he learns to live with this new understanding, benefit from it and grow into a new role for himself, or he rejects it and vilifies it wholesale.

"Women are really not as bad as these misogynists, these bitter, burned men would all have us believe. They're shallow and soulless to think women are all out to get them. They over-analyze everything when they should all just be themselves and let fate or some divine force pair them up with their soul mates. I pity them, really I do."

I've heard all of these regressive rationales from boys as young as 14 to men as old as 75. It's a comfortable ignorance to believe that things are just unknowable and beyond one's control or efforts to really understand. And to make matters worse, there's a long established system of social conventions ready to reinforce and affirm these rationales; ready to reinsert him back into the Matrix and tell him he's unique and special ("not like other guys") and will be rewarded with female intimacy for rejecting it.

CHAPTER 7

HYPERGAMY

THE DISPOSABLES

Martyrdom is the ultimate expression of social proof.

After I'd finished my Chivalry vs. Altruism post, I had to pause for a moment to consider the impact of '*women & children first*' as an operative social convention. Even before the overt rise of the feminine imperative, this female protectionism was in effect, and I'm fairly certain that this was a result of our primal hind-brain wiring to protect our families. Most higher order animals have evolved this instinct so I don't see that as much of a stretch. However, humans being a much more complex species, I think that the social convention of WaCF goes a bit deeper than a simplistic protectionism. In fact, I'd argue that 'familial protectionism' is more of a convenient foil for women (and sympathetic men) who'd rather see men's mortal sacrifice in honorific terms than the much uglier truth.

Tits for Tat

In its rawest form, the sexual marketplace of our early ancestors would've been one where feminine hypergamy and Alpha dominance would've been more or less in balance. Obviously men being the stronger sex would've forcibly put women into a weaker position in the earliest incarnations of the sexual marketplace, but also consider that men fought and killed each other for access to those breeding rights – short version; men were disposable.

As our species began to socialize, collectivize and cooperate, our earliest social conventions would've revolved around the environmental prompts and biological cues that were essential to the survival of their more feral ancestors.

The earliest form of proto-Game would've been a sexual quid pro quo. Can't figure out how to seduce that hot, hunter-gatherer woman in the tribe? Save her ass from being torn limb from limb by a saber tooth tiger and she'll reciprocate her gratitude with open legs. In other words, risk your life and women will reward you with sex in gratitude. Today that may not be a reality in practice, but it's the deductive logic that's led to the psychological internalization and the social doctrines that follow it.

It's such a primal, male-deductive-logic principle that's worked so successfully, for so long, that social contingencies were evolved to both mitigate it and exploit it. Don't believe me? Promise a young middle eastern girl 70 virgins in heaven and see if she'll strap explosives to herself. The downside to this is that men often do "die trying."

All of this kind of brought me around to thinking about the psychological 'software' that's been evolved into our species as a result of environmental adaptations of the past. In War Brides I go into detail about the Stockholm Syndrome women seem to have an inborn propensity for, which logically makes them predisposed to abandoning emotional investments more readily than men. Considering the brutality of our feral past, evolving a capacity for quick emotional abandonment and reinvestment would've been a valuable survival trait for women (thus insuring a perpetuation of the species), however, in the present it serves to complicate newly developed social dynamics in terms of parental and ethical considerations.

Likewise, men have evolved into the disposable sex as a result of that same feral past. In today's environment it's very easy for men to draw upon ethical indignation about our disposable status, but it's not primarily due to social influences. To be sure, social influence has definitely exploited men's disposability, but the root of that devaluation (in contrast to women's) really lies in our evolutionary past and our biological make up. Men have always been disposable – so much so that women evolved psychological contingencies (War Brides) to cope with that disposability.

As socialization and acculturation progressed, so too did the social rationales for men's disposability. It became honorable to sacrifice oneself, ostensibly for a greater cause, but subversively as a means to recognition.

Martyrdom is the ultimate expression of social proof.

Appreciating the Sacrifice

Unfortunately, as is women's biological imperative, once a man's martyred himself women seek a suitable substitute within the week. Two years after I posted it on Rational Male and I'm still getting a lot of response on my Appreciation post, and predictably most of the criticism is rooted in assuming my intent was to illustrate women being inferior to men in terms of sincerely appreciating the sacrifices he must make to facilitate her reality.

The inability of women appreciating men's sacrifices isn't an issue of who's better than who, it's merely an observation of facts and corollaries. What I think critics fail to recognize is that I'm simply relating the observed mechanics; any conditionality they choose to apply to those mechanics are their own opinions and biases.

"Yeah Rollo, it's pretty fucked up that women have some inborn ability to 'switch off' their emotions for you in favor of a higher SMV male…"

You're right it's pretty messed up. It's also unethical, insincere and duplicitous when you also consider the planning involved in dissociating her emotional investment in favor of a new investment; but all of these are social conditions we apply to the underlying mechanic. It's also pretty fucked up that men's lives intrinsically have less value than women's – but we can apply esoteric principles of honor, duty and courage to men killing themselves and engaging in the dynamic of their own disposability.

We can also apply principles of cowardice and betrayal to men who refuse that sacrifice in favor of self-preservation, but these are qualification of social conventions that we establish as a culture.

The biomechanics are what they are, irrespective of the social paint we color them with. It's not that women lack an intellectual capacity to appreciate men's sacrifices, it's that this isn't their evolved psychological predisposition. The social constructs which tells her to expect a man's sacrifice, which normalizes his martyrdom, have evolved to better dissociate her own investment in her biological imperatives (i.e. Hypergamy).

In English this means evolution has prepared her socially and psychologically for his sacrifice, and readies her to move to a better provisioning should one present itself in her surroundings. Likewise, men putting themselves in harms way is rooted in our competing for resources – in this case breeding rights.

Ravenous wolves tearing apart an elk aren't evil; they're doing what nature has prepared them to do in order to survive. This isn't to give anyone, male or female, some biologically determined free pass for bad behavior, it's just to understand where this behavior originates and how it came to be what we make of it today.

WAR BRIDES

Reader *Nas* had an interesting question regarding female duplicity:

"Evolution has largely selected-for human females with a capacity to form psychological schema that preserve an ego-investment that would otherwise afflict them with debilitating anxiety, guilt, and the stresses that result from being continuously, consciously aware of their own behavioral incongruities. Evolution selects-for solipsistic women who are blissfully unaware of their solipsism."

Can you please expand on this Rollo? I find it fascinating.

OK, baton down the hatches, we're heading for dangerous waters. What I'm getting at here is suggesting that women's propensity for solipsism is a psychologically evolved mechanism. In other words, it helped women to cope with the harsh realities of the past, to develop a more focused sense of self-interest.

To really grasp this you need to understand women's brain function and chemistry. I'm not going to get too detailed in this, but suffice it to say numerous studies show that a female brain is hard-wired for emotional response and communication on a more complex level than men. I think this is pretty much an established point for my readers, but if you disagree, well that's going to have be the topic of another post.

Given the harsh realities that women had to endure since the paleolithic era, it served them better to psychologically evolve a sense of self that was more resilient to the brutal changes she could expect be subjected to. Consider the emotional investment a woman needs to put into mothering a child that could be taken away or killed at a moment's notice.

Anxiety, fear, guilt, insecurity are all very debilitating emotions, however it's women's innate psychology that makes them more durable to these stresses. Statistically, men have far greater difficulty in coping with psychological trauma (think PTSD) than women. Why should that be?

On the face of it you may think that men's better ability to rationally remove themselves from the emotional would make them better at coping with psychological trauma, but the reverse is actually the case. Women seem to have a better ability to accept emotional sacrifice and move on, either ignoring those stresses or blocking them entirely from their conscious awareness. Women possessing a more pronounced empathic capacity undoubtedly served our species in nurturing young and understanding tribal social dynamics, however it was also a liability with regards to a hostile change in her environment.

Stockholm Syndrome is far more pronounced in female captives (the story of Jaycee Duguard comes to mind), why should that be? Because women's peripheral environment dictated the need to develop psychological mechanisms to help them survive. It was the women who could make that emotional disconnect when the circumstances necessitated it who survived and lived to breed when their tribe was decimated by a superior tribe. This is also known as the War Bride dynamic; women develop an empathy with their conquerors by necessity.

Men are the disposable sex, women, the preserved sex. Men would simply die in favor of a superior aggressor, but women would be reserved for breeding. So it served a feminine imperative to evolve an ability to cut former emotional ties more readily (in favor of her new captor) and focus on a more self-important psychology – solipsism.

Now, here is where I'll step off the diving board and into the theoretical. It's my purview that a lot of what men would complain are duplicitous acts of indifference towards them are really rooted in this innate feminine solipsism.

That's a bold statement, I realize, but I'd argue that what men take for inconsiderate indifference in a break up or in ruthless shit tests is really a woman tapping into this innate, self-preserving solipsism. Combine hypergamy with the chronically hostile environments of the past and you end up with a modern day feminine solipsism.

Add to this an acculturated sense of female entitlement, social conventions that excuse this 'duplicity', and a constant misdirection of intent by women themselves, and you come to where we are now. As if that weren't enough, throw in the element of hypergamy and the countdown in terms of fertility and long term provisioning that a woman must deal with before hitting the imminent Wall, and now you have a fuller picture of the conditions and stresses that necessitate this solipsistic nature.

Ever wonder why it is a woman can 'get over you' so quickly after a break up from a relationship you'd thought was rock solid for so long? Ever wonder why she returns to the abusive boyfriend she hopes will change for her? Look no further than feminine solipsism.

After reading all of this I can understand if anyone thinks this is a very nihilistic observation. Let me be clear, this dynamic is real by order of degrees for individual women. A woman's conditions may be such that she's never needed to tap into this reserve.

Also, we are dealing with subconscious elements of her personality here, so it would come as no surprise that feminine solipsism wouldn't be cognitive for most women – thus offensive and denied. I'm not asking that anyone accept this idea as gospel, just that the dots do connect very predictably.

MRS. HYDE

Women's Sexual Pluralism

In a study I linked by Dr. Martie Hasselton there was a very salient point that kind of gets passed up since the focus of that social experiment was more about isolating variables in women's physical preferences for males. That point was illustrating women's pluralistic sexual strategies – short term breeding strategies whilst in her sexual peak, progressing to long term sexual strategies as her sexual agency becomes less valuable and subject to the rigors of competition anxiety in the SMP.

According to strategic pluralism theory (Gangestad & Simpson, 2000), men have evolved to pursue reproductive strategies that are contingent on their value on the mating market. More attractive men accrue reproductive benefits from spending more time seeking multiple mating partners and relatively less time investing in offspring. In contrast, the reproductive effort of less attractive men, who do not have the same mating opportunities, is better allocated to investing heavily in their mates and offspring and spending relatively less time seeking additional mates.

From a woman's perspective, the ideal is to attract a partner who confers both long-term investment benefits and genetic benefits. Not all women, however, will be able to attract long-term investing mates who also display heritable fitness cues. Consequently, women face trade-offs in choosing mates because they may be forced to choose between males displaying fitness indicators or those who will assist in offspring care and be good long-term mates (Gangestad & Simpson, 2000). The most straightforward prediction that follows is that women seeking short-term mates, when the man's only contribution to offspring is genetic, should prefer muscularity more than women seeking long-term mates.

Over the course of a woman's life the priorities and criteria a she holds for a 'suitable' mate fluctuate in response to the conditions she finds herself in. The criterion for short term coupling are much easier to demand when a woman is in her peak fertility phase of life and thus places these prerequisites above what she would find more desirable for a long-term pairing. The extrinsic male-characteristic prerequisites for short-term sexual strategy (hot, quick Alpha sex) preempts the long-term qualifications for as long as she's sexually viable enough to attract men.

Thus it follows that as a woman exceeds or is outclassed of her previous SMV, her priorities then shift to an attraction for more intrinsic male qualities. For the short-term strategy, quick impulsivity and gratifying sensation take precedent. For the long-term strategy, slow discernment, prudence, familiarity and comfort satisfy a desire for security as she exits the competitive stage of the SMP.

The dirty little secret to all of this is that although a woman may abandon one strategy for another depending on the phase of life she's in, nature has seen fit to make sure she never quite abandons one for the other completely. As her environment warrants, she can readily re-prioritize her conditions for intimacy in order to achieve that sexually strategic balance.

This is a very uncomfortable truth for contemporary women in that it exposes the underpinnings of a great many feminized social conventions intended to misdirect men in an effort to maintain superiority in sexual selectivity and effecting these strategies. Men becoming aware of the pluralistic nature of hypergamy is the greatest threat to the feminine imperative.

Nothing is more threatening yet simultaneously attractive to a woman than a man who is aware of his own value to women.

Biomechanics

An even more uncomfortable truth is that women's pluralistic sexual strategy is literally written into their genetics. In a woman's sexual peak, across her ovulatory cycle she will tend to seek out High-Testosterone cued Alpha Men to pursue for her short term breeding strategy during her pro-phase of ovulation. In her menstruation period her preferences switch to preferring the long term security of a docile, secure Beta provider, and thus filters for these traits in her pair-bonding.

I'm elaborating on the genetic aspects here because I think it's important for men to understand the biological mechanics of women's sexual strategies in a broader scope. I endure an endless stream criticism for implying that women are selective sluts. Obviously women in the general whole have the capacity to resist these base impulses to "go slut", however this is the base biological impulse against which they resist by conviction, rationale, sentimentalism or simply being realistic about having a low SMP valuation.

As I've said before, all women have the capacity to throw caution to the wind in order to pursue her short term sexual strategy. Right place, right guy, right ovulatory phase, I was drunk, he was cute and one thing led to another,.. Nature selected for women who could best effect a covert pluralistic sexual strategy.

Due to the cyclic nature of women's sexuality it's a misnomer to think that "women are just as sexual as men", however, to the importance of sexual selectivity dominance, women are much more sexual than most men are led to believe.

The key is understanding that women want to be sexual on their own terms as their cycle dictates. Essentially they are serving two masters in this: they want the freedom to pursue a short term sexual opportunity (as well as the freedom from social repercussions as a result) and also the prudence to filter for a man willing to assume the responsibilities of parental investment and provisioning.

NAWALT
(Not all women are like that)

From a recent discussion thread:

Here is a tip – level headed girls who are intelligent have told me they don't want to get fake breasts, even when they're an A cup. Also some girls prefer to take it a step slower. They don't NEED immediate gratification, they know that a good thing might take time, and here is an idea, you know how women think men are dumb – MOST ARE. That's why they play games – to weed out players!

This was from a guy. I used to believe this, until I understood the fundamentals of female hypergamy. For far too many men it's a comfortable fiction to think that attractive, self-conscious, "level headed" women really have the presence and forethought to 'weed out' what men would rationally think would be the best fit for them.

However, observably and predictably, their behaviors and choices don't bear this out. On the contrary, their behaviors prove the validity of female hypergamy even in the personalities of what we'd consider the most virtuous women. Even the bright, intelligent, good-girl selects for, and sexually prepares herself for, the most immediately accessible Alpha male her attractiveness will command *and* they also filter for the players, and develop bonds with men they believe might provide for their long term security when their necessity dictates that they should. They're the same girl.

Without all the social pretense, on the most root level, women are keenly aware that men's primary interest in them is fucking – everything else is ancillary to sex. The difficulty women encounter in perfecting a long-term sexual strategy is men's singular primary strategy – the value a woman has beyond the sexual comes after she's been sexual.

The Truth is Out There

Almost a year ago Ferd over at In Mala Fide wrote a very eye-opening post about what appears to be an endemic of online Self-Shooters – millions of unprompted, unsolicited young women shooting and posting nude and semi-nude pictures of themselves from a smart-phone. Just image search Google keyword "self shots", you'll get the idea. And it goes well beyond just teenage dalliances with bathroom pictorials; with the rise of convenient digital media creation we get a clearer view of women's true sexual landscape.

Have a look at the sheer volume and frequency with which average women will voluntarily become sexual. Are they all sluts? How many of these women have uttered the words " I want to wait so I know you want me for more than sex?" How many of these women would make great wives in 5-10 years? How many of these women are already (or have been) wife material? How many of these women are thought of as the sweet natured "good girl"? How many guys have considered these girls "Quality Women" at some point? We can look at them with their clothes off and declare them sluts, but would

you know the difference if you saw her in church?
From the same critic:

Most girls will go through an experimental phase at least. I don't think that makes them sluts, necessarily. Depends on degree.

I half agree with this. There is most definitely a phase of life where women will opportunistically leverage their sexuality – usually this is mid-teens to late 20s, but you have to also take into consideration why this sexual attention is such an urgency as well as being so rewarding for a woman in this phase. Hypergamy and a rapidly closing window of SMV spur on that urgency.

I'm also compelled to point out that women in their 30s, 40s and even 50s will still "slut it up" and seek that sexual attention if their conditions dictate that they must return to that agency. Again, refer to the self-shots phenomenon; not all of these girls are 18 y.o. misguided youths experimenting with their sexuality for the first time. A solid percentage of them are post-30s women, and some older than that showing off their 'new' post-divorce body after 3 months training at the gym. Are they still 'experimenting' or are they feeling the need to retroactively solicit male sexual response due to changes in their lives' conditions?

The point I was making is that the "quality woman" meme is entirely subjective to the sexually strategic conditions that a woman finds herself in. As per usual, guys would like to make their necessity a virtue and define whatever is working for them currently as an ideal situation without considering the factors that contribute to it or would radically change it if those conditions were altered. When you met your devoted, soccer-mom wife in her 20s, your first thought wasn't "I wonder if she's a quality woman?" It was probably more along the lines of "I wonder if she sucks a good dick?" At the time, the conditions were different for her, and her personality reflected an adaptation to them.

Now What?

So where does this leave a Man? I think it's determined by where you are yourself in life and what your expectations for yourself are. If you're young and just beginning to find your footing in the SMP then I'd advise spinning plates and enjoying yourself, but with the understanding that you are learning from experience. Maybe that's as far as you want to (responsibly) go, or maybe you entertain the idea of becoming monogamous at some point. Naturally, I wouldn't advise even experimenting with monogamy for any guy under the age of 30, but lets assume you do have the experience and have an understanding of how the SMP and hypergamy work. The most valuable bit of wisdom you can carry into a monogamy of your own decision and your own frame is to understand this sexual pluralism in women. Accept hypergamy as a woman's operative state at all times.

The most common words hear newly divorced men utter is some version of "I never saw this coming in my wildest imagination, we were married for 20 years, we have 4 kids, how could she be over me so quickly?" A lack of understanding the basics of hypergamy is exactly why men are blindsided.

HYPERGAMY DOESN'T CARE

Hypergamy doesn't care how great a Father you are to your kids.

Hypergamy doesn't care how you rearranged your college majors and career choice in life to better accommodate her.

Hypergamy doesn't care how inspired or fulfilled you feel as a stay-at-home Dad.

Hypergamy doesn't care that you moved across 4 states to accommodate your long distance relationship.

Hypergamy doesn't care how 'supportive' you've always been of her decisions or if you identify as a 'male feminist'.

Hypergamy doesn't care about the sincerity of your religious convictions or aspirations of high purpose.

Hypergamy doesn't care about those words you said at your wedding.

Hypergamy doesn't care about how you funded her going back to college to find a more rewarding career.

Hypergamy doesn't care how great a guy you are for adopting the children she had with other men.

Hypergamy doesn't care about your divine and forgiving nature in excusing her "youthful indiscretions."

Hypergamy doesn't care about your magnanimity in assuming responsibility for her student loans, and credit card debt after you're married.

Hypergamy doesn't care if "he was your best friend."

Hypergamy doesn't care about the coffee in bed you bring her or how great a cook you are.

Hypergamy doesn't care about all those chick flicks you sat through with her and claimed to like.

Hypergamy doesn't care about how well you do your part of the household chores.

Hypergamy doesn't care about how much her family or friends like you.

Hypergamy doesn't care if you think you're a "Good" guy or about how convincing your argument is for your sense of honor.

Hypergamy doesn't care whether the children are biologically yours or not.

Hypergamy doesn't care if "she was drunk, he was cute, and one thing led to another,.."

Hypergamy doesn't care how sweet, funny or intellectual you are.

Hypergamy doesn't care if you "never saw it coming."

Hypergamy doesn't care if you're bitter.

Relational Equity

When I started in on the Hypergamy doesn't care,.. post I knew it was going to come off as some unavoidably deterministic rant about the evils of hypergamy.

That post was born out of all the efforts I've repeatedly read men relate to me when they say how unbelievable their breakups were. As if all of the investment, emotional, physical, financial, familial, etc. would be rationally appreciated as a buffer against hypergamy. The reason for their shock and disbelief is that their mental state originates in the assumption that women are perfectly rational agents and should take all of their efforts, all of their personal strengths, all of the involvement in their women's lives into account before trading up to a better prospective male. There is a prevailing belief that all of their merits, if sufficient, should be proof against her hypergamous considerations.

For men, this is a logically sound idea. All of that investment adds up to their concept of relationship equity. So it's particularly jarring for men to consider that all of that equity becomes effectively worthless to a woman presented with a sufficiently better prospect as per the dictates of her hypergamy.

That isn't to say that women don't take that equity into account when determining whether to trade up or in their choice of men if they're single, but their operative point of origin is *always* hypergamy. Women obviously can control their hypergamic mpulses in favor of fidelity, just as men can and do keep their sexual appetites in check, but always know that it isn't relationship equity she's rationally considering in that moment of decision.

This dynamic is exactly the reason the surrogate boyfriend, the perfect nice guy orbiter who's invested so much into identifying with his target, gets so enraged when his dream girl opts for the hot asshole jerk. She's not making a logical decision based upon his invested relational equity. Quite the opposite; she's empirically proving for him that his equity is worthless by rewarding the hot jerk – who had essentially no equity – with her sex and intimacy. He doesn't understand that hypergamy doesn't care about relational equity.

This is a really tough truth for guys to swallow, because knowing how hypergamy works necessarily devalues their concept of relational equity with the woman they're committed to, or considering commitment with. Men's concept of relational equity stems from a mindset that accepts negotiated desire (not genuine desire) as a valid means of relationship security. This is precisely why most couples counseling fails – its operative origin begins from the misconception that genuine desire (hypergamy) can be negotiated indefinitely.

The Rational Female

There are a lot of fluffy little pieces of interpretive Alpha fiction extolling the virtues of Beta men (who are told *they* are the real Alphas only without teeth, pee sitting down and only say sweet things about girls) Irony aside, these female authors still fall prey to two fallacies in their pleas for a better Beta.

The first is as discussed above; the hope or the realistic expectation that women's hindbrain hypergamy can be sublimated in favor of a rational cognitive decision making when choosing with whom to spread her legs for, much less settle down with. The limbic influence hypergamy has over women's decision making processes is a constant subroutine playing in the background. The short answer is this is a mistaken belief that healthy relationships can be rooted in negotiated desire (which is also called 'obligated desire' in the real world).

This then leads into the second fallacy which presumes relationship equity – even the potential for that equity – will make the life time commitment to a "he'll-haffta-do" Beta endurable while repressing her innate hypergamy. Hypergamy doesn't care about relational equity. If it's a consideration at all in a woman's decision making process, it's only for comparative purposes when assessing risk motivated by hypergamy. Some times that risk association is present in deciding whether to accept a marriage proposal, sometimes it's present when she decides another man's genetic potential rivals that of the provider she's already committed to, but in all instances the originating prompt is still hypergamy.

The Rational Male

All of that may sound like I'm excusing men from the equation, I'm not. When men progressively become more aware of their sexual market value, the better their capacity develops to assess long term investment potential with women. The trouble with this model, in its present form, is that the phase at which men are just becoming aware of their true long term value to women (usually around age 30) is almost exactly the phase (just pre-Wall) in which women hope to press men unaware of their SMV into their long term provisioning schema.

As this relates to men, most spend the majority of their teens and 20's pursuing women, following the dictates of their biological impulses, and to varying degrees of success learn from experience what really seems like women's duplicity or fickleness. So it comes as a breath of fresh air for the average (see Beta) guy to finally encounter what he believes is a woman who's "down to earth" and seems genuinely concerned with hearth and family at age 29. Her past character, her very nature, even her single-mommyness can be overlooked and/or forgiven in light of finding what he believes is such a rare jewel.

There's a new breed of White Knight in the manosphere who love to enthusiastically promote the idea of rigorously vetting women as potential wives. It sounds like virtue.

For serial monogamists playing the 'Good Guy' card, it sounds so satisfying to lay claim to having experience and integrity enough to be a good judge or authority of what will or will not do for his 'exacting standards'.

This is really a new form of Beta Game; "look out ladies, I've been through the paces so if you're not an approximate virgin and know how to bake a hearty loaf of bread, this guy is moving on,.." and on, and on, and on. All any of this really amounts to is a better form of identification Game, because ultimately a profession of being a Good Guy is still an attempt to be what he expects his ideal woman would want – a good judge (of her) character.

Know this right now, no man (myself included) in the history of humanity has ever fully or accurately vetted any woman he married. And certainly not any guy who married prior to the age of 30 or had fewer than 1 LTR in his past. It's not that high school sweethearts who last a lifetime don't exist, it's that no man can ever accurately determine how the love of his life will change over the course of that lifetime.

Right about now, I can hear the "wow, that's some pretty raw shit there Mr. Tomassi" from the gallery, and I agree, but ask the guy on his second divorce how certain he was that he'd done his due diligence with his second wife based on all his past experience.

Bear this truth in mind, you do not buy into a good marriage or LTR, you create one, you build one. Your sweet little Good Girl who grew up in the Amish Dutch Country is just as hypergamous as the club slut you nailed last night. Different girls, different contexts, same hypergamy. You may have enough experience to know a woman who'd make a good foundation, but you ultimately build your own marriage/monogamy based on your own strengths or dissolve it based on inherent flaws – there are no pre-fab marriages.

THE HYPERGAMY CONSPIRACY

Rollo Tomassi:

"Hypergamy is a selected-for survival mechanism."

Aunt Sue:

"Hypergamy states that a woman seeks a man of higher status than herself for marriage. Nothing less, nothing more."

Escoffier:

"I don't think that's right.

The theory is more like this, from what I have read. Hypergamy is a woman's natural (which is to say, genetically wired) preference for a higher status male–that is, higher status than herself and also higher status than the other men in her field of vision and also perhaps higher status than men she has known in the past and even (at the extremes) higher status than most men she can personally imagine meeting. That cuts across a range of possible relationships, all the way from a one night stand to marriage. In all cases, women naturally prefer the highest status man they can get. And sometimes they want so much status that they won't settle on any man they could actually get.

*"Status" has a varied meaning in this definition. Certain things correlate with high status, for instance money, prestige, social standing, etc. However a man can have all of that and still be low status because of low status intra-personal behavior (i.e., needy schlumpitude). The highest possible status male would be rich, good looking, fit, well dressed, high social cache, high prestige job (preferably one which involves risk, physical risk being better than mere monetary risk), and also extroverted, dominant, the leader of his group of friends, able to command any social situation, and so on. However, women are wired to be turned on more by the latter **behavioral** traits than by be the former **substantive** traits. So, if you have to choose one or the other, to get women, be socially dominant and a broke societal loser rather than socially awkward and a rich societal winner. But best to be both, if possible.*

As to marriage, sure women want to marry up. But this does not exhaust the effects of hypergamy. Women can marry up–both intrinsically and in their own mind–and still ditch their catch because someone "better" comes along. That is hypergamy at work.

Also, when women are pursuing short and medium term mating, hypergamy has no less force. They always prefer the most socially dominant male they can get. This is often relative (A&B are both a little dweeby but A is more alpha than B and since I want someone NOW I choose A) but sometimes it is more intrinsic (A&B are both a little dweeby and even though A is a little more alpha, since I don't have to have someone NOW, I am going to hold out for the Real Deal).

It's not all about marriage. It's about mate selection across the range of circumstances.

That, at any rate, is how I believe the manosphere understands "hypergamy."

Escoffier makes an astute analysis of Hypergamy in a much broader perspective than Susan's feminine definition-approved "researchers" are willing to recognize. On the fem-centric side we have Sue casually dismiss "Hypergamy" in this context as some fabrication of the Game-set and therefor not a legitimate analysis. A rose is a rose, and as I've stated in prior threads, Hypergamy is a term that should have a much broader definition when considered in context with the feminine imperative and the eminently observable feminine behaviors that manifest as a result of Hypergamy's influence.

That the term Hypergamy should be so wantonly limited in its definition, and in such a way that it serves to deliberately confuse a better understanding of it as an evolutionary impulse on the feminine psyche, speaks volumes about the importance of maintaining its misunderstanding to the feminine imperative.

It's almost ironic that the collective feminine ego should even need to deign to recognize Hypergamy in the terms that it is cast as in Susan's default response. "Hypergamy states that a woman seeks a man of higher status than herself for marriage. Nothing less, nothing more." forces the feminine to at least begrudgingly accept that women are in fact basing their long-term commitment prospects on status (as defined by researchers), and not some ephemeral soul-mate, emotional precept. God forbid men (PhDs or otherwise) should have the temerity to extrapolate any further social, psychological or evolutionary implications that could've influenced that Hypergamy dynamic into existence.

While I wont argue the credentials of the researchers – I often acknowledge all of the same in other posts and comments – I will however make the point that the feminine interpretation (as is everyone's) is subject to bias. And in this case, that bias serves the feminine imperative in keeping the definition of Hypergamy in as closed a way as possible to benefit the feminine.

In the evolving understanding of the motivators that influence inter-gender relations there are going to be terms that describe concepts. AFC's, Alpha, Beta, Hypergamy, etc. are all defined by the concepts they represent.

'Hypergamy' serves well in a much broader capacity, but should the feminine imperative find that broader definition threatening to its purpose it will casually dismiss it as illegitimate. The real question then is, why would that concept be threatening to the feminine? You can delegitimize the term, but the concept is still the operative issue. Why is the concept of that larger scope of the term so offensive to a fem-centric society?

The Conspiracy that Wasn't

One issue many of my critics have is that in exposing these inconsistencies, these oper-ative social conventions and the latent purposes behind them, my writing (really most of the manosphere) seems to take on a conspiratorial tone.

I can fully appreciate this, and it might shock a few readers to know that I reject much of the popularized MRA (men's rights activists) perspective in this respect. I agree with an MRA perspective in a rational analysis to a certain degree, but there is no grand conspiracy, no secret mysterious cabal pushing a negative perception of masculinity – and this is exactly why what I outline on my blog is so pervasive.

There doesn't need to be a unitary group of 'anti-men' bent on some melodramatic goal of world domination; because this feminized ideal is already embedded in our socializa-tion. Fem-centrism *is* our collective social consciousness.

It doesn't need a centralized directorship because the mindset is already so installed and perpetuated by society at large it's now normalized, taken for granted and self-perpetu-ating. AFCs raising AFCs leads to still more AFCs. This generation doesn't realize their own bias because it's been standardized, encouraged and reinforced in them, and society, over the course of several generations now.

What's to question, especially when calling attention to the feminization dynamic leads to ridicule and ostracization?

So to answer the conspiracy question; no, there is no Illuminati shadow conspiracy and that's exactly what makes feminization the normalized and overlooked default.

WOMEN AND REGRET

The funny thing about regret is, it's better to regret something you have done,
than regret something you haven't done.

Paradox on the SoSuave forum had an interesting question after reading War Brides:

I've seen it mentioned here in passing but I would like to know how women handle regret.

How do they handle decisions that may affect their destiny?

Moments like:

Seeing someone on a train, bus, coffee shop, grocery store but not saying hello when the moment comes.

Meeting someone great at a party but not exchanging numbers.

Not calling back a guy

I have seen low IL (interest level) changed to high IL but do women generally waver in their interest level all of the time?

Any observational answer I could offer here is going to have to be adjusted to account for women's inherent solipsism – everything is about her, and everything confirms her assessments as the default. As such, you have to bear in mind that regret, for women, usually begins from a point of how a missed opportunity could've better benefited themselves.

The root of this is grounded in women's constant, in-born psychological quest for security. Hypergamy, by necessity, makes for solipsistic women in order to best preserve the survival integrity of the species. That's not to say women can't sublimate that impulse as necessity dictates, but just as men must sublimate their sexual imperative, women begin at a point of tempering the insecurity that results from hypergamy.

Guilt and Regret

Using hypergamy as a woman's point of origin, this affects how women process regret. At this point I should note that guilt and regret are not cut from the same vine. You can feel guilty about something you did or didn't do, as well as feel regret for something you did or didn't do, but the two are not synonymous. I want to avoid that confusion here from the outset, because guilt is associated with a lingering negativity, while regret comes from different motivations. If you did something you feel guilty about, you probably regret it, but you can regret something you have no feelings of guilt about.

After you finish reading this bit check out the 'Missed Connections' section on your areas Craig's List. Read the differences in tone, vernacular and purpose of both men and women lamenting a missed chance at something they hoped might develop. There's no guilt involved in this wishful thinking, only a regret for not having taken an action.

Women's Regret

Women's experience of regret depends upon the degree or intensity of the encounter in relation to their own conditions. I know that sounds like psycho-babble, but let me explain. If, and to what degree, a woman experiences regret in the situations Paradox is describing, these are directly proportional to her self-worth versus the (perceived) value of the encounter.

At the risk of coming off as shallow again, the fat chick who thinks she blew a shot at a Brad Pitt will regret it more than the HB 9 who happened to lose an "average" guy's phone number. I'm going to catch fire for this I'm sure, but it's really an autonomous response for human beings to make subconscious comparisons and employ a natural ego preservation. While its latent psychological function is to help us learn from experience, generally regret is painful, so our natural response is to defend against it. We tend to regret not capitalizing on situations where the perceived reward value is high. The psychological buffer of course comes in rationalizing the actual value potential of that missed opportunity or minimizing the negative impact of the taken opportunity.

So the debate is really how do women in particular process this reward valuation with regard to men? Again, I'll say it breaks down to subliminally recognizing their self-worth, modified by social affirmations and then comparing it with the value of the encounter.

Even semi-attractive women (HB 6-7) have a subconscious understanding that most inter-sexual encounters they have are mediated by their frequency – how rare was that opportunity? Meaning if a girl is constantly reinforced with male attention (guys asking her out all the time, social media influences, etc.) the rarity of any one encounter is compared against the frequency with which guys are hitting on her. This is female Plate Theory in action. If you happen to be one among many of the throngs of her suitors she's less likely to regret not following up with you in relation to the extraordinary (see Alpha) guy she perceives has a higher value than she's normally used to being rewarded with.

THE PET

One requirement I have of most of the men (and women) I do consults with is that they read *The 48 Laws of Power* (The Art of Seduction is in the class syllabus as well). In the introduction author Robert Greene runs down the ethical implications of understanding and employing the various laws. If you look at the synopsis of the laws you can get an idea of how uncomfortable some of these laws will naturally make people feel. Many of these laws understandably rub the uneducated the wrong way because for the better part of our lives we've been taught to emulate socially acceptable mannerisms and adopt a mindset of cooperation above self interest.

Most people are conditioned to think that deliberate use of power is inherently manipulative, self-serving and sometimes evil. In context this may or may not be true, but in so demonizing even the desire to understand power, not only do we inhibit a better critical understanding of power, but we also make the uneducated more vulnerable to the use of power against them. The 49th Law being: Never educate others of the principles of power, which is itself a form of using power. Never talk about Fight Club.

I bring this up because, just as with the Laws of Power, there will be articles of Game, or foundations of inter-gender communication – complete with all of the underlying motivators – that Men (and women) will be uncomfortable accepting or employing to the point that it challenges some deep rooted emotional or ego investments. Let me be the first to establish that discomfort is part of understanding; truth is supposed to make you uncomfortable in order to inspire you to action.

I should also add here that even though you may not be comfortable in exercising a particular tactic or don't feel confident in approaching an interpersonal situation in some way, it is still vital that you do understand the concepts and methodologies behind why those laws, principles, techniques, attitudes, etc. do work. You may have personal reasons for not wanting to involve yourself in some particular aspect of Game, but it's imperative that you fully acknowledge the mechanics behind that aspect before you decide it's not something you can employ. Declining to use a particular Law or aspect of Game doesn't make you immune to the consequences of it, nor does it invalidate that aspect when others use it for their own benefit, and potentially to your own detriment.

Half the Battle

The primary (though not exclusive) focus of my blog has been devoted to the critical analysis of the mechanics behind inter-gender dynamics, Game-practice, Game-theory, social and evolutionary psychology just to name a few. I can understand the want for practical applications of this field of study, and while in my line of work I have done my own 'field testing' with the majority of what I explore here, I have neither the time, opportunity or resources to develop practices beyond what I offer here. At least not to the degree of which the majority of my readers are able – and that's the good news.

"This is brilliant stuff Rollo, but how do I use this to make my life better with the next girl I sarge, etc.?"

This is a common desire from my readership, and the best I can offer is Knowing is Half the Battle. One size doesn't fit all for everyone in Game or inter-gender relations. Anyone hawking a book giving you an instruction manual on how to have a great marriage or how to pick up chicks is still limited by their own individual experience. In other words, they're not you.

It's for exactly this reason I spend more time and critical thought on the foundations and functions of gender dynamism than pick up artistry. When I get associated with the "manipulative Machiavellian Game gurus" it only serves to highlight an ignorance and lack of any depth of understanding what I focus on here. Game is psychology, sociology, economics, biomechanics, evolution and politics. Game is far broader than simple tricks and techniques. And it's exactly the latent purpose of these applications (PUArtistry) and the mechanics behind their workings that threatens the ego investments of those who's feminized interests would rather see them marginalized and passed off as folly, or usefully ridiculed to shame the curious for fear that the underpinnings might be exposed.

Head in the Sand

Sweetening the poison doesn't make it any less deadly.

I can remember a time in my mid-20s working as a stage tech for a casino cabaret show. The magic act I set up and struck every night involved a Bengal tiger and a black panther. Both of them were professionally handled by trainers, but even though they seemed the most docile of animals I knew they had the potential to seriously fuck me up under the wrong set of circumstances.

The trainers would keep them at distance from the rest of the cast and crew, only myself and one other tech were able to get close since we were the ones wheeling them out in special cages at their particular point in the show. One trainer told me, "the moment you think of them as pets is the moment they'll go feral on you." They would play with these wild animals, and they seemed to have a special connection (almost like a pet), but when you watched them eat, you knew what they were capable of.

I learned a valuable lesson from this when one night I was wheeling the panther out to the curtain. She was in what was basically a reinforced acrylic aquarium on casters with a velvet cloth draped over it. A few minutes before my cue I'd thought the drape was falling to one side and lifted it to even it out. It was then that I was face to face with this "pet" in nothing but faint stage lights and about 4 inches of transparent acrylic between us. She looked at me with those yellow-green eyes and gave me a very low, almost muted growl and flashed just enough of her teeth to let me know this was not a "pet".

It's a mistake (and sometimes a fatal one) to ignore what you know is just under the surface. It's comforting to believe that you've got a special connection, and while the conditions are right, you'll preserve a relationship based on mutual trust and shared affinity. The flaw is in believing that trust, and kinship is unconditional; that the underlying feral motivators are subdued to the point of being inconsequential. It may be that you do have a special bond that goes beyond just the physical, but that relationship is still founded on physical rules that constantly test and influence that individual.

You know better, but the desire for that connection is so strong that you marginalize the natural impulses into feel-good rationalizations. Every divorced man I know has uttered some variation of "I never thought she was capable of this." In their comfort they wondered how they dropped the ball, especially after having played by the rules for so long. Some knew about Hypergamy, others made it their "pet", only their beautiful panther went feral.

Play My Game

It is a far healthier approach to accept the laws of power, the laws of Game, red pill awareness, Hypergamy, etc. and fashion a life around an understanding of them than to convince oneself that they are an exception to them.

There are those who seek power by changing the game – by lowering the basketball hoops in order to better shoot a basket – but in 'leveling the playing field' they only succeed in changing the nature of the competition to better suit their individual abilities, neither improving the game nor themselves. The temporary change of rules only serves *their* inadequacies in that game.

Then there are those who accept the game for what it is, they understand it and they master it (or at least attempt to do so). They understand the need for adversity and the benefits it gives them when they reach the next level of mastering the game – not only in technique, but from the confidence this genuinely and verifiably confers.

Don't wish things were easier, wish you were better.

It's the aberration who seeks to legitimize her cheating at the game as the new way the game should be played. Shoot the arrow, paint the target around it, and you'll always get a bullseye.

CHAPTER 8

THE IRON RULES
OF TOMASSI

IRON RULE I

Iron Rule of Tomassi #1

Frame is everything.
Always be aware of the subconscious balance of who's
frame in which you are operating.
Always control the Frame, but resist giving the impression that you are.

The concept of "frame" is yet another ephemeral idea that had need of a term in the very beginnings of the great masculine awakening that's become the 'community'. If memory serves I think it may have been PUA Godfather *Mystery* who first picked up on what's really a very rudimentary and well established psychological principle.

In psychological terms, frame is an often subconscious, mutually acknowledged personal narrative under which auspices people will be influenced. One's capacity for personal decisions, choices for well-being, emotional investments, religious beliefs and political persuasions (amongst many others) are all influenced and biased by the psychological narrative 'framework' under which we are most apt to accept as normalcy.

The concept of frame covers a lot of aspects of our daily lives, some of which we're painfully aware of, others we are not, but nonetheless we are passively influenced by frame. What concerns us in terms of inter-gender relations however is the way in which frame sets the environment, the ambiance, and the 'reality' in which we relate with both the woman we sarge at a bar and the relationship with the woman we've lived with for 20 years.

One important fact to consider, before I launch into too much detail, is to understand that frame is *not* power. The act of controlling the frame may be an exercise in power for some, but let me be clear from the start that the concept of frame is who's 'reality' in which you choose to operate in relation to a woman. Both gender's internalized concept of frame is influenced by our individual acculturation, socialization, psychological conditioning, upbringing, education, etc., but be clear on this, you are either operating in your own frame or you're operating in hers. Also understand that the balance of frame often shifts. Frame is fluid and will find its own level when a deficit or a surplus of will is applied to change it. The forces that influence that lack or boost of will is irrelevant – just know that the conditions of an operative framework will shift because of them.

Pre-LTR Frame

Often I'll see forum posts or blog comments lamenting some loss of frame – *"Lost the frame, how do I get it back?"*

A lot of times guys believe that because a woman initially gave them indicators of interest (IOIs) or was 'really into them' in the beginning that they had 'frame'. This is another unfortunate misconception about frame – and I partly blame the PUA culture for it – but frame is not interest level (IL). Simply because a woman is attracted to you does not mean she's ready to 'enter your reality'. Her entering your frame may become a by-product of that attraction, but it by no means guarantees it. In truth, under today's social environment, I would expect a woman to resist tooth and nail from rushing into a man's frame. This is why women have psychologically evolved a subconscious propensity to shit test; to verify the legitimacy of a man's frame.

Most Game incongruities develop around a guy's inability to establish frame and opting in to a woman's frame. What's ironic is that on a base level, we understand frame imbalances instinctively. If you feel like you're being led on, or being made to wait for sex, you're operating in her frame. Are you in the 'friend-zone' or did you accept an LJBF rejection? You're in her frame.

Ideally, you want a woman to enter your reality. Her genuine (unnegotiated) desire for you hinges upon you covertly establishing this narrative for her. Famous men, men with conspicuous affluence and status, and men with overwhelming social proof have very little difficulty in establishing frame – they can't help but establish frame in a very overt fashion. A woman already wants to enter that world. She wants an easy association with a man who's unquestionably a proven commodity and offers her hypergamy not just a actualized fantasy, but also a high degree of personal affirmation in being the one a Man of this caliber would choose above other women.

Unfortunately, you and I are not this Man, he's a feminine idealization.

However it's important to understand how hypergamy plays into establishing frame. The Man who impassively accepts women's hypergamous natures has a much easier time establishing frame from the outset. You or I may not be that be that famous guy with an automatic, overt frame control, but we can be by order of degrees depending upon our personal conditions and the conditions of the women with whom we choose to associate.

The default pedestalization of women that men are prone to is a direct result of accepting that a woman's frame is the only frame. It's kind of hard for most 'plugged in' men to grasp that they can and should exert frame control in order to establish a healthy future relationship. This is hardly a surprise considering that every facet of their social under-standing about gender frame has always defaulted to the feminine for the better part of their lifetimes. Whether that was conditioned into them by popular media or seeing it played out by their Beta fathers, for most men in western culture, the feminine reality *is* the normalized frame work.

In order to establish a healthy male-frame, the first step is to rid themselves of the preconception that women control frame by default. They don't, and honestly, they don't want to.

Post LTR Frame

In most contemporary marriages and LTR arrangements, women tend to be the de facto authority. Men seek their wives' "permission" to attempt even the most mundane activities they'd do without an afterthought while single. I have married friends tell me how 'fortunate' they are to be married to such an understanding wife that she'd "allow" him to watch hockey on their guest bedroom TV,…occasionally.

These are just a couple of gratuitous examples of men who entered into marriage with the frame firmly in the control of their wives. They live in her reality, because anything can become normal. What these men failed to realize is that frame, like power, abhors a vacuum. In the absence of the frame security a woman naturally seeks from a masculine male, this security need forces her to provide that security for herself. Thus we have the commonality of cuckold and submissive men in westernized culture, while women do the bills, earn the money, make the decisions, authorize their husband's actions and deliver punishments and rewards. The woman is seeking the security that the man she pair-bonded with cannot or will not provide.

It is vital to the health of any LTR that a man establish his frame as the basis of their living together before any formal commitment is recognized. As I stated in the beginning, frame will be fluid and conditions will influence the balance, but the overall theme of your relationship needs to be led and molded by you.

Even very influential, professional, intellectualizing women still crave the right man to establish his frame in her life. They may fight it bitterly, but ultimately it's what will make for the best healthy balance she can achieve. There's a growing undercurrent of mid-life women questioning and regretting their past decisions to remain single into spinsterhood. And for all their late game rationalizations, the one thing they still simply refuse to accept is acknowledging that a man's frame, the frame their "fierce independence" wouldn't allow for, was exactly the salve their egos so desperately want now later in life.

Gentlemen, you will establish frame in any monogamous relationship you have.

You will enter her reality or she will enter yours.

IRON RULE II

Iron Rule of Tomassi # 2

Never, under pain of death, honestly or dishonestly reveal the number of women you've slept with or explain any detail of your sexual experiences with them to a current lover.

You've been with how many girls?!!

Rational reader Poker ran this one by me recently:

I've been seeing this girl and we've slept together a few times... Today, in bed, I got asked, "How may girls have I been with?" and "Why won't I be her friend on Face-book?"

How many girls question...

Here's how I handled it – would love to know if you think this was handled properly... (using cocky-funny attitude)

Me: "I don't tell that."
Her: "More or less than 20?"
Me: "I have some freedom of information forms in the car – you could fill one out and get your answer in 20 years."
Her: "Don't you want to know how many guys I've been with?"
Me: "No."

The single most disastrous AFC move a man can make is to *overtly* describe past sexual experiences and/or give a number (accurate or not) to how many women he's been with prior to the one he's with.

This simple act, whether you offered the information or she dragged it out of you, **always** comes off as pretentiousness and is often the catalyst for an avalanche of emotional resentment, if not outright emotional blackmail from an insecure woman. This is a rookie mistake that will only take you once to learn.

If a woman puts you on the spot by directly asking you for this information always sidestep this COVERTLY. C&F works wonders in this situation and still keeps the air of mystery and challenge about you.

Her: "So how many girls have you been with?"

You: "You're my first actually"

Her: "Really, how many girls have you been with?"

You:" You mean tonight?"

Her: "C'mon, how many girls have you been with?"

You: "You know, I really lost count after 50″ (or something outrageous).

When a woman asks you this question she is seeking confirmation of what she already suspects – **Never** give her this satisfaction. Remember, when a woman resorts to *overt* communication (covert being her native language) she's generally exhausted her patience to be *covert* and this is a desperation tactic for an insecure woman.

While this scenario may be fraught with potential disaster, it is also an opportunity to encourage her imagination and prompt some competition anxiety.

Her: "How many girls have you been with?"
You: "I have an idea, lets fuck and then you can tell me how many girls you think I've been with, OK?"

A lot of Game rookies think that since they've only been with 1 or 2 women in their lives what's the harm in open, honest, full disclosure? Like most Betas they bought the "open communication is the secret to a good relationship" meme long ago, so the impulse to be upfront is their default response.

They tend not to see the utility in keeping that information, or being ambiguous about it, plants a seed of competition anxiety and stokes her imagination. When she *knows* she's your first, you've just abdicated the frame to her in any kind of relationship.

Second, if she's your 9th then every girl up to 8 becomes a stamp in her collection to use against you in the first fight you have. Every date you take her on she wonders "Did he take #6 here too?" It's as if you cheated on her with every previous girl up to her.

I should also add that this is the first question a BPD (borderline personality disorder) woman will ask you so she can feel horrible about herself for not measuring up to "your standards" and drag you into the emotional hell-pit with her.

IRON RULE III

Iron Rule of Tomassi #3

Any woman who makes you wait for sex, or by her actions implies she is making you wait for sex; the sex is NEVER worth the wait.

When a woman intentionally makes you wait for sex you are not her highest priority.

Sexuality is spontaneous chemical reaction between two parties, not a process of negotiation. It's sex first, then relationship, not the other way around. A woman who wants to fuck you will find a way to fuck you. She will fly across the country, crawl under barbwire, climb in through your second story bedroom window, fuck the shit out of you and wait patiently inside your closet if your wife comes home early from work – women who want to fuck will find a way to fuck. The girl who tells you she needs to be comfortable and wants a relationship first is the *same* girl who fucked the hot guy in the foam cannon party in Cancun on spring break just half an hour after meeting him.

If a girl is that into you she'll want to have sex with you regardless of ASD (anti-slut defense) or having her friends in the room videotaping it at a frat party. All women can be sluts, you just have to be the right guy to bring it out in them, and this happens before you go back to her place. If you have to plead your case cuddling and spooning on the bed or getting the occasional peck on the cheek at the end of the night, you need to go back to square one and start fresh.

I'm probably going to ruffle a few PUA feathers here, but I've never been a proponent of breaking down LMR (last minute resistance) with a woman. Maybe it's a result of experiences in my rock star 20's, but at some point I came to the conclusion that sex with a woman who's organically turned on by me is always a far better experience than one where I had to sell her on the idea of sex with me before the act.

Now don't take this to the binary extreme and assume I mean the only good sex you'll ever have is a first night lay (FNL) with some tart who can't keep her legs closed. What I mean is that if you're still trying to figure out what the magic words are to convince some girl that she ought fuck you after 3 dates – or longer – you're in desire negotiation hearings counselor. You are wasting your time and limiting your opportunity with better prospective women in waiting out a woman who would defer less than 100% of her real desire to have sex with you. The sex will *never* be worth the wait.

A prostitute would be a better alternative.

Genuine desire cannot be negotiated.

Once you get past a certain point in the waiting game, what once had the chance to be an organic, sexual desire becomes mitigated negotiation of a physical act. Just the fact that you're having to make a case for yourself (even covertly) is evidence that there are other factors inhibiting her capacity to be sexual with you.

As I stated, barring a physical inability, this is almost always because of an unmentioned agenda on her part. It may be due to a concurrent boyfriend, it may be a natural internal caution, it may be that your process is telegraphing 'beta' to her, or it may be that she's filibustering you while waiting to see if another, more preferable guy pans out for her, however, none of these are insurmountable if she has a genuine desire to bang you. Many a cheated on boyfriend knows this is true.

In any circumstance, sex with you is not an urgency for her. If she's perceiving your value as high as it should be, she wont hesitate longer than a few dates to become sexual – and she certainly wont tell you she's making you wait. Hypergamy doesn't afford a woman much waiting time with a Man she sees as superior stock.

One of the more frustrating situations I often encounter comes from guys who've been *overtly* told that they're being made to wait for sex until some circumstance or criteria is met for the woman. The standard filibuster (or loss-leader as the case may be) usually comes with the reasoning that she "needs to feel comfortable" before she has sex with a guy. Even more distressing is the guy who was getting laid, only to be told the same thing by an existing girlfriend. If you find yourself in either of these situation there are a couple of things to bear in mind.

First and foremost, sex, by it's nature is uncomfortable. Sex that is motivated by mutual, genuine desire is a tense affair, fueled by testosterone, anxiety and urgency. When two people get together for a first dance (a precursor to copulation), it's rarely if ever an intimate slow dance. It's salsa, it's grinding, it's pumping, it's heat and it's sweat. What it's not is comforting and familiar. It's not a nice warm bathrobe fresh out of the dryer.

Don't take this the wrong way, but sex is threatening. It needs to be, and you need to be considered a sexualized player in her personal sphere. Overtly agreeing to wait for her to become sexual is anti-seductive. It confirms for her that you aren't a sexualized player to her; an Alpha wouldn't wait for sex and she knows this. Worse still, it devalues her SMV as being worth less than of your utmost urgency.

Secondly, always remember why women resort to overt communications (the language of men) – so there is no, or less, margin that her message will be misunderstood. If a woman, point blank says, "I'm not having sex with you until X,Y, and Z happens", what is her **medium** telling you? That there is a precondition that's more important to her than fucking you with genuine, uncontrollable passion.

You want her to be so into you that she's willing to break the rules. The ideal situation is for her genuine passion to be so uncontrollable for you that she'd renounce her religion and throw her convictions to the wind to be with you. That might seem a bit dramatic, but you get the idea. The good news now is that she's being overt, which means she's exhausted her reserves to be covert and, assuming you're not so desperate as to delude yourself, you can NEXT her and move on.

Rapport ≠ Comfort

A lot of "waiters" find all that a tough road to hoe. They want to stick it out and see if things "might develop", and NEXTing their 'waiting girl' seems a lot like throwing the baby out with the bath water after all the time they've invested in building what they think is rapport. Usually this is due to the guy not spinning (enough) other plates that would bear more fruit. However, keep this in mind; *waiting* for sex isn't building rapport.

There's a lot of confusion about rapport, most of which is due to well meaning PUAs conflating rapport with comfort. It's a pretty esoteric term, but rapport is a connection; it's an implied trust between two acting agents who previously had never met or only have limited knowledge of each other. You can have rapport with an animal – that's the connection, it's instinctual.

Comfort comes from familiarity and predictability; all decidedly anti-seductive influences. And while comfort has it's own merits in interpersonal relationships, it is not the basis for genuine, passionate sexual desire. For people (myself included) involved in a marriage or LTR, it's serves our long-term best interest to convince ourselves that sex is better when your comfortable with your partner, however, the reality of it sings a different tune.

Here's an easy illustration: As reported by both men and women alike, which of these circumstances provokes the most intense, memorable sexual experiences ? When a couple plans and arranges a romantic "date night" to 'keep it fresh' and reconnect? Or is it the 'make-up sex' after a horrible breakup, or narrowly averted breakup, where long dormant competition anxiety is brought back into being a very real possibility again? If you said the breakup, you're correct! One scenario is comfortable, the other uncomfortable. One has the element of predictable certainty, the other is chaotic and uncertain, however in both situations there is definitely a working mutually connective rapport operating.

Three Strikes

The problem inherent with coming up with hard and fast Game rules of engagement is that there's always going to be a caveat or special conditions for a guy's particular girl of focus at the time. Even when there's not, guys are prone to think "there's something special about this one." Part of the reason that Plate Theory is integral to Game is that it encourages Men to disabuse themselves of their previous Beta impressions of each woman they accidentally drew interest from as some unique little snowflake. It's hard for your average chump to think of a woman showing base-line rudimentary IOIs (indicators of interest) and NOT think she's predestined for him by virtue of his self-acknowledged scarcity mentality. When you're starving in the desert, Saltine crackers seem like mana from heaven.

Risk & Reward

In Game, there is a subtle balance that needs to be recognized between risks of over-investing in a particular woman with regards to practicality and not throwing the proverbial baby out with the bath water and losing on a potentially rewarding opportunity. Women, as is particular to their own Game, will naturally come down on the side of casting doubt on a man's valid assessment of a woman's potential value, both in long term perspectives and potential sexual satisfaction. This presumption of doubt is a built in failsafe social convention for women; "if only you'd been more patient, if only you invested a little bit more, you'd be rewarded with a great mother for your children and the best pussy of your life – don't blow it now!"

The short version is that it's not in women's best sexual-strategy interests for a man to have sexual options. Women's sexual strategy is very schizophrenic – ideally women want a Man that other women want to fuck, but in order to assess his sexual market value to other women he's got to have exercisable options for her to compete against, or at least display indirect social proof to that effect. So, she needs to limit *his* options while simultaneously determining he *has* those options. Now add to this the hypergamous necessity of maintaining a reasonable pool of potential suitors suspended in doubt of her own SMV in order to determine the best one among them for short term sexual provisioning and long term security provisioning.

Pragmatism

In light of understanding women's sexual strategy, it's important for Men to adopt a mental schema of pragmatism – in the SMP you're really another commodity in hypergamy's estimation. I realize the difficulty most guys (particularly younger guys) have with mentally training themselves for thinking this way, so let me state that I'm not suggesting you kill your romantic, artistic souls in favor of cold calculations. In fact it's vital you do keep that side of yourself intact for the survival of any future relationship and a more balanced human experience. Plate Theory and, really, efficient Game can seem dehumanizing, but what Game denialists fail to grasp is that they're already operating in a dehumanized environment – it's the social conditioning of the feminine imperative that makes men believe that Game is inhumane, because the feminine imperative has made itself synonymous with humanity.

Hypergamy doesn't care if you're a great, poetic soul. Hypergamy doesn't care about your most sincere religious devotions. Hypergamy doesn't care if you're a great Father to your kids. Hypergamy seeks its own level, it wants the best commodity it's capable of attracting and maintaining. Hypergamy is above all, practical, and thus Men, the True Romantics must be pragmatists to enact their own sexual strategy.

I had a lot of shit slung at me when I initially offered up the third Iron Rule. I had the predictable feminine doubt doctrine lobbed at me in response from the beginning. I expected that, but to answer the question more definitively, be pragmatic.

Put it this way, with just average Game, in 3 dates you should be able to determine if her desire level is high enough to want to fuck you.

In 3 dates you'll know if her desire is genuine or if it's mitigated by something else – another guy in rotation, sexual hangups, filibustering, she's in the down phase of her menstrual cycle, etc.

In 3 dates you'll have had sex or you'll have had the "I wanna wait / I need to be comfortable talk."

If you have sex on the 1st date or a same-night-lay, in all likelihood she's really hot for, and into, fucking you based on physical criteria alone.

If you have sex on the 2nd or 3rd date, she's into fucking you and probably wants a relationship, but she wanted to give you a token impression of her not being 'easy'.

If she fucks you after the 4th date, you'll do as her first alternate.

If you're sexless after 5-6 dates you've probably been at it for over 6 weeks and The Medium is the Message. NEXT.

Disclaimers

This rule has proven to be the single most contentious thing I've ever published on The Rational Male. Only my essays on the nature of Alpha has stirred up more controversy. For motivated, hypergamous reasons, my arguing for genuine sexual interest as an indicator of desire on a woman's part never sits well with women. Furthermore, even many red pill men have argued that a woman's immediate sexual interest is the sign of a slut.

My counter to these arguments is generally based in women's observable, organic behaviors. While it may be ennobling to consider that a woman might want to be cautious with whom she has sex, women's biology and hypergamous nature puts that assertion to the test. Similarly it seems prudent for a monogamy minded guy to be discerning about the character of a woman who was an "easy lay" – and likewise he'll make a liar of himself if that natural opportunity arises.

That's going to be a consistent paradox with this rule, but it doesn't make it any less tenable. Even for the more religious minded men, who's convictions compel them to chastity, the rule still provides them with a benchmark for genuine desire. As I outlined in Plate Theory, you don't have to be banging every girl on your roster, but those women should *want* to be banging you. If this is your position, ideally, rule 3 should be modified to filter for genuine, not mitigated, not negotiated desire.

IRON RULE IV

Iron Rule of Tomassi #4

*Never under any circumstance live with a woman you aren't married to
or are not planning to marry in within 6 months.*

You are utterly powerless in this situation. Never buy a home with a girlfriend, never sign a rental lease with a girlfriend. Never agree to move into her home and absolutely never move a woman into your own established living arrangement.

I'm adamantly opposed to the "shacking up" dynamic, it is a trap that far too many men allow themselves to fall into. My fervor against this isn't based on some moral issue, it is, again, simple pragmatism. If you live with a woman you may as well be married because upon doing so every liability and accountability of marriage is then in effect. You not only lose any freedom of anonymity, you commit to, legally, being responsible for the continuation of your living arrangements regardless of how your relationship decays.

I should also emphasize the point that when you commit (and it is a financial commitment) to cohabiting with a girlfriend you will notice a marked decrease in her sexual availability and desire. The single most common complaint related to me in regards to how to reignite a woman's desire comes as the result of the guy having moved into a living arrangement with his LTR. All of that competitive anxiety and it's resulting sexual tension that made your single sex life so great is removed from her shoulders and she can comfortably relax in the knowledge that she is your **only** source of sexual intimacy. Putting your name on that lease with her (even if it's just your name) is akin to signing an insurance policy for her:

"I the undersigned promise not to fuck any woman but this girl for a one year term."

She thinks, "if he wasn't serious about me, he wouldn't have signed the lease." Now all of that impetus and energy that made having marathon sex with you an outright necessity is relaxed. She controls the frame and she's got it in writing that it is for at least a year.

Just don't do it. Relationships last best when you spin more plates or at the very least keep each other at arm's distance.

There was a time when the hip, counter-culture thing to do was flip the establishment the bird and cohabit with a girlfriend, sans the marriage contract. In the swinging post-sexual-revolution 70's, feminism was more than happy to encourage the idea until it ran into the problem of making men financially accountable for all the "free milk" the cows were giving away. However, that not withstanding, there's still a kind of a lingering after effect feeling about "living together" that seems like a good idea to guys to this day.

Of all the reasonable excuses I've heard for men wanting to cohabit with their girlfriends, the most common is that they did so for financial reasons. He (or she) needed a roommate and why not one that they enjoy fucking?

That's the cover story, but underneath it there's the semiconscious understanding that it would be far more convenient to have a continuous flow of pussy as part of the utilities, uninterrupted by the formalities of having to go on dates or drive somewhere to get it. I can't say that, on the surface, this doesn't make perfect sense. Leave it a man to find the most deductive solution to his problem. However, as with most things woman, what seems like the most deductive solution is often a cleverly disguised trap.

Shacking up, just as in marriage, affords a woman a reasonable sense of comfort. It becomes at least a marginal shelter from the competition anxiety that she had to endure while living on her own and dating a guy who still had at least the perceived option to be unpredictable. Not so in the quasi-marriage that living together dictates. And it's just this sense of predictability that allows her to relax into familiarity, and later, into dictating the terms of her own intimacy. In other words, she's in the perfect position to ration her sexuality; to negotiate the terms of her desire in exchange for a living arrangement.

By the same reasoning, most AFCs view cohabiting as an ideal arrangement. Few of them really have the real options, much less the will to experiment exercising them, to see shacking up as anything but a great way of exiting the SMP, limiting potential rejection, and locking down a consistent supply of pussy.

Men who are spinning plates, men with options, men with ambition, rarely see cohabiting as anything but a limiting hindrance on their lives. On some level of consciousness women understand this dynamic; guys with options (the Alphas they'd prefer) wouldn't consider cohabitation. So when a man agrees to, or suggests living together it impresses her with two things – either he's an Alpha who she's won over so completely that he's ready to commit to exclusivity with her, or he's a Beta with no better propositions than to settle into living with what he believes is his 'sure thing'.

What's jarring for a woman is that she may start her living arrangement thinking she's found the elusive Alpha ready to commit, only to later find he was just a clever Beta who reverts back into his former, comfortable, AFC self after they sign the lease agreement.

Now all that said, what makes more sense? To live independently and enjoy the options to live unhindered with a live-in girlfriend, or move her in and have to deal with her every waking moment? Moving in with a woman implies commitment, and whenever you commit to anything you lose your two most valuable resources, options and the ability to maneuver.

IRON RULE V

Iron Rule of Tomassi #5
Never allow a woman to be in control of the birth.

It's called birth control because someone is 'controlling' the birth.

There are presently 41 different types of contraception available for women, for men there are only 2 – vasectomy or a condom – your only line of defense against her 'choice', the only thing separating a man from a lifetime (not just 18 years) of interacting with the decider of altering the course of his life is a thin layer of latex.

Always have protection. I've had far too many guys hit me with the argument that they implicitly trust their girlfriends to be on the pill or whatever, and that she "doesn't want kids" only to be an unprepared Daddy nine month later after 'the accident'. The only accident they had was not being in control of the birth themselves. In fact I'd argue that men need to use *extra* caution when in an LTR since the ease of getting too relaxed with her is present.

Accidental pregnancy is practically a cottage industry now. For a woman without education (or even with) and without means, an 'unplanned' pregnancy may be a pretty good prospect, especially when every law and social expectation weighs in her favor. These are *Professional Mommies*. When I counseled in Reno I knew a guy who married this woman who had 3 children from 2 Fathers who he himself had impregnated with her 4th. She was a Professional Mother.

Flush it

In 2002 the NBA issued a highly controversial and publicized warning to professional basketball players stating that players be advised to wear condoms when having sexual intercourse with women when on road games and to "flush the condom down the toilet" in order to dispose of the semen. This warning was the result of several paternity suits that year involving women these players had slept with by retrieving the condoms from the trash and 'self-impregnating' with the players semen. The NBA had enough occurrences of this kind to warrant a league-wide warning that year. All of these players are now 100% liable for the welfare of these children and their former partners by default because there are no laws protecting men from fraudulent pregnancies.

To what degree is protection implicitly implied? If a man does everything in his power to avoid a pregnancy (barring abstinence or a vasectomy) and can prove his intent and the woman still becomes pregnant, even by fraud, the man is still liable for that pregnancy.

Women are 100% protected and men are 0% protected. I can even go so far as to quote you cases where a man marrying a single mother later divorces her and is still expected to pay future child support for a child he did not father – even without official adoption of the child by the man.

A lot of guys would like to make a moral issue of this but it's not a question of right or wrong, it's dealing with the facts of what *is* in the environment we find ourselves in today. The fact of the matter is that unless men use prior discretion and take responsibility for the birth 'control', not allowing a woman to be solely responsible for it, he is 100% powerless. This means bring your own condoms and flush them yourself, and yes even (especially) in an LTR or marriage. That means standing firm even when she says "take that thing off I'm on the pill and I want to 'feeeeel' you."

Mothers want to be Mothers, otherwise they'd decide not to be. Single Mommies are far too common an occurrence to bet the odds with the rest of your life.

The sexual revolution had far more to do with the development of hormonal means of birth control than the legalization of abortion. Condoms have been around since before World War II, but even in the Baby Boom there were far less unwanted pregnancies or single motherhood than after the advent of the pill. The pill put the control of birth into the hands of women where before it was a man's responsibility to put the rubber on and do so correctly if both wanted to avoid smaller versions of themselves running around the house.

The Choice of Professionals

Abortion rates skyrocketed in the decades after estrogen based birth control was developed, thus prompting a need for legal and clinical regulations of abortions as well as reforming paternity laws in the 70s. There had certainly been abortions (both the medical and back-alley variety) prior to this, but if you look at the increase in abortion statistics both before and after the advent of a convenient form of birth control moderated by the women taking it, it'll blow your mind.

And now even with the vast variety of birth control methods available to women today and 30+ years of safe medical abortions, we still see an increase in single mother families and abortion rates. One would think that these statistics would be lower in light of all this modernization and the 'leaps' women have made culturally since the sexual revolution, but sadly no.

In fact the single mother birth rate has climbed (adjusted for population) since a leveling off in the late 80s and abortion is just as popular as ever even when new methods such as the 'morning after pill' and RU286 are readily available. And conveniently, the social ills as a result are placed squarely on 'dead-beat Dads' rather than the women choosing to have the children.

This isn't a scientific problem, it's a cultural one. Mothers want to be Mothers. Men are only Fathers when a woman decides this for him even in the happiest of marriages. I think (hope) we'll see second sexual revolution once a male form of hormonal contraception is tested and available, but you can bet dicks to donuts that every interested party from the religious to the feminist will fight this method's release to the public at large and come up with every sort of veiled explanation for its demonization in order to put the agency of birth control exclusively into men's control. I sincerely doubt men will "forget to take it" or have their 'accidents' in the numbers women do.

Controlling the Birth

It's a much different task to put on a condom in the heat of the moment (reactive) than to simply swallow a pill in the morning (proactive). It's arguable what the more difficult task is, to remember to take a pill in the morning or to apply a condom at the appropriate time. In the latter situation there are at least two people aware that a condom should be on prior to intercourse; is a woman equally an accomplice in her own pregnancy if she consensually has sex with a guy without a condom? They both know the assumed risks, however a woman forgetting to take her pill isn't reviled as an 'idiot' or negligent as a man not putting on a condom.

Taking her birth control is up to her and rarely would a guy be certain on a daily basis that his partner was faithfully taking her pill. In fact to even ask about it would be presumptuous and bordering on rude if it's a casual encounter. When a man and a woman fail to take the precaution of putting on a condom they're both aware of it. When she fails to take her pill either accidentally or intentionally, she is the sole party responsible for that pregnancy, but in either case she decides the course of the man's life should this occur.

The obvious answer is to put men in control of the birth – wear a condom. However the nature of mens birth control is reactive and even in the case where a man has the condom in his pocket, he can still be thwarted by her only saying, "don't worry about it, I'm on the pill"; the control shifts, but the accountability never does.

Forgive me for belaboring the point, but there are no accidental mothers. Consider fertility statistics and that it takes a considerable amount of negligence for a woman to miss several pills on a regular basis to 'accidentally' become pregnant. One could also argue that even a couple engaging in condom-less sex could still be relatively confident that a woman wont get pregnant even if she's missed several pills regularly. Again my point being that it takes effort to become pregnant. Even without any birth control at all and timing my wife's ovulation cycles for our sex it took us 4 months to conceive our daughter.

This is why I laugh at the accidental pregnancy excuse so common these days. If a woman wants to become pregnant she can do so with impunity and contrive any excuse she'd like about accidents, but the guy is an 'idiot' for not wearing a condom and taking responsibility for his actions, even if he's led to believe she's taking control of her contraception. Yet he is the one penalized both financially and socially because of her choice.

IRON RULE VI

Iron Rule of Tomassi #6

Women are fundamentally incapable of loving a man in the way that a man expects to be loved by a woman.

Men believe that love matters for the sake of it. Women love opportunistically.

This pull quote comes from Xpat Rantings blog. The discourse there is brief, but insightful:

"I really, really, really hope the myth that girls are the hopeless romantics gets kicked to the curb ASAP. Everyone needs to realize that men are the "romantics pretending to be realists" and women; vice versa."

I found this particularly thought provoking – Men are the romantics forced to be the realists, while women are the realists using romanticisms to effect their imperatives (hypergamy). This is a heaping mouthful of cruel reality to swallow, and dovetails nicely into the sixth Iron Rule of Tomassi:

Iron Rule of Tomassi #6
Women are utterly incapable of loving a man in the way that a man expects to be loved.

In its simplicity this speaks volumes about the condition of Men. It accurately expresses a pervasive nihilism that Men must either confront and accept, or be driven insane in denial for the rest of their lives when they fail to come to terms with the disillusionment.

Women are incapable of loving men in a way that a man idealizes is possible, in a way he thinks she should be capable of.

In the same respect that women cannot appreciate the sacrifices men are expected to make in order to facilitate their imperatives, women can't actualize how a man would have himself loved by her. It is not the natural state of women, and the moment he attempts to explain his ideal love, that's the point at which his idealization becomes her obligation.

Our girlfriends, our wives, daughters and even our mothers are all incapable of this idealized love. As nice as it would be to relax, trust and be vulnerable, upfront, rational and open, the great abyss is still the lack of any capacity for women to love Men as Men would like them to.

For the plugged-in beta, this aspect of 'awakening' is very difficult to confront. Even in the face of constant, often traumatic, controversion to what a man hopes will be his reward for living up to qualifying for a woman's love and intimacy, he'll still hold onto that Disneyesque ideal.

It's very important to understand that this love archetype is an artifact from our earliest feminized conditioning. It's much healthier to accept that it isn't possible and live within that framework. If she's there, she's there, if not, oh well. She's not incapable of love in the way she defines it, she's incapable of love as you would have it. She doesn't lack the capacity for connection and emotional investment, she lacks the capacity for the connection you think would ideally suit you.

The resulting love that defines a long-term couple's relationship is the result of coming to an understanding of this impossibility and re-imagining what it should be for Men. Men have been, and should be, the more dominant gender, not because of some imagined divine right or physical prowess, but because on some rudimentary psychological level we ought to realized that a woman's love is contingent upon our capacity to maintain that love in spite of a woman's hypergamy. By order of degrees, hypergamy will define who a woman loves and who she will not, depending upon her own opportunities and capacity to attract it.

Men in Love

I once had a woman ask me this innocuous question in a comment thread:

"Can men really not tell when a woman doesn't love them?"

As would be expected, the male responses to this and her follow up comments ranged from mild annoyance of her naiveté to disbelief of her sincerity with regards to her "want to know." However, her original wonderment as to whether men did in fact know when a woman doesn't love them, I think, carries more weight than most guys (even manosphere men) realize. So I'll recount my comments and the discussion here.

Can men really not tell when a woman doesn't love them?

No, they can't.

Why? Because men want to believe that they can be happy, and sexually satisfied, and appreciated, and loved, and respected by a woman for *who* he is. It is men who are the real romantics, not women, but it is the grand design of hypergamy that men believe it is women who are the romantic ones.

Hypergamy, by its nature, defines love for women in opportunistic terms, leaving men as the only objective arbiters of what love is for themselves. So yes, men can't tell when a woman doesn't love them, because they want to believe women can love them in the ways they think they could.

One man responds:

All right, I keep hoping your rule #6 is wrong, but it hasn't proven to be. So is the big lie that men miss not that women can provide this, but that we don't invest this energy into fellow men? That we don't find men we can be vulnerable with, so that we are emotionally prepared for the trials that women will create in our homes. Is this why so many women tend to isolate their husbands or boyfriends from their male friends early on in marriage or dating?

Presuming this woman was genuinely confused (and I'm half-inclined to think she is) this is exactly the source of her confusion. Women's solipsism prevents them from realizing that men would even have a differing concept of love than how a woman perceives love. Thus her question, "can men really not tell when a woman doesn't love them?"

I don't necessarily think it's a 'big lie', it's just a lack of mutuality on either gender's concept of love. If it's a 'lie' at all it's one men prefer to tell themselves.

Bridging the Gap

Later in the discussion Jacquie (who is one of the two female writers to make my blog-roll) brought up another interesting aspect of bridging the lack of mutuality between either gender's concepts of love:

If it is beyond what a woman is capable of, therefore even if a woman recognizes this incapacity in herself, is there no way to compensate? What if a woman truly desires to try to move beyond this? Does she just consider it a hopeless matter and do nothing? Or is it something she should strive for continuously with the hope that she can at least move somewhat closer to this idealized love? Is it even too much for her to comprehend?

As I was telling the first guy, it's more a lack of mutuality on either gender's concept of love. The original question about whether a man can determine when a woman doesn't love him goes much deeper than she's aware of. I think a lot of what men go through in their blue pill Beta days – the frustration, the anger, the denial, the deprivation, the sense that he's been sold a fantasy that no woman has ever made good upon – all that is rooted in a fundamental belief that some woman, any woman, out there knows just how he needs to be loved and all he has to do is find her and embody what he's been told she will expect of him when he does.

So he finds a woman, who says and shows him that she loves him, but not in the manner he's had all this time in his head. Her love is based on hypergamic qualifications, performance, and is far more conditional than what he'd been led to believe, or convinced himself, love should be between them. Her love seems duplicitous, ambiguous, and seemingly, too easily lost in comparison to what he'd been taught for so long is how a woman would love him when he found her.

So he spends his monogamous efforts in 'building their relationship' into one where she loves him according to his concept, but it never happens.

It's an endless tail-chase of maintaining her affections and complying with her concept of love while making occasional efforts to draw her into his concept of love. The constant placating to her to maintain her love conflicts with the neediness of how he'd like to be loved is a hypergamic recipe for disaster, so when she falls out of love with him he literally doesn't know that she no longer loves him. His logical response then is to pick up the old conditions of love she had for him when they first got together, but none of that works now because they are based on obligation, not genuine desire. Love, like desire, cannot be negotiated.

It took me a long time, and was a very tough part of my own unplugging when I finally came to terms with what I thought about love and how it's conveyed isn't universal between the genders. It took some very painful slap-in-the-face doses of reality for this to click, but I think I have a healthier understanding of it now. It was one of the most contradictory truths I had to unlearn, but it fundamentally changed my perspective of the relations I have with my wife, daughter, mother and my understanding of past girlfriends.

If it is beyond what a woman is capable of, therefore even if a woman recognizes this incapacity in herself, is there no way to compensate? What if a woman truly desires to try to move beyond this? Does she just consider it a hopeless matter and do nothing?

I don't think it's necessarily impossible, but it would take a woman to be self-aware enough that men and women have different concepts of their ideal love to begin with, which is, improbable. The biggest hurdle isn't so much in women recognizing this, but rather in men recognizing it themselves. So, hypothetically, yes you could, but the problem then becomes one of the genuineness of that desire. Love, like desire, is only legitimate when it's uncoerced and unobligated. Men believe in love for the sake of love, women love opportunistically. It's not that either subscribe to unconditional love, it's that both gender's conditions for love differ.

IRON RULE VII

Iron Rule of Tomassi #7

It is always time and effort better spent developing relations with new, fresh, prospective women than it will ever be in attempting to reconstruct a failed relationship.

Rollo, HELP! I fucked up big time and I want her back! How do I get her back?

Easily one of the most common questions I've fielded at SoSuave over the past 7 years has been some variation of "how do I get her back?" It's common for a reason; at some stage of life every guy believes that rejection is worse than regret. Lord knows I tried to recover an old lover or two in my own past. Whether due to infidelity on her part, your own or a regression back to a Beta mindset after initiating an LTR, this is one Iron Rule you should always refer back to.

Never root through the trash once the garbage has been dragged to the curb. You get messy, your neighbors see you do it, and what you thought was worth digging for is never as valuable as you thought it was.

Even if you could go back to where you were, any relationship you might have with an ex will be colored by all of the issues that led up to the breakup.

In other words, you know what the end result of those issues has been. It will always be the 800 pound gorilla in the room in any future relationship. As I elaborated in the Desire Dynamic, healthy relationships are founded on genuine mutual desire, not a list of negotiated terms and obligations, and this is, by definition, exactly what any post-breakup relationship necessitates.

You or she may promise to never do something again, you may promise to "rebuild the trust", you may promise to be someone else, but you cannot promise to accept that the issues leading up to the breakup don't have the potential to dissolve it again. The doubt is there. You may be married for 30 years, but there will always be that one time when you two broke up, or she fucked that other guy, and everything you think you've built with her over the years will always be compromised by that doubt of her desire.

You will never escape her impression that you were so optionless you had to beg her back to rekindle her intimacy with you. The extraordinary effort you would need to get her back is far better spent on a new prospective woman with who you have no history.

IRON RULE VIII

Iron Rule of Tomassi #8

Always let a woman figure out why she wont fuck you, never do it for her.

"Rollo, I'm newly Game-aware, red pill guy and I've been meeting girls with more and more success since my conversion, but I can't help the feeling that the really hot girls I want to get with a so out of my league.

Any suggestions?"

An integral part of maintaining the feminine imperative as the societal imperative involves keeping women as the primary sexual selectors. As I've detailed in many prior comments and posts, this means that a woman's sexual strategy necessitates that she be in as optimized a condition as her capacity (attractiveness) allows for her to choose from the best males available to satisfy that strategy.

This is really the definition of hypergamy, and on an individual level, I believe only the most plugged in of men don't realize this to some degree of consciousness. However, what I think escapes a lot of men is the complex nature of hypergamy on a social scale.

For hypergamy to sustain its dominant position as the default sexual strategy for our society, it's necessary for the feminine imperative to maintain existing, foster new, and normalize complex social conventions that serve it. The scope of these conventions range from the individualized psychological conditioning early in life to the grand scale of social engineering (e.g. Feminism, Religion, Government, etc.)

One of these social conventions that operates in the spectrum of the personal to the societal is the idea of 'leagues'. The fundamental idea that Social Matching Theory details is that "All things being equal, an individual will tend to be attracted to, and are more likely to pair off with, another individual who is of the same or like degree of physical attractiveness as themselves." In a vacuum, this is the germ of the idea behind the 'leagues'. The social convention of 'leagues' mentality is where 'all things are not equal' and used to support the feminine imperative, while conveniently still supporting the principle of social matching theory.

The latent function of 'leagues' is to encourage men to filter themselves out for women's intimate approval.

As social conditions progress and become more complex, so too do men's ability to mimic the personal attributes of providership and security. In other words, lesser men become intelligent enough to circumvent women's existing sexual filters and thus thwart their sexual strategy. These ever increasing complexities made it hard to identify optimally suitable men from the pretenders, and women, being the primary sexual selector, needed various social constructs to sort the wheat from the chaff. With each subsequent generation they couldn't be expected to do all of this detective work on their own so the feminine imperative enlisted the aid of the men themselves and created self-perpetuated, self-internalized social doctrines for men to comply with in order to exist in a feminine defined society.

The concept of leagues is just one of these doctrines. Your self-doubt about your worthiness of a woman's intimacy stems from a preconditioned idea that 'you're out of her league'. The booster club optimist idea that "if you think you can't, you're right" is true, and boundless enthusiasm may overcome some obstacles, but to address the source of the disease it's more important to ask yourself why you've been taught to think you can't.

A lot of approach anxiety comes from your own self-impression – Am I smooth, hot, affluent, funny, confident, interesting, decisive, well-dressed enough to earn an HB 9's attention? How about an HB 6? Our great danger is not that we aim too high and fail, but that we aim too low and succeed.

I'm not debating the legitimacy of the evaluative standards of the sexual market place – it's a harsh, often cruel reality – what I'm really trying to do is open your eyes as to why you believe you're only meritorious of an HB 7. Looks count for a lot, as does Game, affluence, personality, talent, etc. but is your self-estimation accurate, or are you a voluntary participant in your own self-devaluation in the SMP courtesy of the leagues mentality the feminine imperative would have you believe?

The Economy of the League

As I stated above the purpose of fomenting a stratified *league* mentality in men serves to autonomously filter the lesser from the greater men for women to chose from, however, it also functions to increase the valuation of the feminine as a commodity.

Like any great economic entity, the feminine imperative lives and dies by its ability to inflate its value in the marketplace. Essentially the feminine imperative is a marketeer. One of the sad ironies of this, and the last, century is that the feminine imperative has attempted to base women's SMP valuation on a collective importance to the detriment of the individual woman's SMV. For men this is inverted; a man's sexual valuation is primarily individualized, while men as a collective gender are devaluated in the SMP.

What I mean by this is that, as a collective entity women's sexuality cannot afford to be perceived as anything less than the more valued prize. If all vaginas are considered the gold standard then men's sexual default value will always be lower. By this definition men, on whole, are out of women's league.

For further consideration lets assume that average men, most being varying degrees of Beta, are blessed with the 'miraculous gift' of an average woman's sexual attentions. The power dynamic is already pre-established to defer to a feminine frame, so it's small wonder that men would be prone to ONEitis even with an objectively average woman.

This is the intent of the League schema – to unobjectively predispose men to commitment with women who under objective condition couldn't enjoy the same selectivity. It's been postulated that for a healthy relationship to exist the Man must be recognized by the woman to be 1-2 points above her own SMV. This is a pretty tall order considering the feminine imperative's emphasis on women's sexuality being the more valued as default. This is to say nothing of contemporary women's overinflated self-evaluations due to the rise of social media.

Gaming the League

All of the above isn't to say that there isn't a kernel of truth to the notion of leagues; it's just not the "truth" men have been led to believe. For as much as the feminine imperative would have men subscribe to leagues, it equally seeks to exempt women from the same league hierarchy by evaluating women as a whole.

Needless to say men have their own rating systems – most popularly the ubiquitously physical HB (hot babe) 1-10 scale. I should add that it's a foregone conclusion that any rating system men would establish for women in the feminine reality would necessarily need to be ridiculed, shamed and demonized, but you knew that already.

Irrational self-confidence is a good start to circumventing and unlearning the concept of leagues; unlearning this conditioning being the operative goal. The Game-aware Man can actually use the concept of leagues to his advantage with enough guile.

When you approach a woman without regard to a league mentality or even a Zen-like obliviousness to it (ala Corey Worthington, the Alpha Buddha), you send the message that there's more to you than a feminine reality can control. It's exactly this disregard for the influence of the feminine imperative that makes the Alpha attractive; he's unaware of, or indifferent to the rules his conditioning should have taught him earlier.

Just in the attempt of Gaming a woman obviously "out of your league" you flip the feminine script by planting a seed of doubt (and prompting imagination) about your perceived value. Doubt is a very powerful tool, in fact the very concept of leagues is founded upon men's self-doubt. Turn that tool to your advantage by disregarding women's social convention of leagues.

IRON RULE IX

Iron Rule of Tomassi #9

Never *seriously* self-deprecate with a woman you intend to be intimate with.

Apologizing for a lack of Game isn't Game.

One disservice I think most men tend to overlook is an attitude of self-depreciation that they'll resort to as a means of engendering interest in a potential woman by attempting to play to her sympathies.

Case in point (printed with permission):

Subject:
My apologies for being a complete douche

Body:
I actually wanted to call and talk to you tonight, but I just moved into my new place today and lost track of time and now its after midnight. Anyways, I was a complete tool the last time we talked. I thought about what you said to me, and I really have been lame lately. I think back to our first couple of "dates", and I realize what a complete and boring reject I was. Those weren't so much dates as me trying way too hard to impress you as someone that was mature (bad word choice, but I dunno what I was doing) and not myself. Anyways, I now realize I need to get this pole out of my ass and start having fun again in my life. Which is why I have been in a drunken stupor for the last 2 weekends.

I hope we can start hanging out again, because I do enjoy your company. But I promise if we do, I will drink, relax, and not be such a wallflower. I also promise no more gay-ass text messages. I hate when people do that to me, so I can only imagine how retarded i look when I do it.

-Allen

This was an actual email passed on to me from a young woman I counseled after she blew this guy off over the course of three dates, and is one of many emails and IM texts I've gone over time and again with women. This is a textbook example of how men will resort to self-depreciation tactics in order to provoke an "It's OK, I understand" sympathy response from a woman with the expectation that she'll take 'pity' on him for being a "flawed man" and give him a second (or third, or fourth) chance, or any chance at all.

This is a direct manifestation of men being socially conditioned to recognize and acknowledge their weaknesses, and in confessing them they will become strengths, and ergo, attractions (since they mistakenly believe that doing so will make them "not-like-*other*-guys" and therefore unique). "You see? I'm really a sensitive, introspective guy willing to cop to his own character flaws, please love me."

Iron Rule of Tomassi #9
Never Self-Deprecate under any circumstance.

This is a Kiss of Death that you self-initiate and is the antithesis of the Prize Mentality. Once you've accepted yourself and presented yourself as a "complete douche" there's no going back to confidence with a woman.

Never appeal to a woman's sympathies. Her sympathies are given by her own volition, never when they are begged for – women despise the obligation of sympathy. Nothing kills arousal like pity. Even if you don't seriously consider yourself pathetic, it never serves your best interest to paint yourself as pathetic. Self-depreciation is a misguided tool for the AFC, and not something that would even occur to an Alpha.

People seem to get confused about how self-deprecation really functions. I'm not suggesting that a Man take himself so seriously that he can't laugh at himself; in fact a brilliant tactic is to present a prevailing, ambient sense of seriousness, then admit to and laugh at whatever goof it was that removes you from it. Nothing endears a Man more to a woman than to think only she can break through your shell and get you to find humor in yourself. However, true self-deprecation, as illustrated in Allen's (lower case 'a' noted) email, is self-initiated. It's not the "ha ha, look I slipped on a banana peel" sense of deprecation, it's the "I'm a complete douche, but really I'm worth the effort" apologetic sense of deprecation. There is a marked difference between being pathetic and being able to laugh at yourself in good faith.

I'm not advocating that guys never own up to mistakes or wrongs they do; you should sensibly apologize in given situations depending on the conditions and do so appropriately, however self-depreciation is another mental schema entirely.

Humility is a virtue (up to a point), but it's simply not a virtue that a woman you're interested in will ever appreciate in the manner you think they will, and in fact often conveys the opposite intent. Virtuous humility is no substitute for self-confidence.

If you are already involved with a woman, she may develop a socially mandated sense of appreciation, but again this is only up to the threshold of you trading her estimation of your confidence for your ability to address fault on your part. When a woman delivers a shit test based on this, and a guy submits through self-depreciation it's damage done that's not easily undone. Admitting fault is not a strength that inspires women – it's still about the fault. It may be the honorable, necessary, truthful thing to do, but don't believe for a moment women will value you more in the confession of fault.

That said, true self-depreciation is pervasive. Contemporary men have become so steeped in deprecation and male ridicule by popular media that it seems a normative way of attracting women.

The message is 'women love men who laugh at Men'. Thus, you have to be hyper-aware of it and unlearn it. You have to catch yourself in mid-sentence so to speak. Women operate in the sub-communications and when you overtly admit to a lack of confidence in yourself or your collective gender you may as well just LJBF yourself.

That's a strong impression you wont recover from easily if ever. Women want a competent, confident, decisive Man from the outset, not one who's self-image is that of a "complete douche" or even a partial douche. The stereotype of the quirky, but lovable guy who bumbles his way into a woman's heart may work for romantic comedies, but not in the real world. I should also add that when you become hyper-aware of this you can also turn it to your own advantage when dealing with a competitor or you're sarging a girl with a self-depreciative boyfriend or suitor. It's all too easy to reinforce her estimation of a guy like this by covertly confirming it for her, while at the same time playing up your own confidence and value.

All of this is not to say that it's wrong to recognize your own weaknesses and understanding when you're in the wrong. It's simply how you go about addressing it that's the point. There are plenty of ways to assume the responsibilities of fault that aren't self-depreciating. The easiest way is to always adopt the attitude that you're 'getting better all the time'. This mentality fosters confidence and projects ambition, whereas self-depreciation shoves your nose in the dog shit and says "please love me anyway?"

CHAPTER 9

MYTHOLOGY

THE MYTH OF THE LONELY OLD MAN

Is loneliness a disease that necessitates a cure? If men could be made to believe so, think of the potential profit to be made from, and the potential for manipulation of, men.

The real test for a man is how he lives with himself, alone.

Precious few men ever truly allow themselves to be alone and learn real, singular independence and self-reliance. The vast majority of guys (see Betas), particularly in western culture, tend to transition from mother to wife with little or no intermission between. For the most part they subscribe to the feminine imperative, becoming serial monogamists going from LTR to LTR until they 'settle' without ever having learned and matured into how to interact as an adult.

The fear of loneliness is entirely too exaggerated in modern western romanticism. The popularized fear-mythology of becoming the "lonely old man who never loved" is the new 'old maid' myth made popular in an era when a woman's worth was dependent upon her marital status and (at least now) equally as false a premise. But in our brave new 'Generation AFC', men (who've become women) are repackaged and shamed into believing this horse shit as part & parcel of feminized gender role reversal. Thus we get Speed Dating and eHarmony and a host of other "conveniences" to pacify the insecurities that this reversal instills.

I'm going to suggest that most AFCs, most feminized, conditioned males, *like* and embrace the lonely old man myth because it is a Buffer against potential rejection. Does that sound like a stretch? It shouldn't. When used from a feminized perspective this myth is most certainly a 'shaming' social convention with the latent function of getting men to commit to a feminine frame – *"you better change yourself soon, or your soulmate might pass you by and you'll be lonely and destitute in your old age"*. That's the feminized use of the myth, however, the internalized AFC use of the myth is a Buffer. This then becomes his rationale for settling for a substandard LTR or marriage; better to marry a shrew than suffer loneliness.

It's really a triple whammy. There is the feminine reinforced fear of solitude. Then, the self-reinforced expectation of maturity or "doing the right thing". And finally the use of it as a convenient retreat from rejection or potential rejection; and this is what I'm getting at when I refer to it as a Buffer.

Case example: I have a friend who is trapped in a passionless marriage with a woman, who's set the frame from day one. He'd like to come off as dominant with his male friends, but it's clear to most of our friends that his wife owns the frame of the marriage. Prior to meeting this girl our friend was a serial monogamist branch swinger. The LTR girl he'd been with prior to her ran the show in much the same way for almost 5 years. When he was finally freeing himself from her (with a bit of my own help), he started to see the value of being single and independent and began dating non-exclusively for about a 3 month period. After meeting his now wife he gradually tried to find suitable ways to withdraw and become exclusive. Knowing what our reaction would be in so swift a time frame, he began searching for all kinds of rationales to effect this – and settled on the myth of the lonely old man.

His story was the classic one where a guy shakes off his old ways of thinking about women and dating, and almost unplugs from the Matrix, but fails to kill his inner AFC and slides back into his old Beta mentality once he'd secured another 'soulmate'. Here was a guy who'd spent more than half of his 20s in a miserable LTR who managed to briefly unplug for about 3 months before latching onto another ONEitis. Yet his reasoning was "I'm tired of the dating games. I need to settle down. I don't want to be lonely when I'm 60." This from a guy who'd only ever been single for 3 months of his life. It was his Buffer. Of course now he's resentful and pensive about his marriage and lives life vicariously through his single friends, while at the same time self-righteously scolds them for still being single.

The Myth of the Lonely Old Man is a Buffer against rejection. It's a hiding in relationships they're told they must constantly work to perfect, because of the fear of potential rejection. They're pre-set in this idea while still single – they see it as a valid reason and a desirable goal; get married quick, before it's too late. What's worse is that the rationale is unassailable.

The foundation of the myth is associated with maturity, and who's going to tell you not to be more mature? This is how we get the 'Kidult' social convention women like to trot out; "He'll never grow up!" The problem is that this lack of maturity is only paired with a Man's willingness to commit or not to commit to *women's* long term provisioning goals. In the feminine imperative's social construct, maturity means marriage, and marriage means provisioning.

Don't buy into the powder-puff idea that if you don't find your mythological soulmate, or the *ONE* by the time you're 30 and ASAP you'll tempt fate and risk a life of quiet desperation. This contrivance only serves the interests of women who's imperative it is to enjoy their party years in their 20's with as many Alphas as they can attract, only to later have a stable Nice Guy who's petrified he'll live a life of loneliness and desperation, waiting for them at 28-30 to marry and ensure their long term security.

Don't buy this lie. The man who is comfortable with himself and confident in his true independence is the one that women will want to be associated with and to share in it.

How you handle being alone and what you do with the opportunities that freedom allows is the real measure of a man. If you're single and 50 you STILL have options if you're only brave enough to explore them. I know divorced men in their 50s who're dating mid 30s women right now and I know men in their 60s who've been trapped and emotionally blackmailed by their wives for 30 years. Marriage is no insulation from the sexual marketplace.

THE MYTH OF WOMEN & SEX

"Booty is so strong that there are dudes willing to blow themselves up for the highly unlikely possibility of booty in an other dimension. There are no chicks willing to blow themselves up for a penis." – Joe Rogan

One of the single most annoying tropes I read / hear from men (more so than even women it seems) is the "Women are just as / more sexual than men" canard. Nothing stops me in my tracks more abruptly than reading this line parroted back in some form by a self-effacing white knight trying to convince himself, hope against hope, that it could be true. This is a *very* effective feminine social convention, even internalized and spouted back by the likes of more than a few infamous PUAs. This fantasy belongs among the higher order social convention myths like the Myth of Sexual Peak. Just a rudimentary knowledge of female biology is all that's needed to deconstruct the myth.

Women are more sexual than men, but they are repressed due to society or a lack of "trust" with a guy.

Patently false. A healthy male produces between 12 to 17 times the amount of testosterone a woman does. It is a biological impossibility for a woman to *want* sex as much as, or as often as men. Trust that when a woman says, "I don't understand why sex is so important to guys" she's speaking the literal truth. No woman will ever experience 17 times the amount of her own testosterone levels (barring steroids). Amongst it's many other effects, testosterone is the primary hormone involved with stimulating human libido. I should also add that, on average, and barring environmental variables, a mans testosterone only declines 1% per year beyond age 40, so even at age 60 the average, healthy male is only dealing with an average 20% deficit in testosterone.

Critics of this observation like to argue that, for female sexual response and arousal, testosterone isn't the only factor to consider. To which I'll agree, however it is the *primary* factor in sexual response. A woman cannot possibly understand what 12 to 17 times their present amount of testosterone could feel like without steroid use. In fact the first effect female bodybuilders report when cycling anabolic steroids is a 100 fold increase in sexual interest and libido. So in terms of natural female hormonal / biochemical response there is no unaltered way a woman could ever make an accurate comparison to what a man's baseline libido is in relation to her own.

Women's sexual desire is also cyclical. Even at the peak of her ovulatory cycle, when she's at her horniest, she'll never experience what men do 24 hours a day. This is the root of the myth, and the source of the social convention.

Like men, women rely on testosterone to maintain libido, bone density and muscle mass throughout their lives. In men, estrogens simply lower testosterone, decrease muscle mass, stunt growth in teenagers, introduces gynecomastia, increases feminine characteristics, and decrease susceptibility to prostate cancer. Sexual desire is dependent on androgen levels rather than estrogen levels.

I also understand that female sexuality functions differently than male sexuality, but this only reinforces my point. Women's sexuality is cyclic, not only on a monthly schedule, but also over periods of a lifetime (menopause, and peak fertility for instance). There are periods over a month and a lifetime where sexual desire waxes and wanes, (healthy) men's stays relatively constant from puberty to about age 40. Women are slower to arouse, they tend to need more than just visual stimulation, and there is definitely a psychological element (they need a fantasy) necessary. Men only need visual stimulation and minimal feedback to get aroused (i.e. porn).

It should come as no shock that post-menopausal hormone therapies use testosterone to boost women's flagging libidos too. When women are at the peaks of their ovulatory cycles, low and behold they experience a sharp spike in testosterone levels in order to facilitate pregnancy and then it gets flushed out during menstruation. You can debate about how best to get a woman's testosterone flowing, but it's testosterone that's needed to prompt a sexual response.

Now the real question is, why would such a popular myth be such a useful social convention? Think about it. It sexualizes women, while not making them outright sluts. They can avoid the stigma of promiscuity while presenting the fantasy that they are secretly "more sexual" than they are "allowed" to be, if only they could meet a man skilled enough to bring this out in them.

It's a sexual selection convention. The fantasy is that women are really these wolves in sheep's clothing for the right guy. To an extent this is true. Studies do indicate that women in their peak fertility window do in fact aggressively seek out Alpha males for conventional sexual encounters, especially so during the proliferative phase of their menstrual cycles. However, again, the root of this social convention is in the presumption that "women are just as sexual as men", which is simply not the case considering the conditionality that the female sexual response is dependent on.

No self-interested Man is ever going to be encouraged to refute the idea that women are equally preoccupied with, equally aroused as, or equally desirous of sex as men are. We love the fantasy that women are secretly yearning for sex with us, if only society were more open and accepting of feminine sexuality. Yet, in the same breath we'll hear about how slutty and aggressive women have become in the fall of western society by the same guys. It's ironic, but it gives guys hope that if they can find the secret formula to unleashing the sexual beast within every woman he'll find this insatiable she-devil to pair off with monogamously. If women were men's sexual equals, why would they not be prone to the same drives that conflict with monogamy? Imagine a world where women are as horny as men. Think of a gay bath house and you might have a workable model.

Women of course love to encourage and reinforce this social convention because it sounds like empowerment in the face of patriarchal sexual oppression (yes, we'd be more sexual if you'd only allow us to you evil men), while at the same time tacitly acknowledging that, turns men into white knight sympathizers of the cause (i.e. feminine entitlement and primacy).

The point of my starting this topic wasn't to debate whether or not women are sexual at all – obviously they are – however it was my intent to draw attention to the canard that women (and their would-be male identifiers) would like everyone to believe, "women are just as / more sexual than men". No woman can make a realistic assessment about that unless she's had 12 -17 times her natural testosterone levels increased and lived in a man's biological condition. Just on the face of it the assertion is silly, but as I said, for women it's empowering to think that women are "just as sexual" as men. And female-identifiers are all too happy to reinforce that meme because it offers them the hope of getting laid with one of these 'sexually repressed' women.

THE MYTH OF THE GOOD GIRL

Good girls are just bad girls who never got caught.

Allow me relate here a case study I counseled a friend on personally about 6 years ago. I have a very good friend, Rick, that I hired and work with. Though we started out as work associates he became one of my better friends and had the benefit of my personally having unplugged him from the Matrix. He was a good student (for lack of a better term), but in becoming so he went through a transformation process. Like most guys fed on a lifetime of feminine conditioning he patronizingly accepted what I was initially teaching him, but privately, he still clung to his AFC mentalities. That is, until the turning point came.

Unbeknownst to me Rick had entertained a flirtatious "friendship" with a semi-attractive PR girl we were working with for a while. He knew what I'd said about LJBF rejections and "playing friends" with women, so he left me out of the loop on the whole affair. He had "dated" her on several occasions, but beyond the infrequent "kiss while drunk" she kept him at arms distance using the standard filibuster techniques women classically use – "I'm not ready for a relationship", "I'm not looking for a boyfriend", "We're good friends", etc. She did however keep him in her 'attention web' with little carrots of affection for him to pull her cart for about 3 or 4 months. Mind you, Rick was never a chump. He'd hooked up with his share of women, but this cute, "good girl" who was at best an HB7 developed into a ONEitis for him.

This all came to a head when one night she had to do some work with Aaron Lewis (yes, from Staind) while he was doing his solo acoustic act at our casino. To make a long story short, the PR girl ended up buzzed on this night and fucked Aaron Lewis' tour manager in a classic situation of right-Alpha, right-environment, right-conditions. Her mistake was in feeling the need to confess her actions to Rick who'd felt betrayed considering all the investment he'd put into doing what he thought was the right way to go about things. Here was one guy on one night who she fucked in a moment of chemical reaction because "he was hot, I was drunk and one thing led to another,.." versus his 3-4 month personal investment (i.e. Relational Equity fallacy).

This was of course when he consulted me and informed me of everything leading up to it, only now he was at an impasse. She apologized profusely to him and held out (once again) the olive branch of a LJBF rejection. He asked me what he should say, and it was at this point he took the initiative to tell her "no, we can't 'just be friends'." He did what I advised him to do and he walked away from a woman for the first time in his life. This is when all hell broke loose for her. She'd never been met with this response before and all the cards went straight into Rick's hands. She would consistently 'bump into him' at bars or events to "have another talk", she did a complete 180 in her attitude with him all in an effort to "be his friend."

Now I'm exceptionally proud of Rick because, unlike most guys finding the true power of a takeaway, he stuck with it rather than being contented with her chasing him and then giving into the LJBF. He had actually learned a valuable tool that he still uses now – the power of the takeaway.

In addition he also came to understand the principle of understanding a woman, not by what she says, but by what she does (the Medium *is* the Message) – he learned the importance of reading behavior. Of course after about 6 or 8 months she stopped pursuing him "to be friends" and he has talked to her in the interim years, but the frame of their discourse has changed. She has respect for him that she never had when he was the pursuer and never would've had if he'd surrendered to another LJBF.

Good Girls

This girl, at every opportunity, loved to display her 'properness' and would always say she "wanted a man with a good heart" when asked what she looked for in a guy. She was very outgoing as befits a PR person, but at all times she presented herself as someone conscious of how people perceived her and her reputation. Hers was a classic case of basing estimations upon behavior above words. Biology trumps conviction – sexuality, for as much as we think we can, will not go unexpressed. Celibate priests, moralistic conservative statesmen, and the pure-as-the-driven-snow virtuous girl you've got ONEitis for all want to get off, and they'll find a way to do so. According to FaceBook she now lives in Montana with a thoroughly Beta husband who likely has no idea that she had the capacity for raw, feral hypergamy.

One of the trappings of a woman a guy perceives as a 'good girl' is that he'll have a tendency to pedestalize her by default. White Knights are a given, but even hardened PUAs are prone to want to read more into the personality of a 'good girl'. A cute-ish HB8 'good girl' is a recipe for ONEitis because she seems to be above seduction.

"I just want a guy with a good heart" sounds so fairytale perfect and with just the right amount of naiveté applied, she comes off as a girl who truly believes Disney wishes really do come true. To guys with Game she's a jewel in the rough amongst the bitch-shielded mean girls that populate the new hook-up paradigm. To chumpish White Knights she's an archetype – the innocent damsel who needs to be saved from the world before it corrupts her soul and she turns into all the other women who wont date them. Both of them are equally shocked when she spontaneously fucks an Alpha tour manager.

If you haven't done so yet, I highly recommend adding *The Art of Seduction* by Robert Greene to your reading list. In this seminal work he begins by profiling the archetypes of seducers and amongst them we find our 'good girl' is really The Natural; a child like innocence that masks a seductive motive. You may be inclined to think of a good girl as a prude, but this is often in error. The good girl needs to be seductively cute enough to make her hypergamy work for her. Any marginal prudishness is reserved for putting a suitor into stasis long enough to evaluate better options, or in the case of our PR girl, the option to capitalize on an immediate Alpha experience.

The good girl's Game is built around playing to the 'Quality Woman' mythos that men harbor. They want to believe she exists among a sea of vapid, self-absorbed sluts looking to cash in before they hit the Wall. She's not the prudish Madonna and she's not the Whore of Babylon, she's the cute good girl somewhere in between. She's only an HB7-8, not the demigoddess HB9+, so she also emanates the tantalizing potential of attainability. All of this makes for a very idealized, very cemented form of ONEitis until it's graphically dispelled for the guy suffering from it.

Just like all men have some form of game, women have their own game. Since we live in a feminine defined reality, women's game is not considered subterfuge, it's simply how women are, or the feminine mystique. What makes a good girl contrast with 'other girls' is still founded within this feminine social normalization.

The wise practitioner of Game knows what works best for him, but he must also be aware of the Game being used against him. One of the most important aspects of the principle of Amused Mastery is actually having the mastery to be amused. That may sound cryptic, but what it means is having the experience to know what to expect from feminine Game, mastering it and being able to riposte with an amused laugh.

For example, the operative goal of girl-game is to maximize hypergamy, this is a foundation of Game. So in knowing this, you can craft an amused response to any seduction methodology women use on you. The good girl is still looking for an Alpha, and will still stop the good girl car to get out and fuck him should the opportunity arise. When you deal with the good girl or any of her sister's methods always see them beginning with the end in mind.

THE MYTH OF
THE BIOLOGICAL CLOCK

Popular culture likes to teach women and, by association, unenlightened men, that there is an innate biological clock inside each woman that slowly ticks down to a magical period where her maternal instincts at long last predispose her to wanting a child. Perhaps, not so surprisingly, this coincides perfectly with the Myth of Women's Sexual Peak as well as conveniently being the age demographic just post or just prior to when most women hit the Wall.

The concept of a biological clock sounds very convincing on the face of it – it's "biological", and when it comes to feminine social conventions, nothing convinces women more than their bodies, their selves. In girl-world biological reasonings are always suspicious rationales for men's bad behavior, but when applicable to women, biology is "Mother Nature", and you don't argue with that bitch.

Unfortunately, and as fate would have it, the hard science of biology often tends to crash headlong into feminine social conventions. Lo and behold many *Women Underestimate Fertility Clock's Clang*. In 2011 NPR aired an article of the same title. It would appear the cold hard science of women's actual fertility window doesn't exactly coincide with the articles of faith that feminine primacy is teaching them:

A new survey finds a big disconnect when it comes to fertility. The age women think they can conceive a baby is far different from what their bodies are actually capable of. This poses an increasing problem, as more women wait longer than ever to have children.

What's the chance a 30-year-old can get pregnant in one try? Many thought up to 80 percent, while in reality it's less than 30 percent. For a 40-year-old, many assumed up to a 40 percent success rate. It's actually less than 10 percent. And when you keep trying? The survey finds many think you can get pregnant more quickly than it actually happens. It also shows many women underestimate how successful fertility treatments are.

Not only is the myth of the biological clock inaccurate in terms of when a woman should get pregnant, it's dangerously misleading in the odds of becoming pregnant.

"The first thing they say is, 'Why didn't anybody tell me this?'" says Barbara Collura, who co-authored the survey and heads Resolve, the National Infertility Association. She laments that no federal agency pushes this issue, and neither women nor their OBGYNs tend to bring it up. Though, Collura admits that fading fertility is a hard message to deliver.

"Let's be honest, women don't want to hear that they can't have it all," she says. "We can have a great job, we can have a master's degree, we don't need to worry about child-bearing because that's something that will come. And when it doesn't happen, women are really angry."

I wont argue that women actually possess maternal instincts, I will argue that their understanding of when they manifest has been deliberately distorted by a feminine-centric cultural influence. If women are "angry" about the revelation their inability or difficulty to conceive in their post Wall biological conditions presents, their anger is misdirected. Rather than come down from the heady pedestal of ego-invested female empowerment psychology, they'll blame men for not being suitable fathers, or lacking a will to "play-by-the rules" of the feminine imperative by whiling away their time in porn and video game induced comas.

"I just feel like it's something else they lump onto women that we have no control over," says filmmaker Monica Mingo, who's blogged about her decade-long effort to conceive. She says the real issue is society at large, which is pushing back the age people are expected to settle down and have kids. Mingo didn't even meet her husband until she was 32.

"You tell us your fertile years rapidly decline in your mid-20s," she says. "Well, if I'm not dating anyone, and I want to have a family, what's that information going to do for me?"

Well for one thing it might force you to come to terms with the course you want to set for your future life with an informed choice, rather than blaming it on so-called "Kidult" men when you do realize you want kids. I guess that's asking too much when you're in your prime party years at film school. Sorry Monica, time's up, and you did have control over it in your pre-Wall years. All the haggard ghosts of feminism are cackling heartily around the cauldron of boiling good intentions in hell.

What were seeing here is a collision of hypergamy and feminine primacy smashing against the harsh reality of biology. The feminine imperative needs to create a new social convention to make this incongruent reality agree with it's doctrine. It's been done before with the convenient reinvention of sexual fluidity. Blame men for not living up to the tenets of the "having it all" ideology and create a convenient new social convention that shames men in its retro-resolution of the problem it caused for itself.

If there were an actual biological clock, it was ticking its loudest when a woman was 22-24, not conveniently when she needs male provisioning the most, and when her sexual market value is in declination by her mid-thirties.

THE MYTH OF MALE LOOKS

"Your bulletproof Game and charming personality wont make you look any better when your shirt comes off."

Looks.

Assets.

Game.

Have two. Three is best, but if you only have one, Game is the most essential.

I realize that I'm heading into dangerous territory with this, but I maintain that looks are an integral part of attraction – sorry, that's a fact of life – but I've never stated that looks cancel Game. In fact I advocate that learning Game is just as necessary as maintaining a good physique.

The problem is with people who can only think in absolutes. It's always an either-or proposition; Game trumps physique or physique trumps game is horse shit. They're both important and play off each other. There are plenty of average looking guys who pull tail thanks to Game in spite of their looks, and there are also good-looking guys who pull tail without ever hearing what Game is. But wouldn't you rather be the guy with both? The guy who can pull women without compensating for personal deficits?

Consider that greater than 66% of people in western society are overweight (33% are morbidly obese). So it stands to reason that 2/3rd of the guys seeking out the community in order to change their lives, outlook and sexual prospects are going to be struggling with obesity from the outset. Now also consider the preferred belief among guys that looks, at least, matter less than personality, Game, etc. in female attraction. This is *not* a coincidence. For these guys it takes more effort to change their bodies than to change their minds.

"Looks aren't as important for women."

The first thing most men who were previously out of shape will tell you is the marked increase in attention they receive from women after they got in shape. This is perhaps the simplest experiment that puts the lie to this assertion.*

There is a popular misconception men adopt in thinking that "looks aren't as important for women" and that they're more forgiving of a few extra pounds if a guy is witty, humorous and/or embodies some combination of the laundry list of nonsensical adjectives they place on their online dating profiles. This is the male version of the body image acceptance social convention women have been promoting themselves for the past 50 years. Don't worry about getting in shape; money, humor and confidence will make any woman swoon for you. If this were the case the Louie Andersons and Danny Devitos of the world would be swimming in top-shelf ass. I have no doubt that very rich, but out of shape men have a relatively easy time attracting women, but they can't make a woman genuinely desire to fuck him on a physical level. It's just the very commercial version of negotiating desire.

While this may seem like a male-specific social convention, guess again; it's actually a very calculated feminine convention. In terms of feminine breeding strategies and women's schedules of mating, it is far more advantageous for a woman to engage in short-term breeding strategies with Alpha men during the peak of her sexual viability when she knows there is a social structure ready to accommodate her long-term breeding strategy (i.e. provisioning) with future men. In other words, encourage men to think that "looks aren't as important to women" so they'll be more acceptable future providers while breeding in the short-term with men embodying their very specific physical ideal. This is precisely the reason why the "kidult / man-up" phenomenon is so vexing for women today – it threatens this long-term strategy.

Priorities

In accordance with women's sexual strategies, women place an importance upon looks according to their phase of life. The priorities and importance of characteristics that women will consider prerequisites for intimacy shift as her life's conditions dictate.

14 – 24 years old: Looks are *everything*. Yes, some romanticism might help complete the fantasy, and Game is definitely a factor, but the priority for arousal is primarily Darwinian. Women will gladly overlook character flaws or a lack of assets in favor of fucking the physical Alpha while she approaches her own sexual apex. For a brilliant study of this take the time to read Dr. Martie Hasselton's study, Why Muscularity is Sexy linked on the Rational Male.

25-30 years old: Looks are still of primary importance, but other factors are beginning to compete in significance as she becomes increasingly more aware of hitting the impending Wall. While she's still hot enough to command attention, her hypergamic priorities lean more towards the life time provisioning potential and parental investment potential a Man represents. As she gets closer to 30, she knows she has to play her cards well if she is to cash out of the game while she's still able to compete with other women. Ambition, character, assets, humor, personality, etc. begin to be more important in the light of a potential life-time commitment.

30-35 years old: Most single women in this demographic are in varying degrees of denial (aided by social conventions), but on some level of consciousness they realize that they're past their expiration date and securing a commitment is a progressively more difficult battle with every passing year. Looks lose precedent in favor of assets and status.

Game and personality become more prominent, but the primary focus is catching up to the choices she made (or should've made) when she was about 28. Locking down a proven commodity – a Man with a reasonable amount of success and status – is the goal now; not a Man with "potential" for that same success. While the physical is still important, she's more than willing to compromise the physical standards she held at 24 if the Man brings a lot to the table.

35-45 years old: She's well past her expiration date, hit the Wall and is, graciously or not, accepting the fact that she's used goods. Any notion of a list of requisites or priorities are a fond memory now. She may play the Cougar card in an ego protection effort. This may seem like she's back to her primary Looks focus in playing the Cougar, but again, on some level of consciousness she understands that younger Men are doing her the favor by fucking her and in no way expects more than a physical fling. The hope is still, by some miracle, to lock down an aging AFC divorcee in a bad spot, with at least some amount of appreciable assets. Status is nice, looks would be icing on the cake if he's still got them, but provisioning takes priority above even Game or social intelligence.

Making the Change

Changing yourself takes an effort. The greatest obstacle in change is the first one; recognizing and accepting that you need to change. This is where AFCs and Beta males chomp at the bit because they've been told for the better part of a lifetime to "just be themselves" and everything will go according to fate's plan. Then for whatever reason they unplug from the Matrix enough to realize that they've been sold a bill of goods and that personal change is necessary for them. They need to change their lifestyle, change their attitudes, change their outlook, change their minds about themselves and yes, change their physiques too.

But change takes effort and people are lazy. They want the quick fix; the magic pill that makes them happy, successful and sexually irresistible. So they flock to guys selling the best program that promises all that for a minimum of effort. Learning Game demands practiced effort, but it requires far less physical effort than improving one's body, and it's especially daunting for guys unaccustomed to working out. It takes time, energy and dedication all commensurate with how out shape that guy is to begin with.

There are countless "chubby chaser" websites dedicated to catering to this particular "fetish" for men, but not a single one exists for women, why? By that I mean there is a percentage in society of otherwise average, fit men seeking out obese women, yet the standard for ideal masculinity seems to remain constant for females by the lack of *fetishes* for obese males. There is such a demand in society by men seeking fat women that businesses have been developed in order meet it, but there is no similar demand on the part of fit women (or one not sufficient enough to register) seeking overweight men.

Why do you suppose this is? There has never been a "rubenesque" period for Men – where overweight men were consider the feminine ideal – in history. A muscular athletic build has *always* been the masculine standard.

Men define what is feminine and sexy for women, however the inverse is true in that women define what is masculine and sexy for men. The reason women find particular aspects of Men's physiology sexually arousing is because the men in the past who embodied them were rewarded with sex often enough to make those traits psychological subroutines in women's brains.

Yes, Game is vitally important, as is root level, dynamic personal change. I don't think I need to explain just how important this is. However, looks **count**, looks matter.

What I find amazingly ironic is that looks are one of the few areas of change that a Man has *direct* control over – his body. Barring physical disabilities, you have no excuse not to be in better shape. Why wouldn't you want the full package? Stop being so Goddamned lazy and accept that you'll need to exert some effort and sweat to make yourself more attractive and more arousing to women. Game and a positive-masculine mindset are vital elements for your attractiveness and well-being, but they *wont* make you look any better with your shirt off.

*Side Note: I should also point out that for as much as women will assert that a man's penis size is irrelevant to their sexual pleasure, often the first insult they'll hurl at a man in order to shame him is "I'll bet he's got a small dick!" You connect the dots.

THE MYTH OF FEMININE SMV

The manosphere has been awash in articles detailing the sexual marketplace (including my own) and the impact women's short-term vs. long-term sexual strategies have for them for as long I've been writing about gender issues (10+ years). These analyses range from the biological consequences to the insidious, life-damaging punishment a socialized feminine primacy (feminism) inflicts upon unassuming members of both sexes. The most recent manifestations of this have been the social 'shaming' efforts of the Man Up! 2.0 popularizations in mainstream media.

Yes, I'm guilty of cracking this topic more than once, but it bears repeating how feminism, equalism and the feminine imperative conspire to reinvent sexual market value for women.

SMV

In Navigating the SMV I graphed out my own rudimentary overview of how the SMP lays out, as well as sexual market values relative to each sex. Although I began a bit tongue in cheek, in all earnestness I attempted to visually plot out what a persons' life time-line might look like were he or she to have a 'God's Eye' perspective of when their SMV will be at it's apogee, when it builds and when it wanes. As with everything I put to keyboard, my effort was to get to the honest nuts & bolts of the SMP and how our lives' events coincide with that valuation. Here's the breakdown again:

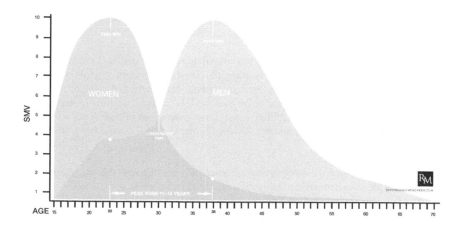

This was an effort in defining a contemporary, realistic view of how sexual market value fluctuates for each sex. I think it's comparatively reflective, if a bit rough, however I approached this graph from a male perspective in that its intent was to educate Men of their SMV potential later in life, and to plan accordingly.

What I didn't account for is feminization's influence on women's (and by association men's) collective understanding of their own SMV. Given the plenitude of manosphere articles devoted to women's distorted and deluded interpretations of their sexual market value I figured this had been done to death; it took a bit of digestion to shake a new thought into my head.

Women Like Men

As if on cue, Team Red vents his frustration from a comment thread:

"Why should money even matter anymore to these women in the long-term when it seems like the majority of them have put their careers first and put marriage/kids off until later on in life? It seems like the dating world is polluted with 30+ year old career women that have been riding the carousel 10-15 years and are now ready to "settle down" and pop out 2-3 kids by ripe old age of 40. What these women seem to have forgotten is the greater risks involved having children so late in life."

I found this comment apropos since it sums up my thoughts on the Myth of the Biological Clock: Women want to *be* men. This is the legacy that a since-decayed feminist social impetus has imparted to the generations of both men and women who've come after the Gloria Steinem's got married themselves, dried up and blew away. Women need to *be* the men of tomorrow. I suppose I should've seen this messaging before, and in honesty I think the greater part of feminized thinking revolves around role reversal, but this is more than reversal. Women want to *be* men.

If a man can wait until his maturation develops, his achievements are more actualized and his SMV peaks at 38-40; equalism says *"why shouldn't you Man-Girl?"*

Whether it's in terms of Dom vs. Sub in sexually fluid relationships, or in terms of respect or social entitlement, Women want to be men. This is what 60+ years of feminization has taught women is valuable, and taught men to accommodate for. In fact men are 'lesser men' for not offering women a 'hand up' to manhood. Feminization in this respect is the ultimate form of penis envy; acculturate consecutive generations of both sexes willing to masculinize women into prominence. This is the heart of the feminine imperative and feminine primacy.

Hypergamy and women's innate psychologies naturally conflict with this socialization effort. Thus we have women expecting masculine equability while simultaneously feeling entitled to traditionally feminine courtesies and expectations. This is what "having it all" means. In the interests of feminine primacy, if it works, use it.

So it should come as no shock that in a desire to be like men, a popularized parallel had to be socialized into women's collective understanding of SMV expectations. In the most literal sense, if men could enjoy a more progressive and maturing SMV then, by the doctrines of equalism, a 'new' woman should also be able to mirror that masculine SMV.

Feminized SMV

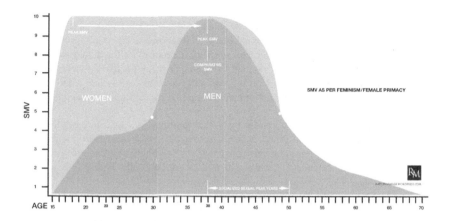

By a combined effort of feminism, feminine primacy and its imperatives women have been socialized and acculturated to believe that their SMV profile encompasses and is synchronous with that of men. Since women are essentially men, Equalism (the religion of feminism) convinces women that their SMV schedule should at least be identical to that of men.

I could have simply recolored the *men* bell curve from my previous SMV graph to illustrate the feminized redefinition of SMV, but that would be inaccurate. It wouldn't account for the obvious benefits women expect to enjoy in their true sexual peak years (22-24) in addition to the masculinized SMV feminization has convinced the modern woman of.

One thing I did find a need to account for was the Myth of Sexual peak. As Team Red laments, and in my post Myth of the Biological Clock, this feminine defined delusion is deceptively close to women's post-Wall valuation. Since men's SMV generally peaks around 38, women needed a social convention that would also make their sexual peak coincide with men's. Thus we read the endless articles about sexual peak inflating older women's sexual prowess above that of the 22 year old 'girl-children' men manifestly prefer for sexual partners. Equalism enforces the delusion that if men are at their most desirable at later stages of life, then so too must be wo-MEN.

Cracks in the Wall

For all its efforts to convince women of a feminized redefining of SMV, there are obvious cracks beginning to show in the social constructs designed to ensure a lasting feminine primacy. Since the last wave of significant feminism was carried along by the Baby Boom generation, women of the consecutive generations are only now beginning to realize the gravity of the "have-it-all" lie.

The institution of gender primacy (masquerading as 'equalism') is largely, and grossly apparent, at odds with women's true sexual market valuation and its progression. Try as it may the feminine imperative has never had an effective counter for the biological motivations that drive SMV – as women age, feminine primacy becomes a victim of its own hypergamy. Thus the imperative must continually redefine its mission, create new social conventions and rely on blaming the men it subjugates for its own inadequacies.

Women are now realizing their true SMV isn't what feminization has convinced them of too late – one crack in the Wall. Another tact is to shame men for their unwillingness to participate in the SMP the feminine imperative defines for, and expect them to participate in. "Man Up you infantile boys!" – and another crack appears in the Wall.

That many a feminist writer can form a prosperous career and celebrity around her inability to come to terms with the conflict between her true SMV and the SMV model the feminine imperative has conditioned into her ego is an indictment of the scope to which the distorted, feminized SMV model has been insaturated into women and our culture.

OF LOVE AND WAR

Generally people of either sex don't like to have love defined for them. The concept of love is loaded with subjectiveness, and not unsurprisingly you'll offend people's interpretations and sensibilities by trying to contain their idea of love in a defined box. This is one of the reasons love is such a great and human idea, but its ambiguity is also the primary cause of much of the human tragedy and suffering we experience.

We see love in religious contexts, personal interpretations, philosophical essays, biological dynamics and a whole slew of other arenas, so it's very easy to understand how universally convoluted, manipulative, and yet also how binding and nurturing love can be according to how well, or how ill our concepts of love aligns with that of others.

In outlining (not defining) a male perspective of love in contrast to a female perspective it's necessary to understand how a man's understanding of love shifts as he matures. A lot of Rational Male commenters wanted to find the base root of that concept in their relationship with their mothers. As Freudian as that rings I wouldn't say it's a bad start. Men do in fact learn their first impressions of intimate, physical and nurturing love from their mothers, and this then forms the foundation of that expected love from their potential wives (or lovers). Even as children are unable to think in abstract terms, there is an innate, base understanding of the conditionality that must be met in order to maintain that motherly love. Yohami posted a great illustration of this with the still face experiment.

Commenter Yohami broke this down thusly:

That circuit gets printed before we learn to talk = before we are able to form abstract and concepts. It's a basic four piece, emotional / behavioral circuit.

There are many ways that circuit can be imprinted "wrong". One is to have the mom (or dads) on the receiving end, making the kid the giver. Other is having him owning the frame. Other is to have the mom (or dads) respond only when the kid acts out. Other is making the kid act out and then silence him / punish him for it. Etc. Shortly, the kid understands the game and starts to play it.

And then you build everything on top.

Your experiences from ages 12-21, of course helped forming you, because you're 35 now and this is a sum accumulative game. But honestly, what happened to you from 12-21, are the same mechanics that were already happening, only adding more external world influence, sex drive, and additional pressures.

I'm trying to locate the source of the pain, and is this: like a compass or a geometrical piece that wants to find equilibrium, the pain wants to find the "good" again (from the good the bad and the ugly), but it only knows to reach that "good" by balancing violently between the bad and the ugly and episodes of rage and if that doesn't work, splitting / self mutilation (cutting out the undesired parts of you, your past, identity, emotions, people, relationships, blocking stuff out, etc)

It's a constant look out for the elusive "good" part of the dynamic.

Yohami continues:

[But] you weren't confident / self reassured about your needs and wants, because you were still negotiating how to even feel "good" and safe, so you didn't develop game nor saw girls / relationships for what they were – but you just added this to the previous unresolved mix, like, seeking the "good" (basic, maternal, paternal love where you're defenseless and you're intimately loved and taken care of and safe) from girls, mixing the defenseless and the sexual aggressive drive and the long time affection longing and the sense of despair of never feeling safe, etc.

From the moment we're born we realize love is conditional, but we want for it to be un-conditional; our idealized state is unconditional love. To be a Man is to perform, to excel, to be the one for whom affections are freely given in appreciation and adoration.

On a base level it's this constant striving for that idealized love-state that helps us become more than we started as, but it comes at the cost of a misguided belief that a woman is capable of, much less willing to love us as we think is possible.

A Place to Rest

Commenter Peregrine John summed it up:

We want to relax. We want to be open and honest. We want to have a safe haven in which struggle has no place, where we gain strength and rest instead of having it pulled from us. We want to stop being on guard all the time, and have a chance to simply be with someone who can understand our basic humanity without begrudging it. To stop fighting, to stop playing the game, just for a while.

We want to, so badly.

If we do, we soon are no longer able to.

This is a realization that men don't make until they are in a 'love relationship' with a woman. For men this is (should be) the catalyst for maturing beyond that want for an idealized unconditional love. At that point they come full circle and understand that the conceptual love they'd hoped they could return to (or could be) with their mother doesn't exist in the woman he's 'in love' with, and ultimately, never really existed between he and his mother from his infancy to adulthood.

There is no rest, there is no respite or reprieve from performing, but so strong is the desire for that unconditional love assurance that men thought it prudent to write it into "traditional" marriage vows – 'for better or for worse, for richer or for poorer, in sickness and in health, to love, cherish, and obey, forsaking all others until death do you part' – in other words, a pledge of unconditional love in spite of all circumstance. Those vows are a direct plea for insurances against a female hypergamy that would otherwise be unfettered were it not made in the context of being before God and man.

In prior essays I've mentioned a 65 y.o man whom I used to counsel, who's wife had emotionally blackmailed him for over 20 years. He'd been married once before and divorced from his first wife after 12 years due to "not living up to her expectations" of financial provisioning. He never made the connection that the women he was 'in love' with had different concepts of what love meant to him. Rather, he evolved his previous concept of love wholesale to match that of women he 'loved', and thus his idea of love was one based upon an endless quest for qualifying for that love. In the first year of his second marriage he lost his job, and was unemployed for about 5 months, leaving his wife as the only revenue source for them. At the end of month 4 of his unemployment, after returning from an interview, he came home to find the locks changed on his home and two duffel bags "full of his shit" were waiting by the door. On top of them was a note written by his 2nd wife which, to the effect, read: "Don't come back until you have a job."

I remember him proudly recounting this story to me at the time, because he said, as pissed off as he was at the time, he was 'grateful' for her kicking him in the ass to be a "better man". By this point his concept of love had been completely altered from his almost identical experiences with wife number one into a model that was entirely dependent upon his capacity to earn his wife's love. Gone were the idealizations of unconditional love for the sake of love, to be replaced with the tactical, opportunistic concept of female love of his new wife. And, he was grateful for it.

After 20 years, at 65 (now 69) and in failing health he had come to realize that his efforts to secure her 'love' indefinitely had never been appreciated, only expected; so here he was facing the very cruel reality that he was losing his health and thus the means to maintain that incessant qualification for her love and affection.

The Reconciling

I get a lot of email and correspondence about the ruthlessness of my, I guess seminal, War Brides essay. Guys have a hard time accepting the amorality of women's inborn capacity to bond with their own captors as a psycho-socially adaptive survival trait, and how this evolved into women's pronounced facility with which they can 'get over' former lovers so much faster than men seem to be capable of.

Women don't like me detailing this phenomenon for obvious reasons, but I think men dislike the notion of their easy 'disposability' because of that same inconsistency in gender concepts of love. Even as martyrs, even in death, that unconditional male concept of love is rebuked by women's, by-necessity, fluid and utilitarian concept of love.

Coming to terms with this is one of the most difficult aspects of taking the red pill.

I get that this seems overly nihilistic, but that's the point. All of the very positive, very beneficial aspects of accepting a red pill reality come at the cost of abandoning the blue pill idealisms we've been conditioned to for so long. Leaving behind that Pollyanna, expectant, blue-pill dream seems like killing an old friend, but unlearning that old paradigm allows you to benefit from a far more hopeful red pill existence.

I'm not debating the genuineness or sincerity of women's capacity to love. What I'm positing here is that women's concept of love isn't what men would be led to believe it is.

The Feminine Imperative

THE FEMININE REALITY

I think one of the basic premises I acknowledge in my essays is one that even some of the more 'enlightened' Men of the 'community' don't entirely grasp. This is the presumption of a feminine reality. Sometimes I refer to this as the feminine imperative, other times I might colloquially express it in terms of it being "The Matrix" for an ease of understanding, but I always presume my readers (even of my comments on other blogs or forums) have a basic understanding of this.

I think I may be a bit mistaken in this.

Everything a man experiences, every social conditioning he receives from the earliest age, every accepted social norm and every expectation of him to qualify as the definition of a mature adult Man in contemporary society is designed to serve a female imperative. Moralist wallow in it, absolutists and defeated white knights existentially depend upon it, and even the better part of relativists still (often unwittingly) feed and serve the feminine purpose. In fact, so all encompassing is this reality that we define our masculinity in the terms of how well we can accommodate that feminine influence.

Our media celebrates it, and brooks no dissent. There is very little dissent, since to peel back the veneer is to be at odds with a reality defined by the female purpose. You feel lonely because you can't understand its influence, and the conditioning you've been subjected to defines the objective solution to curing that feeling. You base the decisions of your future, your education, your career, your religious beliefs, even where you'll choose to live, to better accommodate the feminine influence either in the present or in preparation of accommodating it in the future.

You get married, out of fear for not being found acceptable of it, or from social shame for not yet having accepted your role in service to the imperative. Your children are offered in tribute to it, while in turn you unknowingly perpetuate it in them. You pay tribute in alimony, in divorce proceedings, in the expected sacrifices your career demands to maintain its influence in your own life and in society at large.

Men exist to facilitate a feminine reality.

We can excuse it with moralism, we can attach notions of honor and stability to it, we can even convince ourselves that the feminine imperative is *our* own imperative, but regardless, men still serve it.

Sexual Strategies

For one gender to realize their sexual imperative the other must sacrifice their own. This is the root source of power the feminine imperative uses to establish its own reality as the normative one. From this flows the rules of engagement for dating / mating, operative social conventions used to maintain cognitive dominance, and laws and legalities that bind society to the benefit of the feminine. From this is derived men's default status as the 'disposable' sex, while women are the protected sex. It's this root that the imperative uses to excuse (not apologize for) the most blatant inconsistencies and atrocities of women.

Monogamy and fidelity are only useful when paired with an optimized hypergamy. Without that optimization, they're inconvenient obligations to the feminine reality.

In order to effect this reality men must be convinced of a themselves having a degree of more control than the feminine imperative exerts. They must believe that it is they who are the masters of a reality defined by the feminine, while remaining dependent upon the systems that the feminine reality outlines for them. So they are told they are Kings, brutes, savages, patricians, intellectuals, elites, anything that might convince them that the reality they exist in is privileged and expressly serves their own selfish purpose. Already the 'protected sex', this all encourages the default presumption of victimhood for the feminine.

The crowning irony of the feminine reality is that men should be accused of patriarchy while enabling the very framework of the feminine imperative. The feminine sexual strategy is victorious because even under the contrived auspices of male oppression, it's still the female goal-state that is agreed upon as the correct effort. Satisfying the feminine imperative, achieving the ends of the pluralistic feminine sexual strategy is still the normative condition. Men's goals are aberrant, women's are beatific.

Forgive me if I've waxed a bit too poetic here, but it's important to see the Matrix for what it really is. The next occasion you lock horns with even the most well-meaning woman's (or feminized man's) opinions about life, relationships, marriage, having babies, religion, etc. understand that her perceptions are based in this reality. She's correct because her beliefs line up with what the framework of her reality reinforced in her as correct. Any other frame of reference is either utterly alien to her at best, wicked and evil at worst.

Fem-Centrism

My intent with all this is to illustrate how the reality in which we find things "normal" is rendered by fem-centric influence. Across ethnicities, and encompassing all manner of social diversity, this influence is so insaturated into culture, laws, media, entertainment, from our collective social consciousness to our individual psyches that we simply take it for granted as the operative framework in which we live. I realize this is a tough pill to swallow, because the male imperative does in fact intersect with the female imperative depending on mutual goals. However, the point is that the operative framework, the reality we function in, is primarily defined by the feminine.

I can remember first becoming aware of just the hints of this the first time I watched a popular sit-com on TV with a critical eye. There simply were no positively masculine actors or roles on *any* show, and rather, every male was ridiculed for his masculinity. This then led into other aspects of society and media I was just starting to become aware of. The allegory of taking the *red pill* is one of an awakening. Feminization was everywhere, but my inner, conditioned guilt for even considering the possibility of feminine-primacy was hindering my unplugging from it.

I remember at first feeling guilty about feeling offended by just my noticing this. I felt ashamed of myself for thinking that maybe things weren't as *'normal'* as women would like me to think. What I didn't understand was that this was part of my conditioning; to internalize a sense of shame for questioning that 'normalcy'. A lot of men never get past this programming and never unplug. It's just too embedded in *"who they are"*, and the resulting internal conflict will prompt them to deny the realities of their condition and sometimes actively fight others who challenge the normalcy they need in order to exist.

Once I'd gotten past the self-shame, I began to notice other patterns and interlocking social conventions that promoted this fem-centrism. From the macro dynamics of divorce laws and legal definitions of rape, to the gender bias in military conscription (drafting only men to die in war) and down to the smallest details of mundane water cooler talk in the work place, I began to realize just how overwhelming this influence is on our existences.

Observing the Framework

Recently I listened to an advice radio talk show where a woman called in emotional distress with her husband's actions. Apparently she'd dated the man for a year or two before marriage and they talked about how neither wanted children from the outset. Prior to the marriage both agreed, no kids, that is until about a year into their marriage the wife had secretly gone off the pill and made deliberate efforts in her sexual activities with her husband in order to conceive. Trouble was she wasn't getting pregnant. Only later did the man confess that he'd had a vasectomy so as not to risk having kids with any woman he paired up with.

The ensuing indignation wasn't directed at the woman's admitted duplicity and covert efforts to deceive her husband into thinking she'd had an accidental pregnancy, but rather all the fires of hell were concentrated on this man's alleged deception of her.

This serves as a prime example of how the feminine reality frames the directions of our lives. Publicly and privately, not even an afterthought was spared for the woman's motivation and desperate measures to achieve her sexual imperative because the feminine imperative is normalized as the **correct** goal of any conflict.

A woman's existential imperative, her happiness, her contentment, her protection, her provisioning, her empowerment, literally anything that benefits the feminine is not only encouraged socially, but in most cases mandated by law. Ironically, most doctors require a wife's written consent to perform a vasectomy on a married man; not because of a legal mandate, but rather to avoid legal retaliations and damages from a man's wife. By hook or by crook, her imperative is the **correct** one.

Some will argue that it hasn't always been thus, and that in certain eras woman have been reduced to property like cattle. While that may have some merit I would argue that the perpetuation of this notion better serves the new feminine reality in promoting a need for recognition of victim status and thus a need for restitution. The truth is that even the most ardent supporters of reconciling a "patriarchal past" are still operating in the feminine realty in the now. Other than sultans and emperors, very few men born prior to the dark ages have ever really 'owned' a woman.

Sexual Revolution

I got into a hypothetical debate with an online friend as to what it would mean to humanity (and masculinity in particular) if a new method of birth control was developed with the specific and unique ability to allow men to control conception to the same degree women were given with hormonal contraception in the mid-sixties. I thought it interesting that human effort could create reliable contraception for women in the 60's, yet in 2013 we can map the human genome and yet not figure out how to afford men the same degree of birth control?

Put simply, the feminine imperative will not allow this.

Imagine the social and economic damage to the feminine infrastructure if Prometheus gave such fire to Men? Imagine that balance of control veering back into the masculine; for men to literally have the exclusive choice to fulfill a woman's sexual strategy or not.

The conversation got heated. Men could never be trusted with such a power! Surely humanity would come to a grinding, apocalyptic end if the feminine sexual strategy was thwarted by reliable male contraception. Societies would be sundered, population would nosedive, and the nuclear family would be replaced with a neo-tribalism dictated by men's sexual strategies. Honestly, you'd think the discovery of atomic weapons was on par with such an invention.

The ridiculous, pathetic endemically juvenile and perverse masculinity that 50 years of systematic feminization created could never be trusted to further humanity in pursuing their sex's inborn imperatives.

Yet, this is precisely the power that was put into the hands of women in the 1960's and remains today. The threat that male contraception represents to the feminine imperative is one of controlling the framework of which gender's sexual strategy will be the normative.

Prior to the advent of unilaterally female-exclusive hormonal birth control and the sexual revolution that resulted from it, the gender playing field was level, if not tipped in favor of masculinity due to men's provisioning being a motivating factor in women achieving their own gender imperative. Latex prophylactics were available in the 40's, and this may have afforded men a slight advantage, but both parties knew and agreed to the terms of their sexual activity at the time of copulation.

Once feminine-exclusive birth control was convenient and available the locus of control switched to feminine primacy. Her imperative became the normalized imperative. His sexual imperative was only a means to achieving her own, and now the control was firmly placed in favor of feminine hypergamy. Whether in the developing world or in first world nations, the onus of directing the course of humanity fell upon women, and thus the feminine reality evolved into what it is today.

THE FEMININE MYSTIQUE

Perhaps the single most useful tool women have possessed for centuries is their unknow-ablity. I made that word up, but it's applicable; women of all generations for hundreds of years have cultivated this sense of being unknowable, random or in worse case fickle or ambiguous. This is the feminine mystique and it goes hand in hand with the feminine prerogative – a woman always reserves the right to change her mind – and the (mythical) feminine intuition – "a woman just knows."

While a Man can never be respected for anything less than being forthright and resolute – say what you mean, mean what you say – women are rewarded and reinforced by society for being elusive and, dare I say, seemingly irrational. In fact, if done with the right art, it's exactly this elusiveness that makes her both desirable and intolerably frustrating. However, to pull this off she must be (or seem to be) unknowable, and encourage all of male society to believe so.

The feminine mystique appeals to the feminine psyche for the same reasons 'chick crack' works so well in PUA technique. It appeals to the same 'secret power' dynamic that makes meta-physical associations so attractive (religion, superstition, intuition, etc.) One need look no further than women's innate love of gossip to understand; There's power in secrets for women. It's hardly a surprise that connections with witchcraft have been associated with the feminine for so long. In an historically 'male dominated' culture it follows that the power of secrecy and mysticism would need to be cultivated into the feminine as a resource for influencing the men in control of it. Sometimes that may have ended with a woman burned at the stake, but more often it was a means to becoming the 'power behind the throne' by order of degrees, and depending upon the status of the man she could enchant.

Combine that mysticism with sexuality, and you've got the true feminine mystique – the most useful tool the feminine imperative possesses in its quest for optimal hypergamy.

The feminine mystique permeates inter-gender communication. On every forum response, on every blog comment, on every Facebook post and in any article ever written by women with a personal, feminine investment in the subject, there is a residue of recognizing the feminine mystique. When a woman retorts to an observation of female behavior that betrays female intent, the standard misdirection is *always* saturated in the unknowable, unpredictably capricious, feminine mystique.

The first (and second) rule of Fight Club for the feminine imperative is to protect the mystery of the female – and the sisterhood has no mercy for those who would betray that. The closer you get to truth the louder women screech.

For years I've striven to breakdown confusion and common problems by observing behavior. Women are human beings with the same basic motivations that men are subject to with some greater or lesser variation in their reasoning and methodologies. The point being is that women are every bit as subject to being as mundane or as extraordinary as men are, but the difference is that men don't enjoy a masculine mystique.

With rare exceptions, we don't generally cultivate this sense of mystery because we're not rewarded for it to the degree women are – and honestly, we haven't needed to. But for a woman, if she can cultivate this mystique, her attentions become a reward unto themselves for the guy who is 'lucky' enough to tame her. Rest assured, when you think a woman is crazy, she's crazy like a fox; she's crazy with a reason. Women are every bit as calculating as men, in fact more so I'd argue because they have the mystique to hide a multitude of sins behind. They're not irrational, they're calculated – you just have to develop an ability to read a woman's actions and behaviors and see the latent purpose behind them.

In contemporary times, men are far too ready to write off women as irrational agents. Even Freud was fooled by the hysterics of women's responses and wrote them off as largely incapable, random and duplicitous to their own interests. I can't begin to tell you how frustrating it is to hear an elderly man say "women, I guess we'll never really understand them, huh?" adding a nervous laugh.

How many times have you been asked by a friend, "so, did ya get lucky with Kristy last night?" We don't think much of this passing question, but it's framed in such a way that men autonomously perpetuate the myth of this mystique. It's not luck that gets you laid. I understand that circumstance and being the right guy at the right time most certainly plays a part, but that's not the operative here. However, if due to our preconditioning, we *feel* as though we got lucky, we won the lottery, or walked away with a rare and valuable prize, it doesn't help us to understand what it is we did correctly in a given instance. It perpetuates women as the mysterious prize-givers and ensures they maintain an indirect, primary power role in embodying the prize that is feared to be lost. You were lucky to have gotten sex with this mysterious woman so it must be something rare and valuable indeed.

The feminine mystique discourages questioning the process or the motives involved in inter-gender relations; men are just happy to have had the chance of experiencing the unknowable woman they scarcely understand. When mixed with sexual deprivation, the lucky fate element makes the sex that much more absorbing. It's this luck precognition for men, fostered by women, that leads to the scarcity mentality and often (but not exclusively) ONEitis in men. It serve the feminine if men willingly adopt the feminine mystique mindset with regards to their intimacy. Sexuality is a woman's first, best agency and any social mechanism that contributes to the value of it will always be encouraged.

THE WALL

Throughout this book thus far I've made references to the Wall – the point at which women lose their competitive edge in the SMP to younger rivals. The following was contributed by a Rational Male commenter 'S'. Her comment regarding The Wall made me aware that I hadn't yet gone into too much detail regarding the Wall and its socio-psychological effects upon women:

Yeah, it's a term I have seen before arriving at this blog but have never heard in reality. I always attributed it to a woman losing her looks but to place it at exactly 30 seems to me to be too precise a calculation...as there are many variable to be taken into consideration I would imagine. For example, a party girl, serial tanner and smoker could probably lose her looks long before she reaches 30, whereas a clean living late bloomer might not even realize her potential until her mid to late twenties. I've seen women from my school..the most popular girls (with guys) changed the most in a negative manner and the nerds or just the most unexpected girls have become more attractive over the years. It's freaking odd.

Technically the Wall was a sports term used for athletes who had reached an age where they'd lost their competitive edge. The infamous Wall a woman reaches (or slams into as the case may be) is somewhat of an ambiguous term that was actually coined by catty women long before the manosphere came into existence. It used to be a relatively less combative term that women used for one another in an effort to disqualify an intra-sexual competitor. A woman implying another woman had "hit the wall" was marginally more polite than calling her an old slut, but the latent purpose is still the same – disqualifying a sexual competitor from men's mating considerations.

The Fear of Decay

Underneath the obvious utility of the Wall as an epithet is a more painful truth; the inevitable decay of women's sexual appeal – their first, and for most, only, real agency of power they've ever actualized over men to ensure their long term security needs.

In the heyday of 2nd wave feminism, the sisterhood's message was all about collective empowerment and solidarity, but beneath that was the intrinsic hypergamic need to compete for the best mate their looks and sexual availability could attract. As I've written before, women prefer their combat in the psychological and there are few fears women harbor as deep and as long as losing their sexual agency with men. They know the Wall will eventually come, and they don't like to be reminded of it.

Women's intra-sexual combative use of the knowledge and fear of the Wall did not go unnoticed by men. Therefore the feminine imperative found it necessary to make the truth about the Wall as socially and individually subjective as possible. As with most uncomfortable truths unique to women's weaknesses, the feminine creates social conventions and ambiguities to misdirect men from becoming aware of women's eventual powerlessness over them (i.e. the progressive loss of her sexual agency). The threat of having men become aware of women's Achilles' heel before they could consolidate long-term commitment with their best hypergamic option was too great a risk not to form social conventions about the Wall.

Implications of the Wall

Thus, in an inter-gender social context, the Wall became individualized and subjective for women, and it's within this framework that women like 'S' are most comfortable in addressing the reality of the Wall. "Not all women are like that" (NAWALT), the go-to mantra of feminized subjectivity, is a direct result of subjectivizing the inevitability of the Wall. In fact, virtually every operative social convention women rely upon for empowerment and self-esteem finds its root purpose in avoiding the fear of the Wall. The Myth of Sexual Peak, the Myth of the Biological Clock, the social convention that Women are just as Sexual as Men, are all very complex social rationales with the latent purpose of convincing the majority of men and women alike that post-Wall women can still be equally effective sexual competitors with pre-Wall women.

It's important to bear in mind that all of these complex social conventions are rooted in a fear of the Wall. I'm repeating this point to emphasize the importance this has in a feminized society that's subjected to feminine hypergamy as its most operative doctrine.

When enough women, through cultural forces or personal circumstance, can't capitalize upon what they think is their due, optimal hypergamic male option, then society must be acculturated to believe that women past their Wall expiration date can and should be just as desirable as those in their prime. Think of it as a retroactive social moving of the feminized goalposts. This is the gravity and extent that the fear of the Wall plays for women – feminized society is literally structured around avoiding it.

Defining the Wall

When I wrote Navigating the SMP, the reason I used 30 as the general age women typically hit the 'Wall' is really a combination of factors. Most importantly it represents the threshold at which most women *realize* their lessened capacity to sexually compete with the next generation of women in their 'actualized' sexual peak (22-24).

However, there is a male part of the Wall equation that needs to be understood. 30 is also the general age at which men (should) become aware of their own, longer-lasting sexual market value and potential. This affects women's interpretations of the Wall. Once a Man is aware that he has the capacity to attract the sexual attentions of the younger women he'd previously had limited access to, and understanding of, his actions and imperatives then begin to define the Wall for women who are approaching that threshold. And unsurprisingly this is the point at which Wall-fearing women begin their accusations of men's infantile ego issues, shaming, etc. for preferring younger women than themselves.

When we (and as women in particular would have us) view the Wall in terms of just physical attractiveness we don't see the full picture and relevancy the Wall has for women. It's just as much a psychological issue as it is a physical one. It's very easy (and often fun) to compare pictures of girls we knew in high school with their current FaceBook profile shots at 40+ years old and get a laugh at how bad she hit the Wall. It's also easy for women to point out the notable exceptions to the rule and find a hot 38 year old woman with 3 kids competing in the Ms. Fitness USA pageant. It gives them a sense of hope about their own decay.

However the Wall is much more than just the physical; it's the conditional that accelerates or decelerates a woman's date with the Wall.

Single mother? Acceleration.

Consistent, bad personal habits? Acceleration.

Careerist obsessive? Acceleration.

Obesity? Acceleration.

Do notable exceptions to these exist? Of course, but they prove the rule. And that rule comes in the form of such an overwhelming fear that contemporary society needed to be restructured to help avoid it. The 38 year old, careerist, single mother of 3 competing in fitness pageants is only a hero because of the fear of the Wall.

THE THREAT

Nothing is more threatening yet simultaneously attractive to a woman than a man who is aware of his own value to women.

My use of the word "threat" here isn't to imply malice. I'm sure more simplistic associations with violence or conflict is the natural one, but a "threat" is a challenge – how one deals with it is what's at issue. As I stated in Wait For It?:

Women's sexual strategy is very schizophrenic – ideally women want a Man that other women want to fuck, but in order to assess his sexual market value to other women he's got to have exercisable options for her to compete against, or at least display indirect social proof to that effect. So, she needs to limit his options while simultaneously determining he has those options.

This internal conflict between a want for security and provisioning, and a need for the *'gina tingles* that only the excitement indignation, drama and Alpha dominance can stimulate is the fundamental root for women's shit tests. From Plate Theory VI:

Essentially a shit test is used by women to determine one, or a combination of these factors:

a.) Confidence – first and foremost
b.) Options – is this guy really into me because I'm 'special' or am I his only option?
c.) Security – is this guy capable of providing me with long term security?

Women's shit testing is a psychologically evolved, hard-wired survival mechanism. Women will shit test men as autonomously and subconsciously as a men will stare at a woman's big boobs. They cannot help it, and often enough, just like men staring at a nice rack or a great ass, even when they're aware of doing it they'll still do it. Men want to verify sexual availability to the same degree women want to verify a masculine dominance / confidence.

For a woman, to encounter a man with a healthy awareness of his own value to women, this constitutes a threat. Here is a man for whom's attention women will demonstrably compete for, **and** he knows this. This is the most basic affront to the feminine imperative; to be unplugged, of high sexual market value and to derive a sense of confidence from being consciously aware of it.

Therefore, in order to promote and actualize her own sexual strategy, his self-confidence *must* be challenged with self-doubt, because if such a man were to use this knowledge to his own benefit he may not select her from a pool of better prospective women. Thus, in various ways, both consciously and subconsciously, she must ask him "Are you really sure of yourself? You think you're so great? Maybe you're just egotist? Don't tempt fate."

In this example we can see the conflict inherent in women's sexual strategy; she wants the Alpha dominance of a confident Man, but not so confident that he can exercise his options with other women well enough to make an accurate estimation of her own SMV.

Ambiguity in men's assessment of a woman's true sexual market value is the primary tool of the feminine imperative.

The same characteristics that give him his confidence and acknowledged sense of worth are exactly the same things that women want to be associated with. Even the most controlling, domineering wife still wants to tell her friends that the AFC she married is a "real Man", and even after privately berating him, will defend him as such because anything less is a reflection on her own self-image. She wants to be with a Man that other men want to be, and other women want to fuck, because it confirms for her that she's of an equal or higher value to attract and be associated with such a Man.

Women don't want a man to cheat, but they love a Man who could cheat.

That is the threat and the attraction. Women want a Man that has confidence in his own value; that's sexy, but the more he self-realizes this the greater the anxiety is that she'll be found wanting as he better understands his options. So it becomes necessary to develop social conventions that are standardized across the feminine gender that limit the full recognition of masculine self-value. Thus masculinity is ridiculed, men become characterized as slaves to their sexuality, and masculinity becomes doubted by virtue of itself.

In a global sense, the feminine imperative relies on the same ambiguity women will individually employ to confuse the efforts of men to assess their true SMV. By means of social conventions, the feminine imperative psychologically forces him to doubt his own SMV and women become the arbiters and definers of it to suit their own sexual strategy.

Race to Awareness

Because of women's relatively short window of peak sexual viability it is imperative that men be as unaware of their slower, but progressively increasing SMV for as long as possible in order for them to achieve the prime directive of female hypergamy; realize the best genetic options and the best provisioning options she has the capacity to attract in that peak window. If Men become aware of their SMV before a woman can consolidate on her options with monogamous commitment her sexual strategy is defeated.

The mistake (and the binary retort) is to think this need for contrivances was concocted in whole as some grand sisterhood conspiracy. This just proves an ignorance of social constructs. For a social convention to be such, it necessitates being repeated by society *without* a formal conception – meaning we learn the contrivance from seeing it, internalizing it and repeating it ourselves without forethought.

The best social contrivances are inconspicuous and rarely questioned because they've been learned without having been formally taught. This is why I think encouraging men *not* to bother trying to understand women is in itself a social convention. Don't look at that man behind the curtain, just accept it for what it is, enjoy the show, you're better off that way, the Mighty Oz has spoken.

This is the threat that Game represents to the feminine imperative. Widely shared, objective assessments of Men's SMV and how it develops is the antithesis of the female sexual strategy. Women's greatest fear is that they could become the 'selected' instead of the 'selectors'.

POSITIVE MASCULINITY
VS. EQUALISM

If you type the word "equalism" in a blog's text box you get that annoying little red line underneath it indicating that you misspelled something. In other words, the English language doesn't officially recognize that word in any dictionary (yet). I suppose this is apt since for the last 50+ years the effort to feminize society has always used the abstract concept of gender equalism as something ambient in the background of the agenda. It doesn't have an official definition because, collectively, were supposed to take it as a given; something that should just be considered *"common sense"*. To be sure, feminization's plea for a more *humane* restructuring of society has always been couched in terms like "equality", which sounds comforting when spoken, even if the intent is distraction.

However, that's not the "equalism" my computer wont recognize. I sometimes see it creeping in from the edges on blogs decrying some nefarious, neo-liberal social agenda, or I see it written as some corrupting element keeping conservatism from realizing it's 'true' potential, but what I don't see is a very good accounting of it. Equalism needs to be brought out of the shadows – if at least so I don't have to see that damn red line anymore.

New Gender Definitions

Masculinity has been redefined by people (men and women) who have no concept of what its original definition was. The behaviors and characteristics that constitute what is uniquely masculine aren't being challenged; they've been redefined to fit the purposes of an agenda. In 1905 no one wrote articles on how to "be a man" or bothered to analyze the fundamentals of masculinity. Men knew from their socialization what was masculine and women responded to it.

Traditionally, women define what is masculine and men define what is feminine. The characteristics that made a man desirable were ones that presented the opposite to what men similarly found desirable in femininity. Men and their biology defines what in the feminine that arouses them, women react to this and behave accordingly (knowingly or not).

The root of the AFC endemic lies in the fact that as recently as 50 years ago there has been a concerted effort to "de-masculinize" society, not only in mass media, but down to how we educate and condition our youth to assume masculine and feminine roles. What *is* being challenged is the predisposition of males in predominantly western culture, to even consider what masculinity is. A rugged, stoic, heroic definition of masculinity is losing ground, but is that a good thing? The equalist certainly believes so.

When men become feminized, are we leveling any playing fields or are we progressing towards androgyny and homogenization of gender? The equalist hails this as a triumph of a new gender paradigm. Why should masculine traits be of lower value than feminine traits?

The very characteristics that define traditional masculinity – independence, self-confidence, rugged individualism, physical strength, risk taking, problem solving and innovation – we are now to believe are (or should be) the aspirations of women to the point that ridicule of the singularly feminine female is the order. In expecting women to be just as masculine as men, while simultaneously expecting them to still embody a feminine ideal, not only does this puts undue, unrealistic ideals upon them, but also devalues the merits of their own femininity.

That's not to say, given this new gender dynamic, that women are discouraged from claiming their femininity in addition to their masculinity. On the contrary they're encouraged to "handle their business as well as any man" *and* "still be a sexy, vivacious woman" every man should want.

Yet in opposition to this post-modern gender dynamic, men are not encouraged to embrace their masculine side We are told to "man up" for sure, and yet our masculinity (as we define it) is a flaw; we're poisoned by our testosterone. Our higher aspiration ought to be becoming more feminized, sensitive, emotional, empathetic, nurturing, etc,.. We should "feel comfortable waxing our legs" stripping away the hair that is the result of our poisoning testosterone. Interestingly enough there are few cries in society to have women cultivate their leg or armpit hair.

Yet the 'masculine' that the feminine imperative would have us strive for doesn't encourage anything resembling traditionally masculine traits in a male's personality. In fact it's ridiculed to such a degree in mass media and larger society that it's literally akin to a disease.

While women are congratulated for embodying masculine traits with an acceptance of her feminine character, men are conditioned to believe that feminine traits *are* masculine traits and any traditionally masculine characteristics that manifest themselves in us are the unfortunate byproducts of our 'flawed' biology.

The true crime of this gender redefining is the real "double standard" that men should be so feminized as to loathe their innate masculinity, yet still be held liable for uniquely male, traditionally masculine responsibilities and accountabilities by virtue of them being male. It's the male Catch 22 again; hate your masculinity, but be held responsible for not "being man enough" to solve uniquely male problems, then be shamed when a masculinized woman steps in to do so and then be ridiculed for not being as masculine as she is. That's the cycle. This is self-perpetuating negative masculinity that has led to generations of AFCs.

Needless to say, all of this convolutes what masculinity was, is and is intended to be. Before you can set out a plan to live out what I call Positive Masculinity you first have to take into consideration why masculinity has value and should be encouraged as well as cultivated in yourself, your sons and society as a whole. I'm an adherent of the 'build it and they will come' school of thought in this regard, but understanding how traditional masculinity has been redefined by social contrivance and distilling it back down to it's core fundamentals is imperative in getting back to masculinity as a positive.

So where do you start? With yourself. You must change your mind about yourself as a "m"an and begin thinking of yourself as a "M"an. The first step is to unlearn what feminized conditioning has taught you to the point of it becoming an ego-investment in your personality.

You need to become impervious to convenient accusations of "misogyny" or 1950's caveman thinking whenever you assert yourself. The truly positive masculine Man sets himself apart from the Matrix in spite of a world set against him – this unconscious meta-acknowledgment is what makes a woman (and other men) attracted to you as a vibrant, responsible, but firmly confident masculine Man.

You have to genuinely live it in order to set an example of it. That doesn't mean you're an uncaring, tunnel vision robot, unwilling to learn from anyone or anything, it means that in spite of a world calling you "egotistical", "caveman", "fragile ego", "macho", "infantile", "Jerk", "misogynist", etc., you unwaveringly, provably, live out and exemplify the positive merits of being masculine.

AFTERWORD

I would be remiss in my duties as a new author if I weren't to give credit where due, and especially after such a long and involved process of developing the concepts you've just read. In the essay, The Evolution of Game I made an attempt to detail just how Game (now for lack of a better term) had branched into other aspects of Men's lives and how Men have used it to meet their relational needs and improve not just their sex lives, but also their professional and familial lives.

The following is a list of blogs I frequent and have found very useful and engaging in helping me mold the ideas in this book. Some of the authors have become personal friends and others informal colleagues of the manosphere.

First of course is my own blog The Rational Male: therationalmale.com. Most of what you've read thus far can be found in its original form in the Year One link page. Here you can find most of the essay in this book, but these are a small fraction of the essays from 2011-2012. At the time of this publication there is also a Year Two collection of essays. I presently have more than 320 posts. If there is a topic specific to your interests that I covered in this book and you'd like to find further reading, or if there was some topic you think I may have covered, please feel free to search and browse. If not, you can always request a topic or ask me something specific by using the About page.

The SoSuave forum is where most of my earliest ideas took root. I may have 320+ posts on The Rational Male, but I have well over 5,300 post on this forum where I am still a moderator: www.sosuave.net/forum/index.php

Among the manosphere I'm accounted among one of the Three 'R's, Roosh, Roissy and Rollo. I'm honored and humbled by this association. While I believe my involvement in Game has been at least as long as them both, these two bloggers are easily the most influential in the 'sphere with regard to Game as a concept and as a practice. I'd like to extend my personal gratitude to RooshV for indirectly encouraging me to compile this book. Roosh can be found at http://www.rooshv.com/ and Roissy (or one of his many aliases) can be found posting as Heartiste at http://heartiste.wordpress.com/

From a purely practical and practicable approach to Game Nick Krauser at http://krauserpua.com/ is one of the best. Nick is the author of many PUA guides and focuses primarily on approach and seduction, but is also very deep in his understandings of the psychological and social mechanics behind the technique. His story of transforming himself from what he was into who he is now is inspirational. I owe Nick a solid for making Rational Male a point of influence in his interview on London Real.

Of all the bloggers I've encountered since starting The Rational Male and becoming a fixture in the manosphere, no one has had more profound an impact on me than Dalrock: http://dalrock.wordpress.com/ I'm impressed with Dal because he's the one Man in the 'sphere I can bounce off ideas of common morality and how they relate to Game concepts and know he and I are on the same wavelength. Dalrock is the best blogger in the Christo-Manosphere because he gets the concepts of Game and hypergamy and then accurately applies them in a Christianized context. For the sake of clarity and to avoid the impression of a moralistic bias, that would otherwise color the objective deductions I attempt to make, I intentionally avoid contexts of morality and strive to define my analysis in as amoral a way as possible. Dalrock bridges this gap for readers who are uncomfortable with such an antiseptic approach to Game. If you've read through The Rational Male and found yourself agreeing and accepting of the concepts, but feel as though they challenge your personal or religious convictions, I'd encourage you to read through Dalrock's offerings.

I sincerely hope reading this book has changed your mind about how you previously perceived inter-gender dynamics. Maybe you've agreed with the entirety of the book, maybe you have some rebuttals or questions. I encourage that discourse and so too does the manosphere for the greater part. People with questions don't scare me, it's people without any that do.

If this book has helped you become more *aware* I'd love to read about. If you think I've upset the gender applecart by proposing dangerous ideas, I'd also love to read about it. What's important is that the manosphere has this discourse and that you add your ideas or concerns to it to help it evolve into a better awareness for all Men.

Rollo Tomassi –

therationalmale.com

Made in United States
North Haven, CT
08 November 2022